ART, CRAFT & DESIGN

A PRACTICAL GUIDE FOR TEACHERS

**KEY STAGES
1 & 2**

Diana Brown

JOHN MURRAY

Other titles in the **Key Strategies** series:

Planning Primary Science, Revised National Curriculum Edition by Roy Richardson, Phillip Coote and Alan Wood

Primary Science: A Complete Reference Guide by Michael Evans

Physical Education: A Practical Guide by Elizabeth Robertson

From Talking to Handwriting by Daphne M. Tasker

Helping with Handwriting by Rosemary Sassoon

Planning Primary Geography by Maureen Weldon and Roy Richardson

Planning Primary History by Tim Lomas, Christine Burke, Dave Cordingley, Karen McKenzie and Lesley Tyreman

English Speaking and Listening by Gordon Lamont

Music: A Practical Guide for Teachers by Alan Biddle and Lynn Dolby

Planning Primary Design and Technology by Roy Richardson

© Diana Brown 1997

First published 1997
by John Murray (Publishers) Ltd
50 Albemarle Street
London W1X 4BD

Layouts by Ann Samuel
Artwork by Art Construction
Cover design by John Townson/Creation

Typeset in 10.5/12pt Rockwell by Wearset, Boldon, Tyne and Wear
Printed by G. Canale & C. S.p.A., Torino, Italy

A CIP catalogue record for this book is available from the British Library
ISBN 0–7195–7170–7

Contents

Introduction   vi

CHAPTER 1: Drawing   1

    knowledge and understanding through drawing   1
    ages and stages   2
    Strategies for drawing lessons   3
    organising a drawing lesson   3
    observing directly   4
    using a sketchbook   6
    expressing ideas through illustration   7
    expressing feelings   8
    making visual stories   9
    making problem-solving drawings   11
    Drawing equipment and techniques   12
    drawing supports   12
    pencils   13
    coloured pencils   14
    pen and ink   15
    charcoal   18
    chalks and soft pastels   20
    wax crayons and oil pastels   21
    scraperboard   23
    wax scraffito   25

CHAPTER 2: Painting   27

    knowledge and understanding through painting   27
    ages and stages   28
    teaching resources and discussing paintings   28
    responding to artists' style of painting   29
    Strategies for painting lessons   30
    illustrative and imaginative paintings   30
    painting from direct observation – portraits and still-lives   31
    painting landscapes   32
    painting abstract pictures   33
    Painting and colour   33
    artists' colour choices and styles   33
    colours made from locally found materials   34
    the early restricted palette   34
    new colour theories   35
    colours and washes   36
    Painting tools and techniques   39
    painting surface (support)   39
    brushes and brush strokes   42
    Choosing paints   44
    gouache   45
    watercolour   46
    acrylics   48

CHAPTER 3: Print-making   50

    knowledge and understanding through print-making   50
    ages and stages   51
    General printing equipment   51
    Types of print   53
    direct prints   53

prints with rollers	55
raised-relief prints	56
rubbings	58
shaped and incised blocks	60
monoprinting	67
stencil prints	71
transfer prints	79

CHAPTER 4: Collage and relief · 82

Paper collage	82
paper collage techniques	85
Mixed collage	90
making a mixed collage design	91
Fabric collage and embroidery	91
making a fabric collage picture	93
quilting	95
Modelling in relief	97
using plastic materials	97
modelling with papier mâché and laminated paper	98
modelling with plaster	99
Plaster casts	99
making a plaster cast	100

CHAPTER 5: Sculpture · 102

knowledge and understanding through sculpture	102
ages and stages	102
talking about sculptures	103
Construction	103
construction with card and paper	104
construction with found material	107
construction with wire	109
construction using plaster of Paris	112
construction with laminated paper and papier mâché	114
soft sculptures	116
Carved sculptures	119
carving soft materials	119
carving wood	121
Modelling	121
modelling materials	122
modelling techniques	123
slab-pots	124
thumb-pots	126
coil-pots	127
using a kiln	128
glazing	128

CHAPTER 6: Textiles · 130

knowledge and understanding through textiles	130
working with yarns	131
ages and stages	131
Yarn wrapping	131
yarn-wrap pictures	132
God's eyes	132
cords	133
tassels	134
pom-poms and candlewick	135
stick-weaving	137
french knitting	138
Knotting and knitting	138
macramé	138

plaits and braids	139
knitting	140
Weaving	141
weaving patterns	142
equipment and techniques for weaving with yarn	143
picture weaving	145
Dyeing textiles	146
dyes made with local objects	147
commercial dyes	147
tie-dyeing	148
paper tie-dyes	149
different tie-dyes	149
dyeing the tie-dyed cloth	152
Batik	154
making a batik design	155
dyeing batik in the traditional way	157
batik painting	158
silk painting	160
CHAPTER 7: Art elements	162
ages and stages	162
looking at art works	163
reviewing and modifying work	163
Colour	163
mixing colours	164
relating colours to each other	166
colour groups	167
Showing form through tone	169
shading	170
highlighting	171
shadows	171
recording tone in children's work	171
Textures and patterns	172
looking at textures and patterns in the environment	173
line in texture and pattern	175
decorative patterns and borders	176
patterns based on symmetry	178
repeat patterns	180
Composition – arranging shapes, lines and colours	183
symmetrical and asymmetrical compositions	183
support shape	184
invisible lines	185
focal points	185
Recording shapes and forms – proportion	186
looking at structure beneath the surface	187
life portraits	189
making portraits without a model	191
using a grid	192
Recording shapes in space – perspective	193
Perspective – basic rules	194
More technical rules of perspective	196
drawing the edge of a cylinder	196
drawing the sides of a cuboid	196
lines of perspective and the vanishing point	197
APPENDIX: Health and safety	198
INDEX	200

INTRODUCTION

The National Curriculum for art, craft and design makes many demands on teachers' knowledge, skills and resources. How can teachers who are not art specialists, organise art lessons to respond to these wide-ranging demands when time is so limited?

Art, Craft & Design offers teachers ideas on how to teach many exciting art techniques, skills and concepts, as well as involving children in learning about their cultural heritage and improving their visual literacy. Most important, it outlines practical strategies for integrating these aspects of the curriculum. Using these strategies, teachers will be able to fulfil the requirements of the National Curriculum within the time allocated to art in their school's teaching programme.

A rich resource of techniques and examples is provided and teachers can select those most suited to their own pupils' needs, interests and stages of development. The first six chapters provide information on drawing, painting, print-making, collage, sculpture and textiles. All the art elements of colour, form, texture, pattern, line, shape and space are discussed thoroughly in Chapter 7.

Within each chapter, teachers who have little knowledge of an art technique will find the sections on Equipment and Basic techniques informative and easy to follow. Teachers who are familiar with a particular technique can turn to the Activity sections (tinted panels) for a rich variety of tried-and-tested ideas to supplement their own programme and to ensure a progression of work in each medium. In Ages and stages there is information on what children at different ages and stages might be expected to know and what they can be expected to learn for each technique or concept.

Health and safety – crucial for teachers dealing with new techniques and materials – is referenced throughout the book (marked with a marginal symbol), with detailed recommendations in the appendix.

The National Curriculum asks teachers to create 'activities that bring together requirements from both the Knowledge and understanding and Investigating and making of art'. This book integrates Knowledge and understanding within the framework of different media, techniques and art elements. It helps teachers to avoid a series of one-off lessons on Knowledge and understanding unrelated to children's art production. Instead, teachers are shown how Knowledge and understanding is an integral part of an art programme ensuring progression of skills.

The sources of art work examples are the popular Ginn,[1] Shorewood,[2] Oliver & Boyd,[3] Philip Green Educational[4] and Goodwill reproduction series.[5] These are suggestions; the discussions and activities can be used as a bank of ideas for any pictures that are available in school.

[1] Ginn *Approaches to Art* discussion book (1992)
[2] Shorewood Fine Art Reproductions, 27 Glen Road, Sandy Hook, CT 06482 USA
[3] Oliver and Boyd, Longman House, Burnt Mill, Harlow, Essex, CM20 2JE
[4] Philip Green Educational Ltd, 112a Alcester Road, Studley, Warwickshire, B80 7NR
[5] Goodwill Art Service, Freepost, Didcot, Oxon, OX11 9BR

DRAWING

Main NC focus

PoS 8d
Children should be taught to experiment with (and develop control of [KS2]) tools and techniques for drawing

Introduction

Drawing is a very popular way of making visual images. Children begin to draw before they can talk, and adults who may feel they have no artistic skills often find pleasure in their own private drawings or doodles. Bruce Robertson in *You can draw* (1986) described drawing as 'a thought with a line round it'. Many primary children reveal more in their drawings than they do in their writing.

Teachers can offer children a wide variety of drawing materials, subjects and techniques to encourage them to communicate their ideas and imaginative visions effectively. This chapter includes:

- Strategies for drawing lessons (page 3) organising a drawing lesson (page 3); observing directly (page 4); using a sketchbook (page 6); expressing ideas (page 7); expressing feelings (page 8); making visual stories (page 9); making problem-solving drawings (page 11)

Figure 1.1
Elephant in the jungle, in wax crayon and paint wash.
Y2

- Drawing equipment and techniques (page 12)
drawing supports (page 12); pencils (page 13); coloured pencils (page 14); pen and ink (page 15); charcoal (page 18); chalks and soft pastels (page 20); wax crayons and oil pastels (page 21); scraperboard (page 23); wax scraffito (page 25)

PoS 9d
Respond to and compare different styles and traditions

Knowledge and understanding through drawing

It is good to begin each lesson by looking at an artist whose work is in the same medium that the children will be using. Artists sometimes draw with predominantly pure lines and sometimes with heavy areas of tone, or colour. Corot's drawing *Girl in Beret*, Shorewood 194DR, is linear in form, while Ruben's *Saint Magdelene*, Shorewood 117DR, is drawn with rich areas of tone.

DISCUSSING ARTISTS' DRAWINGS (Y1–Y6)

PoS 9e
Describe and express opinions about works of art

What is the first thing you notice about the drawing? What is the drawing showing us? Is the drawing in pencil, ink, charcoal, pastel or crayon? Are the lines heavy or soft? (Y1–Y6).

Are the lines delicate or strong? Was it an exploratory drawing, a direct observational drawing or an imaginative drawing? What drawing materials have been used and how has this influenced the work? Is there any tonal variation? (Y3–Y6).

Look at the same artist's drawing several times throughout the year (Y5–Y6).

ACTIVITY

PoS 7e
Use knowledge of artists'
work

1 a) Ask children to study carefully a drawing that has many different types of lines. Then ask the children to draw lines using the ideas from the drawing or make 'follow-my-leader lines' (Y1–Y6). Examples are:

- Draw a long, light, twisted line; a short, straight line. Draw it again and again. Make a line hop, skip and jump; make it jump and then fall down. Draw a line quickly, then slowly; make as many circles as you like; change the circles by adding lines.
The aim of this activity is not to try to produce lines identical to those in the original drawing. It gives an idea of the variety of lines that can be drawn and children should feel free to develop their lines as they wish (Y1–Y2).

b) Ask children to make a 'fluid' line using a smooth constant pressure on their pencil; an uneven line using short, quick strokes; a line that varies in thickness and tone by changing the pressure on their pencil; make a thick line and vary its tone by using the side of the lead and then altering the pressure (Y3–Y6).

2 Use portraits by Holbein as references for drawing a head. Either copy the whole drawing, or just the face, and add modern clothes and hair style (Y5–Y6).

Ages and stages

Lowenfeld's theory about the stages through which children's drawings develop is based on age. He also recognised that there could be a significant overlap at the 'changeover' ages.

1 The first stage of *scribbling* spans ages two to four years.

2 The *pre-schematic* stage takes place between ages four to seven years. Children begin to develop their scribbles into symbolic images (without much concern for realism). Each person or object in the drawing occupies its own space, and everything the child has noticed about the person or object is in the image. Aspects important to the child are exaggerated in size.

3 The *schematic* stage takes place between ages seven to nine years when children have developed their symbols and continue to reproduce them as a formula for each image.

4 The stage *dawning realism* takes place between ages nine to 11 years when children start trying to make their images more realistic.

5 The final stage of *pseudo-naturalism* takes place between ages 11 to 13 when children concentrate on achieving realism.

Most teachers find from personal experience that many children do not fall completely into any one of these five categories. Children in Y1 may incorporate elements of well-observed realism in a schematic drawing, and Y6 children may continue to include schematic elements, particularly in imaginative drawings.

Despite these reservations, Lowenfeld's stages are useful for reminding us of the importance of symbolism in children's work at KS1 and KS2. Children need the opportunity to practise, modify and increase the range of their visual symbols so that they can eventually go beyond convention and produce personal visual images.

Figure 1.2
In this pencil drawing of a baby in a pram by a child in reception, parts are realistic and parts are schematic. The rabbit is beautifully observed and the sides of the pram are recorded with the correct perspective and shape; the rest of the drawing is schematic.

Strategies for drawing lessons

Organising a drawing lesson

If the main focus of a drawing lesson is to teach the techniques of a particular drawing medium such as charcoal, use only charcoal in the lesson to ensure the new techniques will be tried and reinforced. If the focus is on an art element such as texture, provide a choice of materials.

USING PRACTICE PAPER

Give children the opportunity to experiment in drawing lines, tones and textures at the start of a lesson. If possible, use off-cuts of the same quality paper as for the drawings, since cheaper paper will not react in the same way. Which lines and shapes would be good for showing smooth or rough textures? How can they control the depth of colour and the width of a line? During the lesson, refer back to their experimental lines and shapes.

USING PRACTICE PAPER

At the end of a lesson, ask the children to evaluate the techniques that they had used successfully, and those in which they needed more practice.

PLANNING SHAPES AND SPACES

PoS 2c
Design and make images and artefacts

Children at KS1 can usually make fluent and attractive shapes that 'grow' on the paper.

Most children at KS2 lose this intuitive skill. They often find it useful to plan the position of shapes and spaces with a quick, light pencil sketch. This helps to avoid cramped shapes and chopped-off sections.

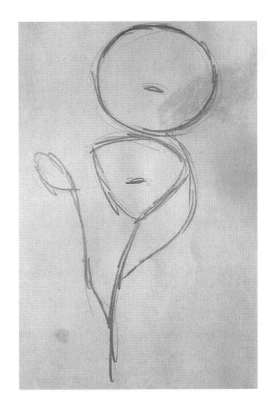

A very soft-leaded pencil (2B), used with light pressure and relaxed grip, is the best tool for sketching a drawing plan. Encourage children to construct their plans from shapes rather than single outlines. Squinting helps children to see main shapes in objects by reducing the clarity of detail. Children at the end of KS2 should be encouraged to look for shapes between shapes.

Once a simple plan has been sketched quickly, encourage the children to use their pencil lines as a guide only. Over-elaborate plans can result in a great deal of erasing which ruins the surface of the paper. Over-detailed plans made with pencil also do not take into consideration the special qualities of drawing in inks, pastels or chalks.

Figure 1.3
Pencil sketch of the main shapes for an ink drawing of flowers. Y5

Limiting the initial pencil sketching to five or ten minutes helps children to concentrate on the main structure (although it is important to be flexible). Complex drawings always need to be planned in more detail, and sometimes children become so absorbed in their initial pencil drawing, they are reluctant to progress to pen or pastels. In this case, just accept that the ink or pastel drawing has become a pencil drawing.

ACTIVITY

1 Use dots to draw a vertical or horizontal line freehand (Y5–Y6). (Drawing with a ruler gives a 'dead' feeling.) Make a dot where the line will end. Look along the edge of the paper and make another dot where the line begins. Join up the dots freehand. For lines over 12 cm in length, use more dots. This method also works for angles and for curves.

ACTIVITY **2** Emphasise an interesting shape drawn on dark-coloured paper by carefully cutting around the outline (Y5–Y6). Stick the shape on to light-coloured paper, and add textures in oils or soft pastels.

Observing directly

<u>KNOWLEDGE AND</u>
<u>UNDERSTANDING</u>

Dürer's drawings from direct observation are famous for their sensitive response to texture, mood and light. The fur on his *Young hare* (Shorewood 185DR) looks so real that children often try to feel the surface of the drawing. Dürer's *Praying hands* (Shorewood 163DR) is another highly textured drawing.

ACTIVITY

PoS 7e
Use knowledge of artists'
work

1 Bring in a pet that has fur (a rabbit, guinea-pig, etc.) so that children can try drawing the texture of fur in the style of Dürer (Y1–Y6).

2 Ask an old person to pose so that children can draw one of their hands (Y5–Y6). Some children might need to draw softly around their own hands to obtain a rough shape before beginning the textures.

<u>AGES AND STAGES</u>

PoS 2b
Record observations

Figure 1.4
Puppy, in charcoal. Y1

Looking at an object with the teacher and enjoying its features is an important start for every direct observation lesson. Although schematic images predominate at KS1, children still enjoy drawing from direct observation if they are interested in the subject. At KS1 children generally have more confidence in their abilities in art than those at KS2, and will often feel at ease with quite difficult subjects. A class of Y1 children made some wonderful drawings of a wriggly puppy; a subject that most Y6 children would have felt nervous of tackling.

PoS 8f
Review and adapt the
work

Some children at KS2 feel so unsure of their abilities in art, they will ask their teacher to start the work or to do a difficult part of their drawing; all of which would further undermine their future self-confidence. Direct observation has the advantage of presenting an object to observe and discuss, so that the problem can be worked through together, without adult imposition or interference. Experimenting with lines and textures on spare paper, or planning the drawing with soft-pencil lines will all increase children's confidence.

<u>CHOOSING AN OBJECT</u>

PoS 4a and d
Investigate pattern and
texture . . . shape, form
and space

Choosing an object that relates to other areas of the curriculum helps to engage children's interest. Knowing about the structure and function of an object also helps to increase their confidence. Natural objects are easier to draw than made objects. The rigid symmetry and hard lines of many made objects makes it very obvious when a line is inaccurate. The shape and texture of a natural object is more forgiving.

It might be thought that simple, untextured objects would be easier for Y1 children to draw but usually the results are disappointing. The children will either complete the picture in a few seconds or create imagined decorative patterns to add interest to their drawing. Choosing unfamiliar objects, or objects with interesting shapes and textures, also helps children at KS2 to get away from schematic images.

Trees seen from the school playground make wonderful subjects. A weeping willow can be likened to someone in mourning, an oak to a strong wrestler and a pollarded willow to a witch. Encourage children at KS2 to show foliage as textured shapes, or areas of light and shade.

Observing rocks submerged in water in a glass container helps to bring the colours into sharp focus.

Animals are difficult to draw because they tend to move. Use a snail, caterpillar, beetle, tortoise or sleepy cat. Transfer fish to smaller glass containers, or use a fish from the fishmongers.

Small plastic farm animals or soft toy animals give children the chance to draw the form of an animal from many different viewpoints at their own leisure.

Other natural objects that make good subjects are: shells, coral, plants, leaves, flowers, fruit, vegetables and wood.

Made objects need to have interesting shapes and details – musical instruments, crushed drinks cans, soft travel bags.

ACTIVITY

1 Introduce a familiar, yet complex object, for example a bicycle (Y2–Y6). First ask children to draw the subject from memory. This increases the intensity of their observations when they are allowed to see the subject.

2 Try contour drawing (Y5–Y6). Contour drawing involves drawing at an extremely slow pace, keeping the drawing tool in contact with the paper at all times. There is no need to erase as adjustments can be made as the drawing develops slowly. The aim is to allow children to spend most of their time observing the object, instead of the drawing.

3 Ask the children to choose something in the room that they have not looked closely at before and draw it from more than one angle, using different drawing media (Y5–Y6).

CHOOSING GROUPS OF OBJECTS

PoS 8e
Experiment with visual elements

Collect a group of objects that are related – different types of fruit, toys, kitchen equipment, things from the tool shed, wood and leaves. Some of these things can be combined – a jug of flowers with fruit at its base – or make a deliberate contrast – a rusty can among flowers.

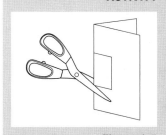

Figure 1.5
Making a simple viewfinder.

ACTIVITY

1 Use a viewfinder to isolate a section of a complicated subject, or still-life (Y4–Y6). Cut a rectangular hole roughly 1 cm by 1.5 cm in the centre of a piece of card. The viewfinder can be moved further away from the eye to frame a smaller area. The drawings often have a photographic quality.

2 Display a large still-life that includes several high objects such as a chair, an umbrella, a tall plant or a flag (Y5–Y6). Divide the piece of paper horizontally into four sections. Ask the children to make a drawing with ink in one section and oil pastel, charcoal and chalk in the other three. This is a dramatic way of exploring and comparing the different characteristics of each medium.

LOOKING AT OBJECTS

PoS 7b
Use resources to stimulate ideas

Children's first impulse is to explore objects by touching them. Examining the details of an object with a magnifying glass, turning it around to view it from all sides, is an invaluable way of getting children to observe closely.

The more detailed the discussion, the more detailed will be the work. If there are a limited number of objects, a group of children could examine them and describe to other groups what they feel and see. They could discuss the function or origin of the object and whether this can be predicted from its shape.

Once the objects have been examined thoroughly, they can be placed so that all the children have good viewing positions. Ideally, children should be able to see the object without moving their heads – being able to glance easily between their drawing and the object. During a drawing session encourage children to spend more time looking at the subject than looking at their paper.

DRAWING OBJECTS

Children need to be reminded to draw what they can see and not what they think they can see, or would like to see. Observing the shape of the spaces in between the objects – negative spaces – will help children at the end of KS2 to check the accuracy of their sketches.

DRAWING LANDSCAPES

Drawing outdoors needs careful organisation. Rest several sheets of paper on a thick piece of card or Plasticine board. Use a bulldog clip to anchor the paper at the top edge, and an elastic band across the bottom edge to stop the paper from flapping in the wind. Alternatively, plastic clipboards are very light to carry.

ACTIVITY

PoS 7c
Work on a variety of scales

1   Use a large scale with children who have a cramped style of painting or drawing. Draw with charcoal, chalk, oil pastel or a very soft-leaded (3B) pencil on a large piece of paper taped to an easel, or the wall. Ask the children to work standing up, with their feet firmly planted on the floor, so they can make sweeping movements from the shoulder.

Small objects such as screws, flowers, pencil sharpeners and twigs look imposing on this scale.

2   Usually, large objects are drawn on a large scale. Try reversing this and portray large objects such as a tree or a landscape on a small scale. Small, delicate pictures should be drawn with a 'loose' style. Instead of working from the shoulder, try to produce a fluid drawing action, using the wrist.

Using a sketchbook

KNOWLEDGE AND UNDERSTANDING

Artists often make multiple sketches before deciding on a final design or position (Watteau *Three negro boys*, Shorewood 207DR; Picasso *Mother and child*, Shorewood 128DR). They also use sketches to record and explore ideas (Ingres *Iliad study*, Shorewood 150DR). Children often find it reassuring to look at the incomplete doodles that filled Gauguin's sketchbook, (1884–1888, The Louvre, Paris).

AGES AND STAGES

KS2 PoS 8b
Pupils should be taught to record observations and ideas, and collect visual evidence and information, using a sketchbook

A sketchbook is a vital piece of equipment at KS2 and also proves very useful for children in Y2. It provides a visual record of a child's interest in particular images and acts as a reference point for future artwork. Children often want to depict a tree, for example, in their pictures. Without a reference, many will unthinkingly draw a schematic image – a circle-on-a-stick. If they have sketched different trees outdoors and recorded them in their sketchbooks, they can then refer to this collection of different sizes and shapes.

Assure children that their sketchbook is a private record so the drawings need not be perfect or complete.

This is a good way of encouraging children to take risks with their drawings; to try difficult subjects and experimental techniques.

EQUIPMENT

Tip!
Make small postcard-sized sketches; these are less intimidating to produce and can yield an enormous amount of information. Try drawing with the drawing tool continuously on the paper. This keeps the drawing moving and helps children to gain confidence in sketching quickly.

SKETCHBOOK
A sketchbook should have a strong back and secure binding. Light cartridge paper is a good choice of paper. It is useful to have a size that fits into a school bag for school trips. Alternatively, several sheets of paper can be stapled to form a small sketchbook.

PENCIL SHARPENERS
Pencil sharpeners can be placed in small, zip-lock plastic bags for sketching outdoors so that shavings can fall directly into the bags.

DRAWING TOOLS
Soft-leaded pencils are ideal for sketching – they are easy to pack and can produce both fine lines and subtle areas of tone. Coloured pencils or oil pastels can be used for colouring and are waterproof in case of rain.

Felt-tip pens have the problem of drying out and will bleed if they become wet. Chalk and charcoal are superb for sketching but can be very messy on long trips. Soft pastels are too expensive to risk losing.

ACTIVITY

Tip!

Before going on a sketching trip, practise in the classroom drawing animals that are likely to be seen, using photographs or artists' drawings. This will build-up children's knowledge of how each animal is structured before they have to deal with the difficulties of sketching animals in motion.

1 Encourage children to make sketches of different views of the same object. Sketch the foliage on branches, as well as the tree shape. Sketch groups of trees and observe how they overlap and grow together.

2 Buildings. Complex objects, such as a building, are best drawn individually so that children are not overwhelmed with detail. Make small-study drawings of interesting features, such as an arched doorway or a shuttered window. Children at KS2 can be reminded to keep the vertical lines parallel with the sides of the paper.

3 People. Choose people who are waiting or resting. Encourage children to be satisfied with a few, quick lines.

4 Animals. Animals are a favourite subject for children's drawings. Unfortunately, the animals rarely remain still long enough for a detailed study to be made. Encourage children to spend most of their time looking, and then to make a quick sketch of the whole animal, before adding details and textures. Just a brief sketch of the shape is enough.

PoS 2a
Express ideas and feelings

Expressing ideas through illustration

Illustrative drawings show people, objects or events from fictional and factual narratives. An illustration can contain an enormous amount of information and is just as valid a means of communication as writing. Learning about this is a very important aspect of visual literacy.

<u>KNOWLEDGE AND</u>
<u>UNDERSTANDING</u>

PoS 7f
Respond to and evaluate art

Illustrators such as Edward Ardizzone (*Stig of the Dump*) and Thomas Henry (the *Just William* books) were chosen by authors because their visual images reflect accurately the ideas and atmosphere of the text narrative. Illustrators such as Beatrix Potter, Maurice Sendak, Shirley Hughes and Raymond Briggs wrote the narrative text as well as drawing their own illustrations.

Children could show their favourite illustrations and talk about why they like them.

ACTIVITY

PoS 7e
Use knowledge of artists' work

1 Look at Pienowski's silhouette drawings and use the same style to illustrate a different story (Y3–Y6).

2 Compare the heroic style of the war illustrators of the Soviet Union with the more realistic British official artists of the Second World War (Y5–Y6). Henry Moore (*Shelter scene*, Goodwill 2(20)); Laura Knight (*The balloon site, Coventry*, Goodwill 1(6)), Bernard Meninsky and Edward Ardizzone are examples. Cut out a headline from a newspaper and illustrate it as propaganda and also in a realistic style.

<u>AGES AND STAGES</u>

Most children at KS1 need little outside stimulus to illustrate exciting incidents in their lives. If children do need help in thinking of a subject, it is best to suggest a subject that involves them directly. 'How about drawing a picture of you playing outside your house?' instead of 'How about drawing a picture of a house?'

PoS 8c
Develop a range of source material

Children at KS2 need more help. They often benefit from looking at previous sketches from their sketchbook or from using direct observation. Reference books are useful for information on the structure and textures of an object, and for ideas on composition and lighting; but encourage children to modify and adapt the images so that their drawings benefit from their own creative input. A city skyline could incorporate building shapes from many different photographs.

Figure 1.6
'I am playing outside my house', in felt-tip pen. Y1

ACTIVITY

1 Illustrate an incident in a book. Choose a passage that has drama and is central to the book's narrative (Y1–Y6). (Avoid showing children the storybook pictures immediately before their own drawings.) Suggest that they concentrate on a particular event or emotion and illustrate it clearly and vividly.

2 Use a drawing to frame a piece of writing (Y3–Y6). Skeletons dancing around information about the body; a dragon coiled around a fairy story are examples.

PoS 7b
Use resources to stimulate ideas

3 Illustrate aspects of history, geography or science (Y3–Y6).

• Cut out the photograph of a contemporary face and add an historical costume.

• Make a word picture (Y4–Y6). Make a line drawing of a subject in very faint pencil.
Keep the drawing very simple in shape and outline. Collect together words that are related to the subject. Check the spellings are correct as these words may be repeated many times in the drawing. Practically any subject lends itself to this type of drawing: animals, people, machines, buildings, landscapes. Use ink to write out the words along the lines. When the ink has dried, erase the pencilled guidelines.

Figure 1.7
A 'word face', words written in pen on pencil guidelines. Y4

 Fully integrate drawings into text by using a special computer program: Pagelink and PaintSpa for KS1 and Revelation 2 DrawPen for KS2.

PoS 2a
Express ideas and feelings

Expressing feelings

<u>**KNOWLEDGE AND UNDERSTANDING**</u>

PoS 9b
Recognise visual elements

Artists use different qualities of line to express emotion in their imaginative drawings. The haughtiness of the rider is reflected in the proud curves of the drawing in Rouault's *Equestrienne*, Shorewood 197DR. Kollwitz's *Germany's children are hungry* uses curved, submissive lines, Goodwill 5/44.

<u>**AGES AND STAGES**</u>

Fantasy is the prime motivator for much of children's drawings at KS1. Children are willing to start a picture not knowing how it will end, and are guided by their reactions to the images as they produce them.

Vocabulary to help children describe the visual aspect of their work could include: dark, light, gloomy, bright, strong, weak, faint, bold, soft, hard, flowing, free, confident, broken, scribbled, tight, sweeping.

At KS2, children express their feelings towards the world in their drawings with less verve and confidence. Children at this stage often benefit from radically new approaches to help them release images that express feelings – the use of abstract line, shape or colour; and the use of music, dance or visual images as a stimulus for ideas.

At KS2, descriptive vocabulary could include: meandering, angular, fluent, delicate, hesitant, cramped.

<u>**EXPLORING LINES AND SHAPES**</u>

PoS 4c
Images are made using line and tone

Drawings that express feelings are very dependent on the quality of lines. Lines can jerk in violent movements, soothe with flowing shapes, lay down restfully, stand up rigidly. Increasing the range of lines that children can draw will increase the control they have over the images they want to express in their drawings.

ACTIVITY

1   In dance lessons children often explore with their bodies the lines and shapes that convey emotions, for example, sharp, jagged, angry shapes contrasting with smooth, flowing, relaxed lines. These ideas can be successfully linked to visual imagery in art (Y1–Y6).

2   Drawing lines and colours (Y3–Y6). Make dark, light, heavy, thin, jagged and parallel lines. Make colour patches in a sketchbook of colour mixes that convey specific emotions.

• Ask children to grit their teeth and think aggressive thoughts while they make an angular, jagged line. Listen to lyrical music while making flowing, fluent lines. Use these lines to make marks and shapes that express moods and feelings. Can they make an 'angry' shape, a 'lazy' line, a 'tight' texture?

Figure 1.8
The sharp zig-zags of the lightening and the chaotic lines of the water make this a violent and exciting drawing. Dragon in chalks. Y3

• Draw or paint a hurricane using twisting, whirling lines.

3   Listen to sounds such as a dripping tap, the clatter of a sewing machine and the tap of footsteps (Y5–Y6). Make lines, textures and shapes that represent these sounds.

PoS 2c
Design and make images and artefacts

Making visual stories

Visual stories challenge children to make simple, economical drawings to show an event or sequence of events as clearly as possible.

<u>KNOWLEDGE AND UNDERSTANDING</u>

PoS 9c
Relate art to its time and place of origin

Children enjoy looking at works of art that tell a story. The Ancient Greeks used visual images on the sides of their vases to record the deeds of their Gods and heroes. Goodwill (series 7, set 70) have a set of artists' works that show visual stories.

Comic-strip images fascinated Pop artist Roy Lichtenstein (*Whaam!*, Goodwill 3(22)) and are a great source of interest to children. Children who are interested in making moving pictorial sequences could look at nineteenth century multiple-exposure film (Thomas Eakins *Man walking*, 1885). Duchamp developed this idea in *Nude descending a staircase no. 2*, Shorewood 1282; Boccioni in *Unique forms of continuity in space*, Goodwill 3(22) and Balla in *The car has passed*, Goodwill 2(11).

ACTIVITY

PoS 7e
Use knowledge of artists' work

1   Ask children for their interpretations of an artist's picture before giving any background information (Y1–Y6). It is valuable for children to see that different interpretations can be made of the same images.

2   Collect cartoons and photographs of political figures from newspapers. Match photographs to cartoons, and see which features the cartoonist has chosen to exaggerate (Y3–Y6).

<u>AGES AND STAGES</u>

Visual stories challenge children at KS1 to work in a logical time sequence and need to be kept quite brief. (A moving object is particularly difficult to depict. It involves analysing a movement and breaking it down into separate stages and should not be tried until KS2.) By Y6, children can make quite long sequences if the drawings are kept very simple.

The cartoon characters that appear in children's drawings at KS2 are often direct imitations of commercially drawn cartoons. Some children practise and practise these to a state of perfection and naturally feel very proud of their competence. These children may need careful weaning from direct imitation so that they can create original and highly individual cartoon characters.

MAKING A SEQUENCE

ACTIVITY

PoS 4d
Investigate shape, form and space

1 Create a visual diary (Y1–Y2). Every day record something that has happened at home or at school. Use a variety of materials.

2 Make story cards (Y1–Y2). Use four or five card rectangles (about the size of playing cards) to tell a simple story. Write a word or short sentence, with an illustration, on each card. Keep the cards together with an elastic band. Ask children to exchange cards and arrange them in order.

3 Make a sequence of cartoon drawings to form a story without words (Y5–Y6). Subjects could include a burglar in a house, an argument, a journey. If the school has access to a single-frame cine-camera, make an animated cartoon using the children's drawings.

MAKING A SEQUENCE OF CONTINUOUS MOVEMENT

ACTIVITY

1 Trace hand actions in sequence on a large piece of paper (Y3–Y6). Draw around the hand with a felt-tip pen as it moves in stages across the paper, opening or closing the fingers. Slightly overlap the images and record a gradually clenching fist or a hand catching a ball.

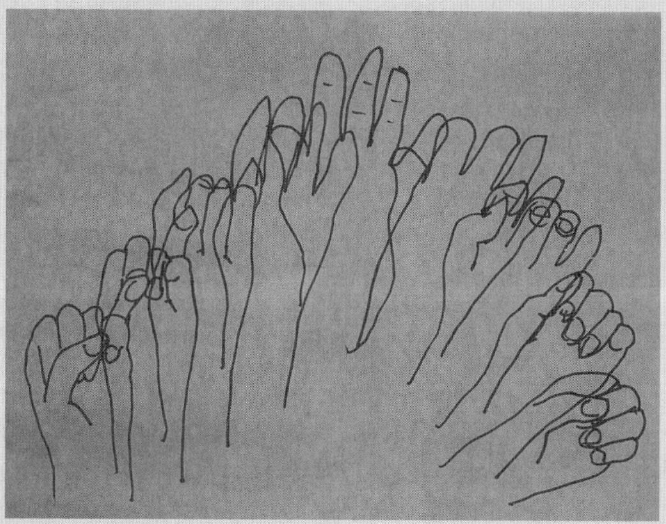

Figure 1.9
A gradually closing fist using felt-tip pens. Y3

2 Draw six frames getting closer and closer to an object (Y3–Y6). Use children's knowledge of a creature's habitat to zoom in from a general view, for example from a tree to eggs in a bird's nest.

VISUAL JOKES

ACTIVITY

PoS 2a
Express ideas and feelings

1 Draw a literal interpretation of a well-known saying, for example, raining cats and dogs, time flies, time drags.

2 Find words with another word inside them and draw an appropriate picture. 'Ant' is hidden in all these words: plant, pendant, phantom, anti-war, anti-septic, antique, elephant.

Figure 1.10
A plant, in ink. Y4

CREATING A CARTOON CHARACTER

ACTIVITY

1 Practise drawing different eyes and mouths to show expressions of anger, fear, disdain, joy, determination, surprise (Y4–Y6).

2 Exaggerate the personality of a person in a magazine by giving them bulging eyes or an outrageous moustache (Y4–Y6). Practise a variety of noses and hair styles. Draw arms and hands to make exaggerated gestures.

3 Look carefully at a photograph or drawing of a figure or animal (Y5–Y6). Draw an image, remove the original and then draw it again from memory.

Simplify the structure so that it can be drawn in basic geometric shapes. Hands, for example, are usually reduced to a mitten shape, or a thumb and two or three fingers. A frog could be reduced to a ball with legs, and two bulging eyes. Give it human characteristics such as sitting down or eating an icecream cone.

 Use a computer program to produce simplified drawings that can be repeated easily. ArtSchool for KS1 and Revelation2 for KS2 SmArtoons. *Cartoon* by Newman College. *Kid Pix* ESM ES320.

PoS 2c
Design and make creative images and artefacts

Making problem-solving drawings

Drawing is a way of thinking. We doodle before making decisions because drawing makes us ask questions and helps us to record answers. Encourage children to share ideas and make modifications.

KNOWLEDGE AND UNDERSTANDING

PoS 5b
Examine styles from past and present

The Ancient Greeks and the Romans used drawings to work out and record engineering problems. The advent of the Renaissance and the Industrial Revolution created an even greater demand for clear, explanatory drawings. Leonardo da Vinci's drawings of his inventions make good examples of this type of drawing.

Drawing also forms the basic tool for artists who wish to work out a problem in their work. It may be a composition for a painting, tapestry or print (da Vinci *Head of a woman*, Shorewood 145DR; Picasso *Mother and child*, Shorewood 128DR). It is interesting that artists used drawing primarily for analysing problems before beginning a painting.

The Heath Robinson drawings of the 1930s and '40s are created from an hilarious marriage of imagination and logic (Robinson *The automatic egg rationer*, Oliver and Boyd Card B24).

AGES AND STAGES

In general children at KS1 do not have enough knowledge about the quality of materials to use drawing for planning out work in other media. At this stage, it is much more important that they work out their ideas at a practical level. They do, however, enjoy making drawings of fantasy machines.

At KS2, children will gradually increase their use of drawing for exploring ideas for other art materials, as they learn these materials' strengths and limitations. Explanatory drawings will also be used to record their work in science, and they continue to enjoy the inventive logic of complex fantasy machines.

Figure 1.11
Mars Bar machine, in ink.
Y2

WILD AND WONDERFUL
TECHNOLOGICAL DESIGNS

These are some suggestions for drawings in the tradition of Heath Robinson:

- the ultimate Swiss army knife
- multi-functional school desk
- lazy cat mouse-trap
- personalised hang-glider
- sweet-making machine
- nappy-changing machine
- bicycle that protects the rider from the rain
- car that minimises pollution in the streets
- vehicle that will fly as well as travel on land and sea
- vehicle that will take you to the centre of the Earth
- machine to wake you up in the morning.

Drawing equipment and techniques

PoS 8d
Experiment with tools and
develop techniques

Styles of drawing are strongly influenced by the medium that is used. The broad sweeps of colour and dramatic use of tone from soft pastels and oil pastels can give a drawing an almost painted quality; drawings in chalk and charcoal have rich tonal variations; while pencil, ink or scraperboard drawings may rely solely on line.

Drawing supports

AGES AND STAGES

PoS 4d
Investigate shape, form
and space

Children at KS1 enjoy drawing in sand, on walls and on pavements as well as on more conventional paper. It is sometimes thought that children at this stage lack the fine motor skills to make small drawings, but children usually come to school after several years of drawing experience. All ages need opportunities to work on different scales.

Children at KS2 generally have a less sure way of placing their drawing on the paper. Large pieces of paper are useful for children who find it difficult to locate their drawings in the centre – the paper can be trimmed down later. If children's drawings are cramped, a pavement art lesson in the school playground often 'loosens' their style. A photograph could record the work.

PAPER

Very slightly rough paper is the best surface for the majority of drawings. Cartridge paper is ideal. The more texture or 'tooth' on the surface, the more layers of colour can be applied under heavy pressure. A light pressure on textured paper gives a grainy effect.

Most children prefer white paper for drawing but try coloured sugar paper with stronger-coloured drawing media, such as oil pastels and soft pastels; the background can be treated as one of the colours of the drawing.

PAPER SIZE
Paper is sold in standard sizes. The 'A' standard is the one that is used most commonly. 'A0' is the largest size, and each size is half the size of the previous sheet.

A0: 84.1 × 118.9 cm	A4: 21.0 × 29.7 cm (drawing-pad size)
A1: 59.4 × 84.1 cm	A5: 14.8 × 21.0 cm
A2: 42.0 × 59.4 cm	A6: 10.5 × 14.8 cm
A3: 29.7 × 42.0 cm	A7: 7.4 × 10.5 cm

ERASERS

Too much erasing will ruin the paper surface, causing ink to bleed and preventing colours from building up in chalks, crayons and pastels. Use soft rubbers with the minimum of pressure.

Pencils

Pencil is the medium perhaps most closely associated with drawing. Surprisingly, the pencil is a comparatively recent drawing tool. In 1564, a type of carbon called graphite was discovered in Borrowdale, in the Lake District. At first it was mistaken for lead but it was later mined as a drawing tool. As graphite was so expensive, it was mixed with clay and, later still, encased in a sheath of wood.

KNOWLEDGE AND UNDERSTANDING

Artists use pencil as a 'thinking' tool – it is easy to carry in the pocket and is always ready for trying out ideas. Pencil with its soft, subtle shading is also a favourite medium for portrait drawings. Ingres (1780–1867) is famous for his pencil portraits. Reproductions of pencil drawings are not easy to find in teachers' art resource packs although Goodwill do an excellent example (Escher *Drawing hands*, Goodwill 3(28)). Fortunately conte crayon drawings use very similar techniques (Velazquez *Portrait of a girl*, Shorewood 519DR; Quast *Four fools*, Goodwill 2(13)).

AGES AND STAGES

A pencil is one of the first drawing tools that children use but they will still need time to explore its potential. Soft, medium and hard pencil grades can be introduced as early as Y1. Children will make mostly linear pencil drawings at KS1 and they could start including some areas of tone early in KS2.

Figure 1.12
Holding a pencil correctly.
a) sketching position;
b) detail position; c) grip for
broad strokes.

Teachers of children at KS1 will want to make sure that the orthodox way of holding a pencil is well established before they introduce any variations. At KS2, the sketching position and the detail position can be both be introduced gradually.

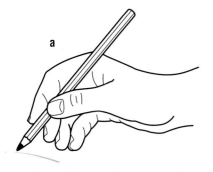 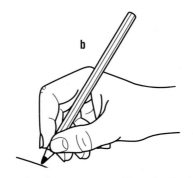 

As children aim for more realism in their drawings at KS2, erasers tend to be used with great enthusiasm. Unfortunately, this can ruin the surface of the paper and erase useful lines along with superfluous ones. Encourage children to use soft, exploratory pencil marks that can be left as an integral part of the drawing, or erased when the drawing has been completed.

CHOOSING PENCILS

PENCIL GRADES
The higher the clay content of the lead, the harder the pencil grade. Good quality pencils are marked with a grade. This is important information so ask children to sharpen a pencil at the opposite end to the grade letter.

- ■ B: soft
- ■ H: hard
- ■ HB: between H and B.

The higher the number before the letter, the more extreme the degree of hardness or softness. 8B is the softest and 10H is the hardest.

A good range for primary school children would be grades 2H, HB, 2B and 6B.

THE PENCIL SHAFT
Hexagonal pencils do not roll off tables easily. They also give a good grip which is useful when shading with the side of the pencil. Wedge-shaped pencils are useful for shading large areas of paper but are difficult to use for general drawing.

DRAWING TECHNIQUES WITH PENCILS

ACTIVITY

PoS 4c
Images are made with line and tone

1 **Experiment with different pencil grades (Y1–Y6).**

- **See if children can tell the difference between the grades by scribbling with different pencils on scraps of paper (Y1–Y4).**
- **Use different grades of pencil in the same drawing – the harder one for distant objects, and the softer one for the foreground (Y5–Y6).**

2 **Use tone to indicate the colour of an object (Y5–Y6). It is surprising how much information about colour can be given by the use of different tones of black. Purple would be a dark tone, red would be a medium tone and yellow would be a light tone of black.**

3 **Use aqua-pencils for subtle tones. These look like ordinary pencils but are water soluable. (Y5–Y6).**

- **Create both lines and areas of shading. Dip a brush in water and use it to soften the lines and produce areas of different tones on shaded areas.**
- **If the shading does not give enough depth of tone, scribble some lines on a scrap of paper. Pick up the dense tone with a wet brush from the scrap of paper and apply it to the drawing.**

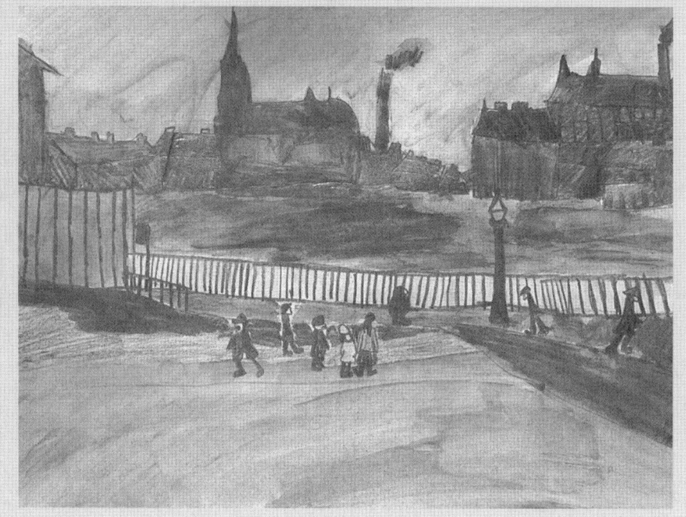

Figure 1.13
Lowry-style drawing, in aqua-pencil. Details were emphasised after the drawing was dry, in pencil. Y6

PoS 4b
Colour is applied and experienced

Coloured pencils

The colours in coloured pencils mix easily, avoiding the need to buy large sets of colours; although different shades of grey are very useful for showing tone. Soft grades are more versatile than hard grades. Pencil crayons can be used to add detail to gouache paintings after the paint has dried.

KNOWLEDGE AND UNDERSTANDING

PoS 9d
Respond to and compare different styles and traditions

David Hockney draws using coloured pencils. His *Marinka nude* and *Study for two vases* in the Louvre have delicate areas of shading in addition to areas of dense, vibrant colour.

DRAWING TECHNIQUES WITH COLOURED PENCILS

PoS 8d
Experiment with tools and develop techniques

Layering colours

A more lively and interesting drawing can be produced using layered colours rather than colours from the packet. Yellow and red produce orange; blue and yellow make green. Depth of colour can be controlled by pressure on the pencil tip. A third colour could be added to create other colour layers.

Create shading

Layering deeper depths of the same colour, or overlayering with different greys creates interesting shading. On a large drawing, lay down layers of colour with a continuous scribbling action. Wide spaces between the scribbles will lighten the colour tone.

ACTIVITY

1 Use aqua-pencils and soften and blend colours with a damp brush (Y2–Y6).

2 Mix colours by cross-hatching one colour over another (Y5–Y6). Lay down a colour in one direction. Then layer a different colour on top in the opposite direction. Vary the spaces between the lines to get different intensities of colour.

3 Find the easiest direction for a pencil stroke by practising on a piece of scrap paper (Y5–Y6). Try to keep this direction when blocking in areas of colour. Downward strokes give the impression of smooth surfaces.

Pen and ink

Ink drawings vary from fine-lined delicate drawings, to bold drawings with wide, sweeping lines; depending on the tool employed.

Many teachers are wary of spills involving indelible ink, especially at KS1, but with a little planning this risk can be minimised. If ink drawings still seem too messy, there are pens available that are already loaded with ink – ball-point pens, felt-tip pens and marker pens.

KNOWLEDGE AND UNDERSTANDING

PoS 5c
Include work from a variety of cultures

The Chinese have used ink for both writing and drawing and have raised each one to a fine art form (T'Ang *Return of Duke Wen*, Shorewood 110DR; Shunsho *Cat licking its paw*, Ginn 7). The smooth lines of brush and ink are also used by European artists (Kandinsky *Lyric – man on horse*, Shorewood 515).

Van Gogh's ink drawings are full of textural interest (Van Gogh *View from the wheat fields*, Ginn 14); Gaudier-Brzeska's *Cat*, Ginn 6, is very linear in design; while Beardsley's ink drawings exploit the drama of large dark areas and fine textures. See, for example, Beardsley (1904) *Design for the title page of 'The Yellow Book' in 'Under the hill'* (Paddington Press, UK).

ACTIVITY

PoS 7e
Use knowledge of artists'

1 Use coloured chalk to make a drawing and then add lines and details in ink of the same colour, in the style of da Vinci (Y5–Y6).

2 Use a traditional feather, or reed quill, after looking at the marks made by Van Gogh (Y5–Y6). Quills can be bought at art specialist shops. Feather quills can be made from large, naturally discarded feathers (not plucked); feathers from crows are the best. An adult will need to slice across the feather tip with a craft knife, remove some of the soft centre and cut a small slit up the shaft.

• Divide a sketchbook page into small squares and fill the squares with texture marks from Van Gogh's drawings (Y5–Y6). Use this as a reference for future work.

3 After examining drawings by Beardsley make linear drawings with highly textured areas and areas of pure black (Y5–Y6).

AGES AND STAGES

Children at KS1 make linear drawings; these are particularly suited to ink. Tone is very difficult to achieve with ink and most children will need to wait until the end of KS2 before they try hatching techniques.

Children at all stages need time to experiment with drawing tools, especially dip-pens. Y1 children could spend time practising different marks, and then overlay washes with vivid sweeps of coloured inks.

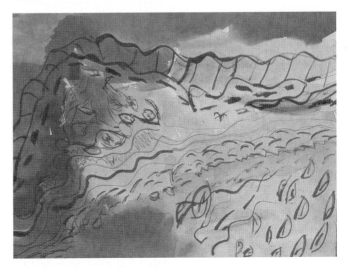

Figure 1.14
Indian-ink patterns, with a coloured ink wash. Y1

Most children at KS1 will need a ready-mixed wash, as it is very easy to ruin a delicate line drawing with colour that is too heavy. An ink drawing involves a bold commitment because the line cannot be altered. This teaches children to observe carefully and closely and to think about what they are drawing.

Children at KS2 who worry about the permanence of ink may need to plan out their drawing in detail in pencil. If their hands shake when they apply the ink, ask them to use small, broken pen strokes, going over the pencil lines slowly and carefully. Children in Y5 or Y6 may feel confident enough to plan out a direct observational drawing in ink. They should hold the pen very loosely and make small dots and lines on the paper.

GENERAL EQUIPMENT

Ink drawing is similar to pencil drawing in needing very little equipment – just a pen, ink and paper.

INKS

Waterproof ink can be bought in bottles for dip-pens, or ready-loaded in marker pens and ball-point pens. Inks can be bought in a wide variety of colours and give a dense line. Sepia ink gives a drawing an antique appearance. Waterproof inks can be used with paint washes to make a very attractive picture, with well-defined lines and delicate colours.

Water-soluble inks are available in bottles for dip-pens and ready-loaded in felt-tip and fibre-tip pens. Powdered coloured inks, such as Easibrush, can be mixed with a little water for brightly coloured drawings.

PAPER

Ink works best on good quality cartridge paper with a smooth surface. A soft or rough surface causes ink to spread unevenly, and pen nibs to catch on the surface. Thin paper will wrinkle as ink dries.

ORGANISATION

Use a very small volume of ink in a shallow, stable container, for example a painting palette. Position the palette correctly for left- and right-handed children. A left-handed child and a right-handed child can share a palette.

Shake excess ink from a traditional dip-pen on to a paper towel placed under the ink container. This helps to prevent drips of ink spoiling the drawing. There is no need to do this with bamboo or wooden skewers as they absorb excess ink.

INK BLOT

Small blots are inevitable, but sometimes a badly placed blot can ruin a drawing and needs to be removed. A small, dry blot can be hidden with Tipp-Ex. For a large, dry blot, scrape off the ink layer with the side of a craft knife. Blow off any black pieces of paper as the scraping progresses.

For a large wet blot, use the corner of a piece of blotting paper to soak up the centre. Then lay small, damp pieces of fresh blotting paper over the stain and apply pressure until all the ink has been absorbed. Use a damp brush to soak up the stain. Let the area dry and then use a soft eraser to remove what colour is left.

DIP-PEN

METAL NIB

This is the traditional artists' tool for ink drawings. Different sized nibs provide a variety of drawing lines. Downstrokes and strokes made with strong pressure produce thicker lines; side strokes or strokes made with light pressure produce thinner lines. Avoid smudging by working from the top of a page down.

FOUNTAIN PEN

Fountain pens draw a variety of textures and lines and make a good substitute for a dip-pen whilst drawing outdoors. Waterproof inks cannot be used as they block the pen. Use a loose, relaxed grip and always make practice strokes on a piece of paper before beginning a drawing.

IMPROVISED DIP-PEN

An excellent alternative to dip-pens is a wooden or bamboo kebab stick, meat skewer or tooth-pick. They are inexpensive and hold enough ink to produce a continuous long line. They can produce a variety of line widths without the bother of changing nibs. A thin line can be produced

Figure 1.15
Driftwood, using a kebab stick to make many different types of lines, in ink. Y5

from the tip, a slightly thicker one from the blunted tip and a thick line from the cut end. Snapping the middle section so that the wood frays gives a combed effect (excess ink should be blotted on newspaper). Children also enjoy experimenting with sticks found in the playground or garden.

ACTIVITY

*PoS 4a and b
Investigate pattern,
texture and colour*

*PoS 4b
Investigate colour*

1 Add details and textures to a large ink drawing with prints (Y1–Y6) (see Chapter 3). This avoids trying to create repeated detail with a pen.

2 Add colour to a drawing (Y1–Y6).

• If the drawing is in waterproof ink, add colour by washing over the drawing with thin watercolours. Erase pencil marks first, and keep the washes light.

• Add areas of poster paint if the drawing has strong, dark lines (Y5–Y6). Give careful thought to balance and composition so that a delicate drawing is not swamped by areas of heavy colour.

Figure 1.16
Beetle, in ink and watercolour. Y2

OTHER PENS

FELT-TIP PEN

Felt-tip pens are inexpensive, but they soon dry out if the tops are not replaced. Most children will have felt-tip pens in their pencil cases, so it is probably more cost-effective for a school to provide supplementary colours and emergency supplies for when children run short. A series of grey tones are very useful for showing tone in KS2. White patches should be left for highlight effects.

Colours can only be mixed by adding one on top of the other and the joining lines show quite distinctly. These lines can be softened using a damp brush.

MARKER PEN

Marker pens use spirit-based inks that dry almost instantly solving problems of smudging. Marker pens do not make drawings with subtlety of line or detail, but their bold lines can be used to make vivid and dramatic drawings. Turn the wedge-tipped pens to make thick and thin lines and use them for filling large areas.
At the end of KS2, children could try using a candle for lines and areas that should be left white, and diluted black paint for tonal variations.

CARE!

Work on a pad of newspaper to prevent the indelible ink marking the table top.

BALL-POINT PEN

Ball-point pens are suitable for sketching as they have a smooth and relatively constant ink flow. Sometimes the ink becomes blotchy and the variety of marks that can be made is limited. Drawings in ball-point pen can be combined with washes of ink because the lines do not bleed.

ACTIVITY

1 Make felt-tip pen drawings on greaseproof paper (Y1–Y6). This gives colour an attractive translucency. Mount the drawing on coloured paper, or tape it to a window.

2 Draw flowing lines (Y1–Y4).

- Make patterns to imitate Indian embroidery. Stick large, flat, round sequins on to coloured paper and surround them with linear patterns.

- Draw large and small dots on a piece of paper. Draw lines in felt-tip pens around the dots; avoid touching the dots.

Charcoal

KNOWLEDGE AND UNDERSTANDING

PoS 5b
Examine styles from past and present

Charcoal is the oldest form of drawing material. Drawings on cave walls in Altamira, Spain are made in charcoal and the size of many of the drawings – between one and a half and two metres wide – demonstrates how sympathetic charcoal is for drawing on a large scale (cave art *Two reindeer*, Shorewood 1741).

ACTIVITY

1 Make charcoal cave drawings on brown paper, or plaster of Paris 'cave walls' (Y1–Y6).

2 Map the size of an original cave drawing on a wall in the playground and draw on the same scale (Y5–Y6). Take a photograph of the drawing before washing the wall.

AGES AND STAGES

PoS 4c
Images are made using line and tone

Children at KS1 usually start a drawing in charcoal or chalk without any preliminary planning which encourages vigorous lines and shapes. Charcoal is particularly useful for introducing children at KS1 to sketching outdoors. The dense, thick marks make children focus on important details and textures, and encourage a bold style.

By Y3, most children want to do some planning before they start a charcoal drawing but they should limit this to a few broad lines – a detailed pencil plan stunts the drawing. The soft texture of charcoal makes it an ideal medium for children at KS2 who may be beginning to develop a cramped drawing style. Some children will take more risks if they draw on newspaper. Charcoal is also excellent for children at KS2 who wish to show tone in a drawing.

EQUIPMENT

Charcoal can vary in hardness. If possible, provide a variety of grades, but the softer ones are more versatile if only one type can be bought.

STICK CHARCOAL

Stick charcoal is generally packed in boxes of ten or 20, in either thick, medium or thin sticks. Thin sticks are best for line drawings and thick sticks for shading large areas. Long pieces will need to be broken into manageable sizes for children at KS1. Use the sides of small pieces for making thick lines.

COMPRESSED CHARCOAL

Compressed charcoal is produced in uniform sticks, similar to chalk sticks. It is made from powdered charcoal mixed with a binding agent. It is less fragile than stick charcoal but the marks are less easy to remove when a mistake has been made. Compressed charcoal can be bought in varying shades, from light grey to a black that is deeper than that of stick charcoal. This makes it very useful for shading, highlighting and showing aerial perspective, when shapes become paler and lighter in shading as they recede. It is difficult to make thin lines with compressed charcoal, so use them in addition to thin stick charcoals.

Figure 1.17
Industrial scene, in different colours of charcoal. Y5

CHARCOAL PENCIL

Sticks of compressed charcoal surrounded by wood or rolled paper are graded according to hardness. Because the sides cannot be used, a charcoal pencil is better for drawings requiring many linear patterns and textures, such as fur and feathers. It is ideal for sketchbook work outdoors as it leaves children's fingers relatively free from colour. Children who hate the messiness of charcoal sticks prefer charcoal pencils.

PAPER

Choose paper with a slight tooth. White shows the dramatic tones of charcoal. Coloured paper makes smudging less obvious and can add to the atmosphere of a drawing.

FIXATIVE

A fixative helps to stop smudging when a drawing is finished.

ERASERS

Charcoal is one of the easiest drawing marks to remove from paper. Use a soft tissue to remove any powder and then use a putty eraser or soft bread to erase any remaining marks.

DRAWING TECHNIQUES USING CHARCOAL

PoS 7c
Work on a variety of scales

Draw on a large scale if possible. Ideally, drawing paper should be pinned to an easel so that the child's arm can move freely from the shoulder. If all the class is drawing and paper has to be on the desks, ask the children to stand up to distance themselves from their paper.

Begin with soft pressure. This prevents initial over-use of charcoal and mistakes are easier to erase. Build up dark areas on the drawing by layering marks until the desired depth of colour is achieved. Avoid excessive pressure on charcoal sticks. They can break quite easily and spread over the drawing.

Children are often discouraged by the degree of smudging on their drawing when they use charcoal. Emphasise that charcoal has always been enjoyed by artists as an exploratory medium. Shadowy 'mistakes' can form an interesting background to a finished drawing. There are, however, several ways to minimise smudging.

■ Keep the steadying hand away from the drawing area to prevent it from smudging the lines.

■ Blow any excess dust away instead of wiping it away with a hand which will rub it into the paper.

■ Tape the drawing to a board and prop it up at an angle so that the dust can fall from the drawing.

ACTIVITY

1 Make direct observational drawings in charcoal (Y1–Y6). Mistakes are easily erased and this encourages children at KS2 to draw without any preparatory sketching in pencil. Decide on the position of the main shape, look carefully at the details and only then begin the drawing. This helps to keep the lines of the drawing confident and spirited instead of hesitant and weak.

2 Use a finger or a damp, fine brush to gently smudge and soften lines; a cotton bud can be used for small areas.

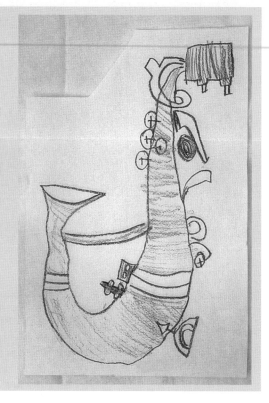

Figure 1.18
Saxaphone, in charcoal. Y2

Chalks and soft pastels

KNOWLEDGE AND UNDERSTANDING

PoS 9c
Relate art to its time and place of origin

Chalks and soft pastels are comparatively recent drawing tools. They were very popular with the French Impressionist artists Morisot, Renoir and Degas who used them to make soft flesh tones and areas of highly textured colour (Renoir *Female nude torso*, Shorewood 165DR). Mary Cassatt's *Mother and child* (Scholastic Publications, *Art and craft* magazine, April 1994) has dense areas of colour, whereas in *Berlin street scene*, Shorewood 549, Kirchner used scribbled lines.

AGES AND STAGES

PoS 4b
Investigate colour

Soft pastels come in an extensive range of soft pastel colours but, unfortunately, they are expensive. Their softness encourages a free and fluid drawing style so they are particularly valuable for children at the end of KS2. For younger children, a good compromise is to supplement the basic colours in the chalk box with a few soft pastels which can be blended to produce a wide variety of colours. Different shades of grey are also very useful for shading and highlighting. Whatever the age, encourage children to use the cheaper chalks for large areas of colour and the soft pastels for smaller details and colour blends.

EQUIPMENT

PoS 8d
Experiment with tools and develop techniques

CHALK
Although colours are limited, chalks are inexpensive and are readily available in schools. Chalk drawings look particularly effective on coloured sugar paper.

SOFT PASTEL
Colours are very pure but the sticks are very crumbly. Keep soft pastel sticks in shallow boxes, or trays lined with corrugated paper, to prevent them from rolling loose on the table top.

PASTEL PENCIL
Pastel pencils are soft pastels protected by a shaft of wood. They feel harder on the paper than pastel sticks and the sides cannot be used for sweeping areas of colour, but they are useful for detailed work and do not deteriorate as quickly as soft pastel sticks.

PAPER
Paper should have a rough surface to hold the chalk particles in place. Sugar paper is ideal.

DRAWING TECHNIQUES WITH CHALK AND SOFT PASTEL

It is better to build up areas of colour rather than fill in outline drawings. Light pressure at the beginning allows other colours to be overlayed without clogging the paper. Use a finger to gently smudge and soften lines and to blend colours. A cotton bud is useful for blending small areas.

Some smudging is inevitable but chalk marks are very easy to remove from paper. A soft tissue removes any powder and a putty eraser removes the remaining mark. Soft pastel marks are not as easy to remove as chalk. Use an old stiff brush to take away as much colour as possible and then rub the area with a putty eraser.

ACTIVITY

1 Draw with chalks on damp paper (Y1–Y6). Use a sponge to dampen the surface of the paper. Alternatively, dip the tips of the chalks in water and draw on to dry paper.

2 Practise blending with coloured chalks (Y2–Y6). Produce the background of a drawing first – an underwater scene, a sunset sky or desert sand dunes. Add details in darker chalk colours. If the background is very dark, add details in charcoal silhouette or collage.

Wax crayons and oil pastels

Wax crayons and oil pastels lack the fine lines of pencil and ink, and are not as free-flowing as soft pastels, charcoals and chalks. They do have the advantage of superb covering qualities – oil pastels, especially, make a thick and 'creamy' line. In addition they are cheap to buy, clean to use, easily held, do not smudge, are comparatively robust and do not have a sharp point. Both resist water which suggests whole new areas in drawing techniques.

KNOWLEDGE AND UNDERSTANDING

PoS 9c
Relate art to its time and place of origin

Artists began to mix fatty substances with powdered colour in the sixteenth century, but wax crayons as we know them were not produced until the early nineteenth century. They quickly became very popular for drawing as they produced smooth, rich colours that did not smudge, and lines that could be varied from a fine, delicate line to a bold, thick stroke (Mbuno *Machwili*, Goodwill *Contemporary African art*; Smith *Beech in his chair*, Goodwill 3(28); Kissmer *Silk*, Goodwill 3(28)).

AGES AND STAGES

PoS 4b
Investigate colour

Sorting the colours of crayons or pastels helps to make children at KS1 aware of the full range of hues and tones. Young children find it difficult to sustain the pressure needed for solid blocks of colour and should be encouraged to make linear drawings which can be washed over with inks or paints. Oil pastels are easier to use with resist pictures than wax crayons.

Children at KS2 should plan their colour layers so that they start with the lighter hues and finish with details in black. At the end of KS2, they could plan the positions of white areas and leave them without any colour (as long as the paper is white). By the end of KS2 children will be able to cover large areas of the paper with solid colour.

Figure 1.19
A tribute to Matisse, with strong blocks of colour, in oil pastel. Y5

EQUIPMENT

WAX CRAYON
Wax crayons are supplied in sticks of various thicknesses. The thicker crayons are easier for some children

in Y1 to grip and will not snap under the strong pressure needed for resist drawings (see page 23). However, they are frustrating to use when children want to draw details. The more subtle colour ranges come in the thinner crayon sticks.

Wax crayons do not blend easily. As they are relatively inexpensive, try to buy as many different hues and tones as possible to encourage subtle variations in colour. Crayola crayons come in a range of 64 colours.

SHARPENER

Sharpeners are specially produced for both thick and thin crayons. If drawings are to achieve any subtlety of line the crayons need to be sharpened. Make sure the small shavings are carefully folded up in a piece of newspaper and thrown away. If they fall off the table, they break into tiny pieces and stain the floor.

OIL PASTEL

These are supplied in sticks and in a wide variety of colours. They blend more easily than wax crayons but not as easily as soft chalks; so a fairly wide range of colours is needed.

A white oil-pastel stick helps to blend colours together by rubbing over the layered colours, although it leaves them looking lighter. Because white is used for blending colours, an extra supply would be very useful. Blender sticks look like transparent oil pastel sticks and blend colours without altering tone.

PAPER

White cartridge paper provides a background that brightens colours and provides enough tooth for the colour to adhere. Coloured sugar paper will give a more subdued effect.

DRAWING TECHNIQUES USING WAX CRAYONS

PoS 8d
Experiment with tools and develop techniques

Draw on a thick layer of newspaper. This gives a more even flow of colour. Drawings need to be large so that details can be achieved with the thick tip of the crayon – even sharpened crayons are too blunt for fine details. Vary the pressure on the crayon to achieve soft or rich tones of colour.

The colours mix to some extent on smooth paper if they are given sufficient pressure, but they do not blend easily. Dark wax crayons contain a higher proportion of wax that makes them softer. This means that they can be used over a light-coloured crayoned background. Use them for details and to liven-up areas of a drawing.

ACTIVITY Make a translucent wax crayon picture (Y2–Y6).

• Wipe cotton wool dipped in cooking oil over both sides of a wax crayon drawing. This looks best with drawings that cover the paper with a blanket of colour. The oil prevents the paper from being taped to the window, so glue it to a large sheet of polythene and then tape this to the window.

• For a large design such as a dragon, cut the body into sections and let several children colour in the textures and patterns on the body (Y3–Y6). Use a marker pen to number each piece. It is useful to have this guide, because the oil makes it impossible to distinguish the front from the back.

DRAWING TECHNIQUES USING OIL PASTELS

PoS 7c
Work on a variety of scales

Encourage children to stand up so that a whole arm movement can be used and not just the hand and wrist. Choose subjects that have large masses of colour rather than small details. Extensive areas of colour can be covered easily and quickly, so drawings can be on a larger scale than those done with wax crayon.

Mistakes cannot be erased, so begin the drawing by applying very light pressure. This makes it easy to cover up mistakes with more colour. Not all of the drawing needs to be filled with solid colour. Linear sections look very attractive and the colour of the paper can make a valuable contribution to the drawing. Use bold lines or delicate, softened lines.

1   Draw inside a masked area (Y3–Y6). Mask an area with a paper shape and spray ink over and around it with a diffuser, or splatter it with ink from a toothbrush. When the ink has dried, remove the mask and draw inside the white shape with oil pastels.

2   Use a cloth dipped in turpentine to wipe over the surface of a wax crayon or oil pastel drawing (Y5–Y6). Turpentine softens edges and blends colours to give a drawing the overtones of a painting.

MAKING RESIST DRAWINGS

The wax in wax crayons and the oil in oil pastels will resist inks and paint if the colour is applied with enough pressure. This technique allows children to concentrate on a central drawing and then provide a background by sweeping over the picture with a brush dipped in ink or paint. The consistency of the paint needs to be carefully monitored; too thin and the impact of the picture will be lost, too thick and the paint will cover the drawing.

Inks such as Easibrush are much easier to use than paint. They can be mixed to form intense colours and are still resisted by a wax crayon drawing.

Teachers could draw lines in crayon made with different pressures on a piece of scrap white paper. Then sweep over the paper with black ink. This demonstrates how ink will obscure a thin line of colour and only be resisted by one made with strong pressure.

Figure 1.20
Malaysian house and palm tree, a wax crayon resist, in a mixture of coloured inks. Y4

1   Make a 'magic' wax resist drawing (Y1–Y4). Use white crayon or a white candle on white paper. Y1 children could make fairly random marks such as raindrops, stars or sparks from a fire. Others could make a drawing directly on the paper, or use light pencil guidelines. By turning the paper to the light, children can see a faint difference between the candle marks and the white paper.

2   Cover the background with solid areas of colour, leaving the foreground as white paper (Y5–Y6). Sweep over with black ink to create silhouettes, eg: trees in a forest fire, or leads in a stained-glass window.

Scraperboard

Scraperboards are pieces of card covered with a layer of white chalk and then a layer of black paint. Children scrape a design into the black layer just deep enough to reveal the white chalk underneath. The contrasts between a light and a dark colour, and a shiny and a matt surface give impact to the simplest of drawings.

AGES AND STAGES

Scraperboard is relatively expensive so many children never experience the pleasure of this drawing medium. This is a pity as many children who lack confidence in their drawing skills particularly enjoy the dramatic impact of scraperboard drawing.

To economise, the scraperboard can be cut into smaller pieces. These are ideal for simple drawings of mini-beasts or faces. There are also ideas in this section (page 25) to show how children can make their own version of a scraperboard.

Children at KS1 should begin with the easier scraperpaper using a paper-clip as a scraper (the points on other tools are sharp). Metallic-coloured scraperboards are best left until the end of KS2 as the black layer does not always come away as smoothly and easily as it does from white scraperboards.

PoS 4d
Investigate shape, form and space

Children at KS1 will make mostly linear drawings but those at KS2 should be encouraged to remove large areas of the black surface to create a balance between the white and the black. In Y5 or Y6, children could remove the background entirely and bring the subject into dramatic relief, or leave lines of black by removing surrounding areas. They should look for interest and balance in texture, as well as in the areas of black and white.

EQUIPMENT

SCRAPERBOARD

Scraperboard is supplied in black over white, bronze, gold and silver. The metallic colours are useful for drawings of machines, aeroplanes, ships by moonlight or treasure chests.

SCRAPERPAPER

A base of paper rather than card is supplied. It is less expensive than scraperboard and comes with the additional choice of black over a grid of small multi-coloured squares. Scraperpaper is usually easier to use than scraperboard but sometimes there are faulty batches. It is worth sacrificing a section of each sheet to check that the scraperpaper is functioning correctly.

SCRAPERBOARD TOOLS

Figure 1.21
Scraperboard tools: a) for a fine line; b) for a broader line.

Special scraperboard tools produce thick or thin lines. If you can only buy one type, choose tool b.

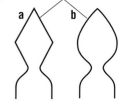
points of contact with the board

H & S

Anything metal that will scrape can act as a substitute, for example nails, the points of scissors, nail files, keys, blunt knives, the edge of a paper-clip or a wedged end of a piece of dowelling.

DRAWING TECHNIQUES USING SCRAPERBOARD

PoS 8d
Experiment with tools and develop techniques

Scraperboard drawing techniques are very different from those used with other drawing media and need to be practised. Give each child an off-cut of scraperboard to practise strokes needed for a drawing. Off-cuts can be trimmings from previous children's pictures, or they may have to be cut from original pieces. This may seem extravagant, but the pieces need only be very small and it really is essential to practise before every drawing. Do this after the design has been planned and transferred so that children can go straight to the drawing after practising the strokes.

TRANSFERRING A DESIGN

Cut out a piece of paper the same size as the scraperboard and sketch out the main lines of the drawing. Paper-clip the paper to the top of the scraperboard. Pressing hard, go over the lines of the drawing. The design will show as shallow indentations on the surface of the scraperboard.

PRACTISING STROKES

The side of the tool and not the point should be used in a sideways, scraping action. The black should come away easily. If it resists, the tool is not being held correctly and will hack holes through to the cardboard backing. The hand needs to keep

Figure 1.22
Bird of paradise. The transferred outline has been used to limit the feathery strokes. Y6

scraping in the same direction so the scraperboard has to be moved around underneath. This makes it very different from a pencil drawing when the paper stays still and the pencil can move in any direction. A piece of paper positioned under the hand holding the tool will help to prevent any finger-prints from spoiling the upper surface.

DRAWING ON SCRAPERBOARD

The traced lines should act as guidelines only. Children tend to make a heavy line around the drawing but a variety of strokes ending at the line will give movement and texture to the drawing.

Focusing on the subject and leaving the background largely unworked increases the impact of the black and white contrast. If it is necessary to indicate a foreground, low density patterns and textures could be used.

Erase small errors by filling the white areas with ink from a black marker pen. The pen marks do show slightly, so generally it is better if mistakes are incorporated where possible into the drawing.

ACTIVITY

PoS 4a and b
Investigate colour and texture

1 Add a little colour (Y1–Y3). Young children sometimes find the black and white a little stark and enjoy adding a touch of colour with felt-tip pens.

2 Add ink details (Y5–Y6). Make texture marks in black ink in some white areas.

Wax scraffito

An inexpensive alternative to scraperboard is for children to make their own wax scraffito boards. The contrast between the top and middle layer is not as clean or dramatic, but the colours glow through the black in a satisfying way. An important advantage over home-made scraperboards is

Figure 1.23
House, in wax scraffito. Y4

that a mistake can be immediately rectified by covering it over with another layer of colour.

KNOWLEDGE AND UNDERSTANDING

PoS 7e
Applying knowledge of artists to their own work

Klee made several pictures based on this scraffito technique, *Fish magic*, Ginn 38, and *The goldfish*, Shorewood 1382.

AGES AND STAGES

Preparatory colouring can be tedious so drawings need to be small, especially in KS1. Young children usually prefer to paint the last layer rather than crayon it, even though it does mean they have to wait for the paint to dry before making the drawing.

MAKING SCRAFFITO PAPER

THE TRADITIONAL METHOD

1 Cover a sheet of white cartridge paper with a thick layer of wax crayon. The crayon could be the traditional white, but any light colour will do. If possible make all the strokes in the same direction.

2 Cover the first layer of wax crayon with a second layer of black or other dark crayon. Crayon at right angles to the first layer of colour.

3 Scratch through the top layer using a scraperboard tool or other scraping implement. Be careful to just take off the top layer. If both layers are taken off the colour will appear only as a faint shadow.

THREE ALTERNATIVE METHODS

1 Make the top layer with black powder paint mixed with washing-up liquid (the consistency of thick cream). It will need to dry before the top layer is scraped.

2 Paint a thick layer of black ink on white paper and allow to dry. Cover the ink with several thick layers of white oil pastel. Scratch the design.

3 Use black Chinese ink to cover a coloured layer of wax crayon (Y5–Y6). At first the wax will resist the ink. Keep applying the ink with a wide brush until it takes. Make sure the wax layer totally covers the paper before starting with the ink, or the ink will seep into the spaces. Allow the ink to dry and the colours are just visible under the black. Plan the drawing to take full advantage of the range of colours underneath.

Tip!

Children often blow away the soft curls of scraped-off crayon and these are very difficult to remove from the floor. Spread large sheets of newspaper under the drawings and carefully gather in the bits at the end of the lesson.

ACTIVITY

PoS 4b
Investigate colour

1 Use themes to decide the colours on the underlayer of wax crayon: reds, oranges and yellows for a bonfire drawing, blues, whites and greens for an underwater scene (Y3–Y6).

2 Divide the background (Y3–Y6). Fold the paper to divide it vertically or horizontally. Choose cool colours for one side and warm colours for the other. Cover with a layer of black crayon. Make a symmetrical drawing with the fold as the line of symmetry. If the line is vertical, draw a mask, a tree or a pair of semi-detached houses. If the line is horizontal, draw an object or scene reflected in water.

3 Soften areas of the black (Y5–Y6). If the top layer is black paint that has been mixed with washing-up liquid, sweep off areas of colour with a cloth before the paint dries. The softer areas of colour contrast with the sharp lines and shapes made with scraperboard tools later.

PAINTING

Main NC focus

PoS 8d
Children should be taught
to experiment with (and
develop control of [KS2])
tools and techniques for
painting

Introduction

In general, when people think about art they visualise paintings, so most children are familiar with the idea of a painting as a work of art. Children are generally very responsive to paintings and willing to give their ideas and opinions. Reproductions of paintings are also comparatively easy to acquire. For all these reasons, paintings make a good starting point for implementing the Knowledge and understanding section of the Programme of Study. The medium of painting is also the most accessible one for colour mixing.

This chapter includes:

■ Strategies for looking at paintings (many of these ideas will also be useful for works of art in other media) (page 30)

■ Painting and colour (page 33)

■ Painting tools and techniques (page 39)

■ Choosing paints (page 44)

Figure 2.1
Three dahlias, in powder paint (powdered gouache).
Y1

PoS 7f
Pupils should be given
opportunities to respond
to and evaluate art, craft
and design, including
their own and other's
work

Knowledge and understanding through painting

The examples of paintings are confined to those found in the more widely available publications, such as Shorewood Ginn, Goodwill Art and Philip Green Educational. Teachers are encouraged to develop their own collections of illustrations using postcards, magazine articles and books.

The amount of time teachers allocate to looking at reproductions of paintings will vary considerably, depending on circumstances and the age of the class. A Y1 class interested in the brightness of red could spend a few minutes looking at Angelico and Lippi's *Adoration of the Magi*, Shorewood 104, where so many figures are dressed in rich reds. At the other extreme, a Y6 class could have a full term examining the history and ideas of the French Impressionist painters, investigating the social context and painting in ways that explore the different contemporary techniques and styles. Other teachers prefer to spend ten minutes on a regular basis at the beginning of most art lessons looking at reproductions.

Ages and stages

At KS1 the subject of a painting is the focus of children's attention – it needs to be understandable, realistic and preferably include some action. Children at this age generally prefer happy subjects and many bright colours. Large paintings are judged harder to paint than small ones, but otherwise assessments are based on very personal preferences and on an expectation that others will think the same as they do.

At the beginning of KS2 pictures are still expected to be realistic but children will also accept that artists paint what they feel, as well as what they see. Sad themes become more acceptable but really disturbing subjects are usually rejected as bad paintings.

By the end of KS2 children can discuss elements of composition; whether the subjects represented are realistic, impressionistic or abstract portrayals; what materials the artist has used and how this has influenced the work.

Teaching resources

It is important to use good quality reproductions whenever possible as children rarely have the chance to see original paintings. Art books and art magazines usually print pictures large enough to look at, if the class is gathered in a group. Posters are ideal for classroom discussion and give a more accurate idea of the painting. Postcards are cheaper and are useful for individual work. Use a metre rule to show children the real size of the painting.

Visits to art galleries are particularly valuable when they are related to work children have been doing in school. Focus on a few themes to encourage children to study paintings thoroughly and quietly. If the art gallery sells postcard reproductions it is useful for children at KS2 to compare the differences in colour between the original and the reproduction. Children can also consider the impact of the frame. Does it add or distract from the painting?

Discussing paintings

LOOKING CAREFULLY

PoS 9e
Describe and express opinions about works of art

If children's comments about paintings are accepted in a non-judgemental way, they will learn to value their own reactions to a painting while remaining receptive to new experiences and images. Getting children to postpone any judgement until the painting has been examined quietly will help with this. After time for looking and thinking, directing the children's attention to the subject matter of the painting is usually an excellent starting point for a discussion.

ACTIVITY

1 Establish the main subject (Y1–Y6). What is happening? What has just happened and is about to happen? What season is it and what is the weather like?

• Discuss whether it is a landscape, still-life, portrait, religious, domestic, narrative or abstract painting (Y5–Y6).

2 Involve all the senses (Y1–Y6). Ask children what they would be able to see, hear and smell if they were in the painting.

KEEPING A DISCUSSION FOCUSED

PoS 9b
Recognise visual elements

Often a pupil will give a personal response to a painting, for example 'I like this painting because I like horses' (Delacroix *Frightened horse*, Shorewood 1225). This describes the child's taste in art and is a perfectly valid response to a painting but it tends to lead to a group discussion on favourite animals rather than focusing on the painting. The teacher could guide the discussion back by asking what kind of horse the artist has shown – its colour and its mood; how the artist has shown the smooth coat, or tangled mane of the horse with different brush strokes and tonal changes.

ACTIVITY
1 Look at a painting which shows a lot of activity (Y1–Y6). Ask children to raise their hand when they have a sentence ready about the painting. Try to achieve a continuous linkage of ideas without a pause.

2 Match pictures (Y1–Y6).

• Make a jigsaw puzzle to encourage children to look carefully at paintings. Mount a picture of a painting on card. Take a photocopy and then cut the coloured picture into a grid of squares. Number each square on the back in case it is misplaced. Build up a collection and exchange with other classes.

Figure 2.2
An art jigsaw.

EXAMINING THE SOCIAL AND HISTORICAL CONTEXT OF A PAINTING

KS2 PoS 9c
Pupils should be taught to recognise ways in which works of art reflect the time and place in which they are made

Children enjoy learning about the historical and social context of a painting. If your school is about to buy a series of art posters or cards, look to see whether they provide information about the medium being used, the date it was made, the dimensions of the work and where it can be seen. Art history books can also give information about the artistic climate of the time, the personal history of the artist and any social and political influences.

The backgrounds in paintings often show interesting details of costumes, jewellery and other artefacts. Van Eyck's *Giovanni Arnolfini and his bride* (1434), Goodwill 2(15), and other Gothic paintings are rich in symbolic and everyday details.

 Use *Art in the National Curriculum* AVP COM5001-2 by Acorn as a reference for pictures of artists' work. CD-ROM Microsoft *Art Gallery* shows paintings from the National Gallery.

ACTIVITY
1 Use a map to locate places where artists lived, or live, and find pictures of local conditions (Y5–Y6). Small groups could become experts on particular artists, finding examples of earlier and later work and comparing them. Ask children to share their expertise with others in the class.

2 Discuss what the paintings tell about the different roles and expectations of men and women, children and adults, people from different ethnic backgrounds (Y5–Y6). Why are there so many nudes of women but not of men? Why were there so few portraits of children when today they make up the largest proportion of family photographs? Why are women and black people so often shown in passive roles?

Responding to artists' styles of painting

KNOWLEDGE AND UNDERSTANDING

PoS 5b
Examine styles from past and present

Looking at paintings of the same or similar subject painted by different artists teaches children that artists make highly personal responses to the world and that, in art, there is more than one correct interpretation. The Goodwill Art Service and Philip Green Educational have a series of packs on specific themes (postcard and A4 size). Using these reproductions, children can compare the media used by the artists, the subject, the feeling each painting gives and what each artist emphasises – colour, line, shape, pattern, texture or composition.

ACTIVITY

1 After comparing a group of paintings, ask the children which painting they would like to have on their wall at home and why (Y1–Y6).

2 Match styles (Y5–Y6). When children become familiar with a group of artists, collect a set of reproductions, two from each artist, and ask them to sort them into pairs according to artist, by looking only at the style.

MAKING A TRIBUTE TO OR PARAPHRASING AN ARTIST

PoS 7e
Use knowledge of artists'
work

Copying paintings can be a valuable part of exploring and identifying with a particular style and was a technique very much in favour with the old painting masters. It can be particularly useful for children who want to absorb skills and processes without having to think about creating an image. Children generally do make some of their own adjustments and interpretations, but if the painting is very close to the original, it could be called a tribute to the artist. Using a painter's style with a creative input could be called paraphrasing.

ACTIVITY

1 Make a tribute painting (Y2–Y6).

• Use strips of card to isolate sections of the painting and examine the brush strokes and colour choice (Y3–Y6). As they gain in confidence, children in Y5 or Y6 may want to paint the whole of a simple composition.

• Use a grid to plan out a group painting on a large scale (Y5–Y6). Try to find a painting with a limited range of colours. Figure 2.3 shows a tribute to Picasso's *Guernica* (Shorewood 134) which was made on 20 sheets of paper, each 70 × 23 cm, with children working in groups of two. It needed a lot of co-operation between the groups to match the edges carefully so that the lines flowed continuously across the painting. They discussed the tonal values in the picture and mixed and labelled the grey inks before starting to paint.

2 Paraphrase favourite paintings.

• Provide a vase of flowers for children to paint after studying Van Gogh's and Rohlfs' sunflower paintings (Ginn 35/36 and Shorewood 560)

Figure 2.3
Guernica, a tribute to Picasso made of 20 sheets of paper, in ink. Y6

Strategies for painting lessons

Illustrative and imaginative paintings

KNOWLEDGE AND UNDERSTANDING

PoS 3
In order to develop visual literacy, pupils should be taught about the different ways in which ideas, feelings and meanings are communicated in visual form

Paintings that tell a story or describe an event have a particular fascination for children. It is valuable to compare painters who have dealt with the same subject in different ways. Children at the end of KS2 could look at the way artists depict war (Picasso *Guernica*, Shorewood 134; Chagall *The war*, Shorewood 1332; Goya *The third of May 1808*, Shorewood 42).

Examples of narrative commercial art are in the streets, in the press and on public transport. Ask the local cinema for any old posters of films that the children might have seen. Posters by Toulouse-Lautrec (Toulouse-Lautrec *Jane Avril*, Shorewood 208) or Joyce Denny (*Women's Royal Naval Service*, Goodwill 1(6)) can be used to analyse why their images capture the viewers' attention.

AGES AND STAGES

PoS 2a
Express ideas and feelings

Children at KS1 usually produce paintings that communicate very personal and immediate interests. They will talk about what they are painting while they are working, sometimes altering the story when asked to talk about it later. This is because the images become independent of their original thinking and inspire a new fantasy. This rich internal response to painting, so typical of KS1, is an essential part of children's early education and should be nurtured throughout KS1 and into KS2, through imaginative and illustrative work.

Whereas children at KS1 seem to be able to concentrate on a particular event or emotion and illustrate it clearly and vividly, children in KS2 often clutter a painting with images. These children should be encouraged to select a focal point that will hold their and other's attention and to eliminate unnecessary detail.

ACTIVITY

PoS 8c
Develop a range of source material

1 Starting points for imaginative paintings (Y1–Y6).

   • Take ideas from poems and stories as a stimulus for imaginative art work (Y1–Y6).

   • Use music such as Mussorgsky's *Pictures from an exhibition* to provide a wide variety of moods and ideas for imaginative work (Y3–Y6). For example, the section called *The dwarf* suggests witches to many listeners.

   • Work from direct observation of an object but place it in an imaginary setting (Y5–Y6). Paint a plant that grows fantastic fruit or flowers; a new species of insect, fish or animal and give it a Latin-type name.

2 Starting points for illustrative paintings.

   • Make a symmetrical painting of a mask, a face, an animal's head, a vase of flowers or a building (Y3–Y6). Paint on one side of a fold and close the paper at regular intervals. The print will be faint but can act as a guide for the main shape.

Figure 2.4
Butterfly, planned by folding the paper over, in liquid gouache. Y3

PoS 2b
Record observation

Painting from direct observation – portraits and still-lives

KNOWLEDGE AND UNDERSTANDING

Portraits are a rich source of inspiration for primary children and there is a wealth of choice. Artists have painted portraits of their patrons (Holbein *The ambassadors*, Goodwill 3(26)); family and friends (Hockney *My parents*, Goodwill 3(26)); workers (Knight *Ruby Loftus screwing a beech-ring*, Goodwill 1(6)); models (Degas *At the dressing table*, Goodwill 2(16)); and of themselves (Turner *Self-portrait*, Goodwill 3(26)); all from direct observation.

PoS 9c
Relate art to its time and place of origin

Painting everyday objects was once thought to be an unworthy subject. Despite this, many paintings of the Renaissance portrayed mundane background objects with great skill and attention to detail, which often serve as background to a portrait. Gradually, these objects became a more prominent element of a composition, until they became the subject or genre in their own right: a still-life. Some still-life paintings are almost photographic in accuracy and detail (Jan Van Os *Fruit and flowers in a terracotta vase*, Ginn 48). Other artists make a very personal interpretation of objects (Braque *Purple plums*, Shorewood 1329; Caulfield *Still-life autumn fashion*, Goodwill 3(24)).

AGES AND STAGES Portraits intrigue children at KS1 and KS2. They enjoy discussing the personality and way of life of the sitter so any information that can be given to them about the sitter is helpful. This gives a good opportunity to talk about the social and political context of the painting.

When it comes to painting portraits themselves, this appeals to all ages. A model might find it difficult to pose long enough, but mirrors allow children to paint self-portraits (see pages 189–192 for various approaches for making portraits).

ACTIVITY

1 Make a portrait of a model in profile, in the style of a Renaissance painting.

2 Plan the painting (Y4–Y6).

• If children need to plan a painting, encourage them to use broad strokes of chalk or soft pencil to plan main shapes and positions. Use the lines as a guide and keep examining the subject.

• Use tints and tones of one colour to distinguish areas of light and shade (Y5–Y6). This need not take very long, but it will help to flesh out a charcoal sketch in an important way. Many children then enjoy the freedom of applying pure colour, knowing that the main decisions of colour tone have been made.

Figure 2.5
Direct observational painting dahlias in the style of Van Gogh, in acrylics. Y5

PoS 2c
Design and make creative images

Painting landscapes

<u>KNOWLEDGE AND UNDERSTANDING</u>

PoS 9d
Respond to and compare different styles and traditions

Landscapes were initially painted as background to religious paintings and portraits (Raphael *The Alba Madonna*, Shorewood 101). In some religious paintings, landscapes began to dominate (Patenier *Saint Jerome in a rocky landscape*, Ginn 24) until, by the end of the sixteenth century, landscape painting had become a genre in its own right. Landscapes were used to record the estates of wealthy families (Devis *Family group*, Ginn 46) but in general, landscapes portrayed an ideal rather than reality. Turner, Corot and Constable broke with this tradition (Constable *Flatford Mill*, Goodwill 3(29)), and the Pre-Raphaelites laboured to portray the absolute truth of nature (Dyce *Pegwell Bay*, Ginn 51). Impressionist and post-Impressionist landscapes were painted outdoors and the artists tried to capture a particular moment of light and movement (Van Gogh *Landscape with cypress*, Goodwill 3(29)).

Other artists such as Cezanne (*Le Chateau noir*, Goodwill 3(29)) depicted landscapes as abstract shapes and colours.

ACTIVITY

PoS 7e
Use knowledge of artists' work

1 Use a viewfinder (see page 5) to isolate a section of a landscape and paint the colours and textures (Y1–Y5).

2 Use the same colours and shapes from a landscape painting as a starting point and then incorporate new features (Y4–Y6).

<u>AGES AND STAGES</u>

In general, children at KS1 paint a landscape as background to an event that has been painted first. However, they do respond to suggestions to create an atmosphere with particular shapes or colours. Children at KS2 can be encouraged to paint a landscape before adding foreground details. This promotes a more fluid line.

ACTIVITY

1 Paint imaginary landscapes (Y1–Y6). A hot, dusty desert, a jungle, an industrial wasteland, a tropical island, wetlands, a country scene in four seasons.

2 If your school has a view of trees, go in the playground and paint outdoors in the style of the Impressionists (Y5–Y6). Use a viewfinder (see page 5) to isolate a section of the view.

Figure 2.6
Tree on a sunny day, painted with a sponge, in liquid gouache. Y3

PoS 2a
Express ideas and feelings

Painting abstract pictures

<u>AGES AND STAGES</u>

Abstract art seems to be more accessible to children than to many adults, perhaps because children are very open to new experiences and also because they enjoy pure line and colour. At the beginning of KS1, children often make paintings consisting entirely of lines and patches of pure colour.

ACTIVITY

1 Paint a picture to show a mood or emotion (Y3–Y6).

• Paint a large area in appropriate background colours and make a series of shoe prints in the shape of a movement: a fight, a nervous shuffle, a happy skipping action, a burglar's tread.

• Discuss experiences in children's lives when they have felt a strong emotion and ask them to relate it to shapes, colour and line (Y5–Y6). It might be a time when they felt lonely at a new school, or frightened when their parents were angry with them; relieved when they made up a quarrel with a friend, or excited on Christmas Eve.

2 Paint visual images in response to music (Y3–Y6). Children often react figuratively to music but some may want to explore a more abstract response with shapes, colours and lines. A deep, loud sound could be shown as a massive purple or black shape; a high-pitched note as a thin, long, blue line.

Main NC focus

PoS 4b
Pupils should be taught about . . . colour matching and how colour is mixed from primary colours (KS1)

How colour is applied and experienced in images and designs (KS2)

Painting and colour

Artists' colour choices and styles

Colour can be the initial stimulus that draws attention to a painting. The ease with which paints can be mixed gives children great control over colour choice. No other media mix so easily. Artists have not always had the extensive range of colours available now. It is very useful for children to learn how beautiful paintings of the past were created with quite a restricted palette and to try to paint with similar colours.

PoS 5b
Examine styles from past and present

Colours made from locally found materials

Pre-historic cave painters used coloured clays as pigments mixed in animal fats to form a paint (cave art, *Standing bison*, Shorewood 1742). Pigments are still extracted from earth, but we also have other sources: metals, plants, animals and synthetics.

Australian Aboriginal paintings were originally made on bark or stone with pigments sourced locally (*Two kangaroos*, Ginn 43). They are now mostly painted on boards with acrylics but the traditional colour range of rich browns, reds, ochres, whites and blacks is still used in many paintings. The dotted designs, swirling shapes and links with traditional myths make this a fascinating subject for children.

ACTIVITY

1 Mix home-made colours (Y3–Y6). Ask children to bring things from home that they think might make interesting colours to paint with – coffee and cocoa powder, strong tea, red cabbage, burned wood, leaves, crushed berries, fruit juices, food dyes, spices. Make a cave painting on plaster of Paris, using these colours.

2 Use paints to mix hues similar to those in the Aboriginal paintings (Y3–Y6). Use brown paper or hessian as a background

Figure 2.7
Horse, on plaster of Paris, in mixed paint. Y4

The early restricted palette

In the Ancient World, Egyptians used only seven colours – white, cinnabar (vermilion), azurite (bright blue), malachite (green), orpiment (yellow), realger (red) and blue frit (*The pool in Nebamun's garden*, Ginn 26; from Thebes *Fragment of a wall-painting*, Goodwill 1(13)). The Ancient Greeks used the same colours as the Egyptians, although paintings on Greek vases were generally restricted to terracotta, black and white. The Romans added verdigris (light green), indigo (blue-violet) and purple to the Egyptian palette.

In the early Middle Ages, ultramarine, madder yellow, vermilion and lead tin-yellow were introduced to the European colour palette. Ultramarine was made from a semi-precious stone and it was the most expensive pigment. This meant that ultramarine was very closely associated with paintings of the Madonna (Poussin *Holy family*, Shorewood 107).

ACTIVITY

1 Use ultramarine as the focal point of a picture portraying something of importance to each child (Y1–Y6).

2 Compare the flat, formal paintings of the Ancient Egyptians and Greeks with the flat shapes of the Cubists in the twentieth century (Y3–Y6). Copy one of the designs and paint it in the same hues. The formal designs need careful planning and fine brushwork.

3 Look at copies of Roman murals. Paint a border pattern using the Roman palette of colours (Y3–Y6).

New colour theories

The Industrial Revolution and the discovery of coal tar dyes led to important changes in the colours of paint available to artists. Pigments became cheaper and more varied. Towards the end of the nineteenth century, painters in Europe began to take a strong interest in the scientific explanations of how colours interact with each other: paints could be applied in their unmixed form next to each other and the eye would do the mixing. This meant that dabs of red and yellow next to each other would be seen as orange.

The Impressionists Morisot, Cassatt, Pissarro, Manet, Renoir, Monet, Sisley, Degas and Whistler were all profoundly influenced by this idea of optical colour mixing. Although the concept of broken colour was not completely new, the Impressionists took the idea to such extremes, that in close-up, their paintings looked like a confused mixture of daubs of colour. From a distance, the eye mixes bright primary and secondary colours. This gives the paintings a characteristic shimmering quality that makes Impressionist paintings so popular. Contemporary public opinion, however, judged their paintings to be crude and unfinished (Morisot *Summer's day*, Goodwill 2(14); Cassatt *Children playing on the beach*, Goodwill 3(21)).

The Pointillists Seurat, Cross, Signac and Henri van de Velde took the idea of optical colour mixing to its logical extreme and created pictures made entirely of small dots of colour. The dots were painted very close together and from a distance the eye blends the dots to create colours far more luminous than those produced by mixing colours on the palette (Seurat *The bathers*, O&B A10; Signac *The Seine at Herbley*, Goodwill 2(15)).

Expressionists such as Van Gogh, Munch and Gauguin used colour in a revolutionary way to express their strong internal emotions:Gauguin *Haymaking*, Goodwill 1(6); Munch *Girls on a bridge*, Goodwill 2(19). Painters such as Matisse, Kandinsky and Derain used wildly exaggerated colours and were given the name of 'wild beasts' or Fauves: Matisse *The purple robe*, Shorewood 1126; Derain *Boats of Collioure*, Goodwill 1(5). More abstract artists such as Chagall, Miro, Klee and Picasso also used colours for their symbolic value while artists such as Arp used colour purely for its own beauty without reference to representational or symbolic value: Picasso *The tragedy*, Shorewood 1073; Arp *Configuration*, Shorewood 1359.

ACTIVITY

1 Look at the Impressionist and Expressionist paintings (Y2–Y6). The interesting colours and exciting brush work in the paintings make them particularly popular with children. Use a viewfinder (see page 5) to isolate sections and try out similar colours and painting techniques. Then progress to a larger area.

2 Try Pointillist techniques (Y5–Y6). This painting technique intrigues children but they need to work on a very small scale or the painting becomes tedious. Use a straw or stick dipped in paint and place the dots very close together.

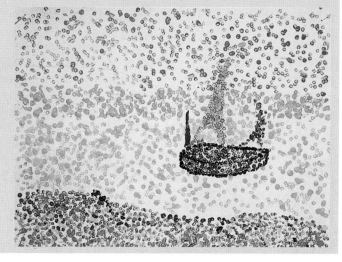

Figure 2.8
Boat, using the Pointillist technique, in acrylic. Y6

Colours and washes

Children at KS1 need to learn about the primary colours and what happens when they are mixed (see below and Chapter 7). If children seem to be producing endless variations of sludge brown, it is worth remembering that muddy colours do have a place on a painter's palette. Paint areas of unmixed primary and secondary colours and use the mixed muddy colours as a foil to the brighter hues.

At KS2 children should learn to predict more accurately the results of colour mixing. They can learn to mix subtle variations of tints and tones, understanding that colours have versions that are warm and cool and how this affects colour mixing. Children at this stage can use colour more consciously for a specific effect. They could use a colour in more than one place to give a feeling of unity to the painting; use warm colours to show areas lit by light and to bring objects closer to the viewer; use cool colours to show shadows and to make objects recede into the background; use a dark background to increase the brightness of light colours in the foreground (see page 168). In Y3 and Y4, this can be done as the painting progresses; in Y5 and Y6 these elements could be decided on before the painting is begun.

MIXING PRIMARY COLOURS

PoS KS1 4b
How colour is mixed from primary colours

Although 'red' is often thought of as a specific colour, there are many varieties of reds. The same applies to the other primary colours, blue and yellow. The specific red and specific yellow will affect the orange that is made when they are mixed.

To mix secondary colours effectively, children will need warm and cool versions of each colour: cadmium red and alizarin red, cadmium yellow and lemon yellow, ultramarine and cerulean blue.

An orangey red (vermilion) and an orangey yellow (brilliant yellow) will produce a truer orange than a purply red (crimson) and a greenish yellow (lemon yellow).

A greenish blue (cobalt blue) and a greenish yellow (lemon yellow) will make a true green.

A violet blue (ultramarine) and a purplish red (crimson) will make a true violet.

Two primary colours that have different biases, for example a purplish red and a greenish yellow, will make a muted or muddy secondary colour. Although not true secondary colours, they are useful neutral colours.

ACTIVITY

1 Draw a linear pattern in thick, black wax crayon and paint mixed colours in the spaces (Y1–Y4). Black emphasises the colour differences and the wax keeps the colours from merging.

2 Paint around a shape (Y3–Y6). Paint a shape such as a dancing figure in a primary colour (blue) in the centre of the paper. Paint a thick line around the shape with a second primary colour (yellow). Mix the third primary colour (red) into the yellow in stages, adding a strip of colour each time to the painting. Finish with a true red at the edges. This idea can also be used for mixing tones (see page 38 and Chapter 7).

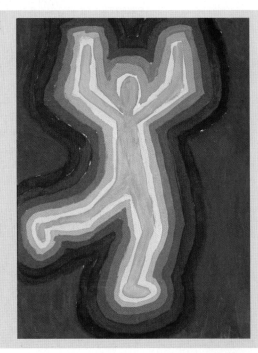

Figure 2.9
Colour mixing around a figure, in powder paint (powdered gouache). Y3

ACTIVITY   3 'Take a line for a walk' (Y3–Y6).

a) Divide a piece of white paper 30 × 26 cm into thirds, so the sections are 10 × 26 cm. Use a pencil to 'take a line for a walk' across the paper, creating large shapes.

b) On each of the thirds, use paint to mix two different primary colours. On the left could be blue and yellow, in the middle, red and blue, and on the right, red and yellow. Never paint beyond a pencil line – this includes both the pencil shapes and the vertical lines dividing the paper into thirds.

c) When the paint is dry, emphasise the 'travelling line' by painting it black, ignoring the folded divisions.

Figure 2.10
'Taking a line for a walk', in powder paint (powdered gouache). Y3

MIXING PRIMARY AND SECONDARY COLOURS

The closer the primary and secondary colours are to the tertiary colour that they produce, the truer the tertiary colour is. A warm red (vermilion) mixed with orange makes a 'truer' orange-red than a cool red (crimson) mixed with orange.

PRODUCING INTERESTING GREYS

Black mixed with white produces a cold grey. Mixing the three primary colours equally produces a dark grey. More blue will make a dark, plum colour; more red, a chestnut brown; more yellow, a dark olive. Complementary colours (blue/orange, red/green, yellow/purple) mixed with white also produces grey.

ACTIVITY   1 Paint a camouflaged creature (Y3–Y6). Create a paper collage background and paint a camouflaged insect or animal on separate paper, carefully matching the colours to the background. Cut out the painted shape when it is dry and glue it to the collage.

2 Match colours (Y3–Y6). Find a piece of patterned fabric or paper. Glue a small section to a piece of white paper. Mix the same colours and extend the pattern to make a larger picture. The original piece of paper could become part of a dress, shirt, hat or landscape.

Figure 2.11
Camouflaged butterfly, in powder paint (powdered gouache). Y3

MIXING TONES

PoS 4c
Images are made using light and tone

By mixing tints (lighter tones) and shades (darker tones), children can increase the range of colours in their paintings.

Different tones are especially important when children at KS2 attempt to make an object look realistic. Tones give a strong impression of light and dark and make the painting 'come alive'. Decide on the local colour (the colour in neutral light) and use this to paint the object. The local colour can also be used to mix darker shades and lighter tints. Add black, or a complementary colour, and a little white to the local colour for shading; add white for highlights.

1 Make tonal stripes (Y1–Y6).

• Choose a primary or secondary colour and paint a horizontal line across the centre of a piece of white paper (Y1–Y3). Mix gradually lightening tints above the line and gradually darkening shades below the line. Make a card window in the shape of a fish, tree, balloon or ball and position it over the tones. Paint the window in the same tones but use contrasting vertical stripes. Children at KS1 may need to separate the two processes and use one shape for recording tints and another shape for shades.

MIXING A WASH FOR BACKGROUND

*PoS 8d
Experiment with tools and develop techniques*

Different colour tints can be mixed by using different amounts of water in the paint (instead of adding white). This method is called mixing a wash. A wash spreads a thin layer of colour over the page. If a wash is used as a background, it will be dry enough to overlay paint in ten minutes. An even blending of graded tints is particularly useful for receding landscapes, seascapes and skies. Unevenly graded washes give an interestingly textured background.

MAKING A WASH WITH GRADED TONE

Wet the paper with water and a clean brush. Load a brush with paint and work the brush backwards and forwards horizontally across the paper, until the bottom of the page is reached. This is the easiest way of making a graded wash and should be used in Y1.

Too much water on the paper causes it to buckle and warp as well as taking a long time to dry. Teach the children to wipe off excess colour from the wash brush before it touches the paper.

Mop-up excess water using the 'vacuum-cleaner' technique. Dry the paint brush by squeezing and pulling it up between a forefinger and the newspaper on the table. Dab the brush in an unwanted pool of wash-paint and it will soak it up. Children as young as Y1 enjoy using this technique.

Tip!

Washes need to be left to dry where they are painted. If possible, paint the wash background just before a break. Children at KS2 could go out and do some sketching in preparation for the foreground. Alternatively, gather the children together to look at famous artists' work and discuss the foregrounds of their paintings. If the washes do have to be moved, keep them as flat as possible.

Figure 2.12
Squeezing the water from a paint brush.

1 Create an irregular distribution of colour.

• Dot paint around wet paper and blend with a brush, or sponge.

• Tilt the paper sideways while the wash is still wet for paintings or clouds moving across the sky.

• Hold a grey/blue wash at an angle so that it drains downwards to depict a rain-drenched sky.

• Lift out areas of colour while the paint is wet using a dry sponge, cloth, brush, screwed-up tissue paper or blotting paper.

• Use more than one colour. Coloured inks make very vibrant washes and dry quickly.

Painting tools and techniques

AGES AND STAGES

The introduction of new painting techniques needs careful thought. Children learn most easily if the teacher can demonstrate a new technique, but teachers often worry that their images will look inadequate. There is also the danger that children, at KS1 in particular, will duplicate any images produced by the teacher. Discussing and demonstrating painting techniques using lines and shapes rather than definite images will put fewer demands on the teacher's artistic skills and at the same time will avoid the danger of stale repetitions of imagery. Some children will be eager to try the new ideas and make them part of their repertoire, others will continue to explore familiar methods.

Figure 2.13
A banana tree in gouache.
Y1

Children at KS2 often become anxious about making mistakes, which inhibits the creativity of their painting. If children can be persuaded to use accidental marks and colours by integrating them into their picture, this can actually add a degree of excitement that would not be there with a predictable painting.

Figure 2.14
Hippo, in acrylic. Y6

Painting surface (support)

PAPER

Paper is the most popular support for painting in schools. It is relatively cheap, easy to store and comes in a variety of thicknesses, textures and sizes. If possible, give a choice of colours: white, black, pastels, bright and neutral colours. White gives a sparkle to the paints, especially if children mix their paints too thinly. Black encourages children to apply paint thickly and makes colours look rich and bright.

Different weights and thicknesses of paper make interesting supports: kitchen paper, brown paper, tissue paper, sugar paper, rice paper, card, cardboard. The different absorbencies make each surface very different. Shiny brown paper will need PVA glue mixed in paint to make it adhere to the surface. Rice paper makes the paint bleed and blend dramatically. Use it for smudgy, painted backgrounds and add details in paper or mixed collage when the paint has dried.

Patterned and textured papers can prove a useful starting point for fresh ideas: corrugated paper and newspaper (skyscraper cities), textured white wallpaper (landscapes), marbled paper and monoprints (water scenes). Paste strips of torn tissue paper on to white paper to provide a multi-coloured background.

ANY REASONABLY SMOOTH SURFACE

Wood, pressed leaves, boxes, pebbles, eggshells, fabric, paper plates can all be used as a support. If the surface is slightly shiny, add PVA glue to the paint, or use acrylics. A layer of white paint will provide a neutral-coloured background.

KNOWLEDGE AND UNDERSTANDING

PoS 9d
Respond to and compare different styles and traditions

Artists painted on to stone for thousands of years (cave art *Group of deer*, Shorewood 1745). Children often equate 'primitive' art with something substandard, so it is worth emphasising that any artist would be proud to achieve such a high standard of painting.

Artists have painted on fabric (Indian painted design, Goodwill 3(30)) but canvas is the traditional support for oil paintings. Paper is preferred for watercolours – Turner's watercolour painting *Sunset tours*, Ginn 16, uses the paper as one of the colours in the painting.

The size of the support also has a major impact on the painting. There may be local murals to show children examples of paintings with large supports. If possible, show the children reproductions of the water lily paintings by Monet, Shorewood 1365, or Louis, Goodwill 3(25), and measure their sizes. With the *Sistine Chapel ceiling painting*, Shorewood 117, Goodwill 3(22), Michelangelo painted directly on to wet plaster using the fresco technique.

These large murals can be contrasted with miniature paintings. Some Chinese artists specialise in miniature paintings using a single hair as a paint brush. There are beautifully detailed miniatures by the Elizabethan artist Hilliard, as well as those by Persian and Indian miniaturists (Hilliard *Queen Elizabeth I*, Goodwill 3(26); *Persian miniature illustrating a poem*, Ginn 45; Mansur *A zebra*, Goodwill 3(30)).

ACTIVITY

PoS 7e
Use knowledge of artists' work

1 Paint on plaster of Paris (Y1–Y6). This makes an intriguing surface on which to paint because it absorbs moisture in the paint very rapidly. Make small painting surfaces by filling old polystyrene meat trays with plaster of Paris. Use the smooth surface or 'rough-carve' it to make it look like a cave wall.

2 Paint on small pieces of card or paper and use them for birthday cards (Y1–Y6).

3 Paint swirling finger patterns on polythene using acrylics or powder paint mixed with liquid detergent and display the painting against the light (Y1–Y6).

4 Make imaginative interpretations of the shapes of pebbles (Y4–Y6). Some could be painted as heads, cottages or crouching animals. Examples of this type of painting can often be found in gift shops.

PoS 1
Working in groups

5 Make a large group painting (Y4–Y6).

• Use a roll of lining paper, or a piece of old sheeting stretched over a wooden frame, sheets of paper taped together, or the side of a large cardboard packing case. Decide in advance how the work will be divided so each child has a meaningful task. Co-operate on colours and tones so that the painting will merge as one.

6 Try painting on an egg shell, a matchbox painted white, a piece of bark, or a pressed leaf (Y1–Y6).

PAINTING ON PAPER – TECHNIQUES

PoS KS2 4a
How colour is applied

PAINTING WET ON DRY

Wet paint is applied to the dry paper. This gives well defined edges and clear shapes.

PAINTING WET ON WET

Wet paint is applied to wet paper. It creates subtle blends of colour and blurred, rather formless shapes. It is a useful technique for landscapes or in specific areas of a painting, for example sky or a lake. Paint can be allowed to dry and then more layers and details added.

PAINTING DRY ON WET

Dry powder paint is swept across wet paper. The paint registers in different intensities of colour – the insides of each stroke are dense, strong colours while the outside edges are blurred and less intense. This effect makes interesting skies and waves.

PAINTING DRY ON DRY

A dry brush is dipped in powder paint and then brushed vigorously on dry paper, in a sweeping movement. This gives a smoky effect suitable for rocket vapour or speed clouds.

PAINTING ON CLOTH – TECHNIQUES

If the fabric is wet, colours bleed and blend into each other to produce subtle gradations of colour and blurred shapes. Dry fabric produces pronounced brush marks that add interesting patterns and textures to a design.

Coloured inks (Easibrush) and paint-on-dyes (Brusho fabric paints) give clear colours which blend easily without leaving any chalky deposits behind. Use them on fabrics that do not require washing.

Figure 2.15
Tree stencil, on sky painted with inks on wet fabric. Y2

Undiluted acrylics or paint with PVA glue added can be used for areas that children do not want to bleed and spread. Coarsely woven cloth such as sacking or hessian gives a highly textured surface to the paints.

Thick fabric dyes can be used on fabrics which will need to be washed. Paint a fixative over the design, put a fabric in a black polythene bag overnight and then wash off the fixative in warm soapy water. Dylon makes a fixative that can be mixed with the dye before it is painted on a fabric. Alternatively, mix acrylic paints with a fabric medium and paint a design on a fabric. Iron on the back of the fabric to set the colour.

ACTIVITY

1 Use a brush for each dye colour and drip colour across a fabric (Y1–Y2). Twist the wrist to obtain curves and lines. If the dyes are colour-fast, rinse in water before drying.

2 Making a T-shirt design with fast colours (Y1–Y6).

   • Use a plain, predominantly cotton T-shirt and paint a design on the front. Protect the back of the T-shirt from staining by laying a wad of newspaper inside the shirt. This also helps to stop the fabric from wrinkling during painting.

   • Draw an outline in thick, black lines on a piece of paper. Place it under the cloth and use it to guide the painting.

3 Sprinkle salt on some of the areas (Y1–Y6). The salt absorbs the dye and makes a mottled pattern. When the dye is completely dry, shake off the salt.

4 Add well-defined shapes to blurred backgrounds (Y1–Y6).

   • Sew or glue fabric collage shapes on to the fabric.

   • Use a positive-stencil (a hole cut in the centre of a piece of card) and dab a design on top of the fabric paint with a sponge. The cut edges of the shape act as a barrier for the dye and limit 'bleeding'. Print details or paint them on with thick dyes. Children at KS1 find card difficult to cut. Paper will produce more satisfying shapes, although there will be slightly more bleeding at the edges.

CARE!

Brushes and brush strokes

Children need time to experiment with brushes and other painting tools. Take a few minutes at the beginning of a lesson to experiment, or devote a lesson to practising different brush strokes to make highly textured surfaces. When children are released from the pressure of having to make a picture, they often become much more adventurous in their exploration of texture and line making.

KNOWLEDGE AND UNDERSTANDING

PoS 9d
Respond to and compare different styles and traditions

Children enjoy examining and comparing the meticulous, smooth brushwork of David (*Oath of the Horatii*, Shorewood 1269) and the whirlwind strokes of Cohran (*Stormy waters*, Shorewood 846), Derain (*Charing Cross Bridge*, Goodwill 2(19)) and Van Gogh (*Starry night*, Goodwill 3(27)). Courbet used a palette knife to spread out the background colours quickly and energetically and then used fine brushwork on top of the background (*The cliffs at Etretat after a storm*, Shorewood 1258). Kandinsky (*Interior, living room in Ainmillar Street*, Goodwill 3(23)) used a palette knife with vigorous strokes throughout the painting.

Try to always include some discussion of brushwork whenever children examine a painting. This encourages them to become more adventurous in their own strokes and, at KS2, to relate the type of stroke to the subject.

ACTIVITY

1 Use the Chinese dry brush technique (Y1–Y6). Dip an old brush in paint and then dab it on newspaper to remove most of the moisture.

• 'Jab' it up and down on the paper to paint foliage or fluffy clouds. Y1 children find it difficult to dry the brush but using the same brush stroke will still make interesting textured areas.

• Make parallel lines (Y3–Y6). Splay the bristles and drag them down the paper. Use this stroke for grass, for painting tone on rounded objects, for fur textures on animals and for grain on tree bark.

2 Try scumbling (Y5–Y6). This is a form of dry brush painting used by European painters. Paint is applied very thickly and lightly across another dry colour so that patches of the under-colour show. This works particularly well on a highly textured surface of thick paint. The handle of the brush can be used to remove areas of paint and reveal colour underneath.

Figure 2.16
Clouds, using the Chinese-style dry brush technique. The wash background is in liquid gouache. The birds were stencilled on when the paint was dry. Y5

AGES AND STAGES

PoS 8d
Experiment with tools and develop techniques

At KS1 children are sometimes restricted to large paint brushes to encourage bold paintings with broad strokes, but they should also have the opportunity to use small brushes.

Give a choice of brushes so children can learn to select for themselves an appropriate size and shape.

The direction of a brush stroke shows in a painting and makes a positive contribution to its atmosphere. Children at KS2 should start to plan the strokes before they begin a painting: horizontal strokes for the sky; swirling strokes for tempestuous water and foliage; strokes which move in the same direction for woodgrain, fur or feathers. Children at the end of KS2 could use a contrasting brush stroke to separate foreground from the background.

Finger painting is often associated with KS1, but children at KS2 also enjoy direct contact with smooth and sticky art materials. This enjoyment can become so strong that it causes their movements to become repetitive and monotonous so that the colours become muddied. Ask these children to try strokes on scrap paper and use them as references during the painting. Other children at KS2 only use two fingers and are reluctant to get involved with the paint. These children will need the option of using a brush.

BRUSHES

Hog-hair brushes are most commonly used in schools because they are hard-wearing and resilient. Squirrel-hair makes soft brushes for applying thin paint and for painting detail. Synthetic substitutes cost much less than the natural products and are suitable for acrylics or in any situation where children may permanently damage a brush.

SIZES

Brushes come in standard sizes. The lower the number, the smaller the brush (smallest 000 and largest 36). Sizes 2, 4, 8 and 12 give a good range for primary schools. If you can only order a limited number of brushes, choose larger rather than smaller brushes. A small brush has a limited number of uses, whereas a large soft brush can be used for a wash and also made into a point for finer detail. Home decorating brushes are very useful for covering large areas and for expressive brush work involving large movements.

Badly treated brushes splay and leave a trailing side piece that is impossible to stroke into place. This prevents children from making an accurate stroke and causes frustration. Children enjoy the idea that brushes are like cats – 'they only like to be stroked in one direction'. The following rules will help children learn to care for brushes:

1 Never leave brushes standing in water pots – this leads to distorted bristles.

2 Use brushes in a smooth stroke. Do not scrub brushes across the paper with bristles splayed.

3 Clean brushes thoroughly but gently. Rinse in clean water; wash in soap and water and rinse thoroughly; re-shape the brush by stroking it gently with the fingers.

Tip!

Keep a set of old brushes for children to experiment with. Splaying and stippling quickly ruins new brushes. Stick tape on the brush handles to keep them separate from the good brushes.

ACTIVITY

1 Press the side of a brush down on to the paper to make separate units of colour (Y1–Y6). Use this for foliage, tiles on a roof, stones on a wall or petals on a flower.

2 Use a very wide brush to start a painting (Y3–Y6). This encourages children to make a solid framework of shapes and colours before starting on detail. Work over the entire picture and keep a feeling of 'an overview' throughout the painting.

3 Use a fine brush to paint a narrow area of background colour around foreground objects (Y3–Y6). Background brush strokes in the defined area will then be freer.

PALETTE KNIVES

Palette knives are broad-shaped, flexible painting knives made from steel or plastic. The blades are wedge-shaped or straight-sided and are supplied in different sizes. The handles are angled away from the blades so that a person can manoeuvre paint freely without touching the paper. A 10-cm blade is large enough for broad sweeps of colour and small enough for applying details. Use a rag or tissue to wipe paint from the blade at each colour change.

Strips of plastic or thick card make inexpensive alternatives to the palette knife. Fold over thin card or thick paper to several thicknesses and use the folded edge to make broad sweeps of paint.

Always use thick paint with a palette knife. Thicken paints with paste, or use acrylics. Spread the paint in a thin transparent layer, or paint in thick dabs and slashes to create a highly textured surface. Cover the background quickly with vigorous and energetic movements.

ACTIVITY	Use a spatula to direct painting strokes towards a vanishing point to heighten the sense of perspective (Y5–Y6).

NATURAL AND ARTIFICIAL SPONGE

Artificial sponge is cheap and can be easily cut to the desired size. Natural sponge produces wonderful textures and soft, natural shapes but it is expensive. Try to buy a variety of sponges so that children can vary the textures in the painting.

ACTIVITY	1 Use a flat surface of sponge to sweep colour across the paper (Y1–Y6). Different pressures will give different depths of colour.
	2 Dab with the edge of an artificial sponge to make interestingly textured lines (Y1–Y6).
	3 Remove most of the paint from a sponge and dab to create a highly textured area (Y1–Y6). Use this technique for foliage, scales, beaches or rocky landscapes.

FOUND OBJECTS

ACTIVITY	1 Make sweeping or dabbing movements with crumpled objects such as cloth, cellophane, tissue paper or aluminium foil (Y1–Y6).

• Layer colours and then use a rag to wipe away areas of wet paint to give variations in colour and texture (Y5–Y6).

2 Use fingers with thick paints (Y1–Y6). The finger-ball and finger-tip are useful for smooth strokes, dabbing and varying the width of the stroke. Dabble fingers for foliage, stroke them for bark and swirl them for water.

• Remove small areas of colour using the tip of a fingernail for texture creating hair or fur effects (Y3–Y6).

• Use finger-tips to make dabs of paint to represent faces in a crowd scene (Y5–Y6).

3 Blow through straws on to thin paint to make a winter tree, or a bonfire (Y3–Y6).

Figure 2.17
Portrait, textured areas made using finger nails, in acrylic. Y3

Choosing paints

PoS 8d
Experiment with tools and develop techniques

Paints were first made in Egypt by mixing coloured pigments with gum arabic; the gum dissolves easily in water and sticks to paper when it dries. This is still the way that gouache ('*goo-ash*') and watercolours are made today. **Gouache** is the most popular paint in schools because of its versatility and price.

While gouache is used for texture and dramatic colours, **watercolour** gives the effect of light, with subtle colour variations. Light penetrates the transparent watercolour to the paper and is reflected back, giving the typical luminous effect.

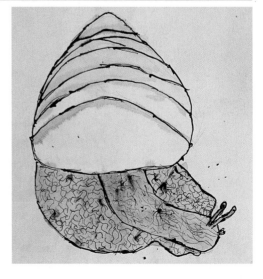

Figure 2.18
Snail, in ink and watercolour. Y3

Acrylics were first introduced in the 1920s. Similar to gouache and watercolours, they are water-based paints, but the colour pigments are not bound by gum arabic. Instead they are suspended in a transparent liquid plastic.

Gouache

AGES AND STAGES

With gouache, each colour has to dry before adding an adjacent colour to prevent the colours from merging. Children in Y1 tend to paint objects that do not overlap or connect so this is not a problem. In Y2, however, children often want to fill their paper with paint and, at this age, waiting for paint to dry is tedious. Painting a wash background is often a good idea (see page 38). A wash dries rapidly and then children can paint the foreground.

Children at KS2 are more willing to paint part of a picture and then leave it to dry so thick paints can be used throughout. Small areas of colour can be painted on top of large areas of colour. A plant, for example, could be painted as a mass of leaves. The complex network of negative spaces where the background colour shows through can then be painted on top of the greens when the paint has dried.

Figure 2.19
A landscape in gouache, painted in stages. Y6

USING GOUACHE PAINT

Gouache paint is supplied in a wide range of colours. A good basic range would be: black and white (for tints and shades), yellow ochre, lemon yellow, brilliant yellow, brilliant blue (or ultramarine), cobalt blue, crimson and vermilion. These colours provide warm and cool versions of the primaries that help in mixing colours accurately.

Gouache is supplied in powder form, ready-mixed liquid paint, finger paint and cake form.

Powder paint is a mainstay of art supplies in most schools. Gouache powder paint is relatively inexpensive and can be mixed to a thick or thin consistency, using varying volumes of water.

Liquid gouache paint is ready-mixed to a creamy consistency and is available in a wide variety of colours. It is relatively expensive but is easier to use than powder paint.

Finger paint is thickened gouache paint especially made for use with fingers to create a highly textured surface. Thick powder paint will crack and flake when it dries but finger paints have a gel or glue added to prevent this. Finger paint can be purchased from educational suppliers, or mixed in school using powder paint, as follows.

■ Mix washing-up liquid with powder paint. Mix in a one to one ratio; then add a little water to make a very thick paint. Use thick paper or card as a base.

■ Mix liquid or powdered gouache with thick paste to get a highly textured surface. Brush marks will show very clearly. Use a comb for water swirls or wood grains.

■ Mix thick paint with a little PVA glue.

Tip!
If a mistake is ruining a painting, start by saturating the paint with water from a sponge. Then blot the paint with tissues. Repeat until the colour has almost gone. Wait until it is dry and then paint over the surface.

Solid paint in cake form is popular because spillages do not occur and very little paint is wasted. The colour lasts longer because children have to work it up using a paint brush directly on the paint blocks. The time this takes makes it a frustrating medium for most children at KS1. Children at KS2 who rub the cake hard to gain enough depth of colour often wear down brushes. They need to stroke rather than scrub the brush back and forth. As it is very difficult to obtain enough colour for large areas of dense colour, these paints are most suited to small paintings, painting outdoors or washes.

PAPER

Paper with a slight 'tooth' such as sugar paper gives an ideal surface. The white base of gouache paint means that it is prominent on coloured, as well as on white, paper. Greys provide a neutral base for most subjects. Not all the paper has to be covered with paint. A well-chosen background paper can add to the colour scheme of a picture.

ORGANISATION

When powder colour containers are stored in a paint trolley, the colour labels on the containers are obscured. The colour cannot be ascertained from looking at the powder – a white powder may be red or blue – so it is useful to colour-code the tops of the pots. Excess mixed paint can be stored in an empty powder paint container with a sign such as a black dot to show it is ready-mixed.

It is important that children have control over the thickness of the paint. However, they tend to add too much water to powder paint and then waste paint by having to thicken the mixture. If there is a long-handled spoon in each pot, the children can ladle the powder into a mixing palette and use a plastic teaspoon to add water.

Ready-mixed gouache in squeezy bottles seems to encourage children to jet great quantities of paint into their palettes. Children need to be taught to squeeze a very small pool of colour into each palette and refill it when necessary.

Watercolour

KNOWLEDGE AND
UNDERSTANDING

*PoS 9c
Relate art to its time and
place of origin*

Watercolour has had a long history of popularity with painters in Europe because it encourages a free, spontaneous style of painting (Constable *Coast scene*, Shorewood 177DR; Gainsborough *Landscape*, Shorewood 156DR; Turner *Landscape*, Shorewood 171DR).

AGES AND STAGES

Watercolour is not an easy painting medium. Children at KS1 tend to mix colours too thickly and then the translucency is lost so it is safer to mix the washes for them. Ask older children, new to watercolour, to test a wash on scrap paper to check before they use it. Watercolour pencil is a useful introduction to watercolour as it gives children much more control over the density of colour.

For both KS1 and KS2 it is easier to use watercolour with an ink drawing. The form is already clear, with sharp linear details and the children can then concentrate on layering colour in subtle washes. Children at the end of KS2 can plan ahead and leave areas of the paper untouched for white. They can also use masking and quite sophisticated texturing techniques.

USING WATERCOLOUR
PAINT

*PoS 8d
Experiment with tools and
develop techniques*

Watercolour is supplied in different forms: dry and moist cake, a thick liquid in tubes, a thin liquid in bottles and water-soluble crayon.

Cake is the least expensive and is easiest to use. There is a basic range of colours and a lid helps to prevent them from drying out. They are very portable and they often have a built-in mixing tray making them ideal for painting outdoors.

A tube of thick liquid is useful for mixing washes with dense colours. It is very easy to squirt out too much colour – only a small dab is needed. The top needs to be securely in place to prevent all the paint in the tube from drying out.

A bottle (of thin liquid paint) is an expensive form of watercolour, but does provide a range of very bright colours. These are water soluble even when dry, so colours can always be blended with a damp brush. It is useful to have a set of bottled watercolours for painting focal points.

A water-colour pencil gives good control over colour density for small paintings. Scribble on a scrap of paper, pick the colour up with a damp paint brush and then apply it to a painting.

COLOUR

A good range of basic colours would be: Cerulean blue, Prussian blue, French ultramarine, Prussian green, Crimson lake, Cadmium red, Indian red, Sepia, Raw umber, Gamboge, Payne's grey and Davy's grey and black.

Avoid white as it muddies colours. Instead, make a colour lighter by adding water. Use black in a very dilute form and very sparingly as a shading tone at the end of a painting. Avoid mixing it with other colours as it makes them dull.

Watercolour is much darker in the palette than it appears on paper. When it dries it changes again to a lighter colour. It is very useful to record two different tonal strengths next to each colour's name on a large chart. If all the children have the same layout of colours in their trays, make the reference chart match the layout and shape of a tray.

PAPER

Good quality paper with a slight 'tooth' such as cartridge paper is ideal. If you can afford watercolour paper for a special painting, buy 'not paper' (not pressed). This is excellent for both details and washes. Paper needs to be white. Watercolour is translucent and relies on the paper being white to gain maximum reflection and glow.

Watercolour will cause paper to wrinkle as it dries. Stretching the paper is the only way to prevent this and is worth the trouble for special pictures.

1 Soak sheets of cartridge paper in a sink or tray of water for a few minutes.

2 Lift one of the sheets of paper out of the water, shaking off any drips. Place it flat on a board and tape down the sides. Thumb tacks can be used as a substitute for the tape (be careful not to tear the paper).

3 Take out another piece of paper and tape it over the top of the first paper. Make a pile of about five sheets before starting a new board.

4 Leave the paper to dry. As it dries, it shrinks and leaves a taut surface that will not wrinkle when it is painted.

BRUSHES

Use soft brushes of a high quality. Chinese brushes have long bristles and carry a large volume of colour for a wash, and the tip is pointed for fine detail. A slight change of pressure will alter the width of the stroke.

ACTIVITY

1 Use light layers of colour (Y3–Y6). Start with light washes, allowing each layer to dry. This will only take a few minutes if the washes are thin. Do not layer more than three colours to prevent a muddy effect.

2 Paint around the outline and then flood the area with paint (Y3–Y6). The outline will help to hold the paint in place.

3 Texturise the wet paint (Y5–Y6).

- Allow the paint to drift into patches and puddles for variation in colour tone.

- Blot some areas with screwed-up tissue paper.

- Sprinkle salt on wet paint for a highly textured finish for sand, rocks, old walls and foliage.

4 Use grey washes for shading at the end of the painting but before adding any fine details (Y5–Y6).

5 Add details (Y5–Y6).

- Use stronger watercolour paint on an almost dry brush.

- Add fine details in pencil, crayon or ink.

- Create dense textures with a well-defined edge by masking surrounding areas with paper and stippling colour with a stiff brush.

Figure 2.20
Leaf, with textured areas made by blotting with screwed-up tissue paper, in ink and watercolour. Y5

PoS 4a
Investigate pattern and texture

PoS 4b
Investigate colour

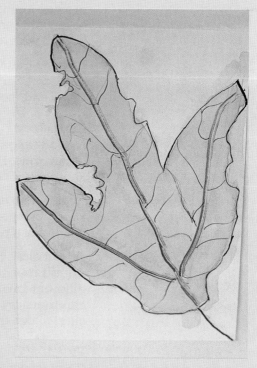

Acrylics

KNOWLEDGE AND UNDERSTANDING

PoS 9d
Respond to and compare different styles and traditions

Acrylic paints were developed in the 1920s for use in industry and it was only in the 1950s that artists began to realise their potential (Ting *Japanese garden*, Goodwill 1(8); Hoyland *Saracen*, Goodwill 3(25)). Many of the hard edges in abstract paintings were achieved with masking tape and rapidly drying acrylics – oil paints took too long to dry.

AGES AND STAGES

PoS 7e
Use knowledge of artists' work

The thick texture of acrylic and its resistance to colour merging means that it shares many of the characteristics of oil paint. The majority of reproductions of paintings children will discuss in school will have been originally painted in oils, yet primary schools cannot use oil paints because of the trouble and expense of cleaning with petrol and diluting with turpentine and linseed oil.

Primary school budgets do not usually allow children of all ages to have access to acrylic paints. If a choice has to be made, it is children at the end of KS2 who most often need the stimulus of a novel and very exciting painting material. Acrylics show brush marks very clearly so encourage children at KS2 consciously to choose subjects with interesting movements and textures – splashing waves, windy skies, fluffy clouds and scaly animals.

USING ACRYLIC PAINT

COLOUR

It is useful to have a cool and warm version of each primary and secondary colour plus a large amount of white and some black and brown. Pearlescent or iridescent acrylics have shimmering colours that look wonderful as butterflies' wings or water. For a more subtle sheen, cover with a wash of thin, non-iridescent acrylic paint.

Figure 2.21
Butterfly, in pearlescent
acrylic. Y3

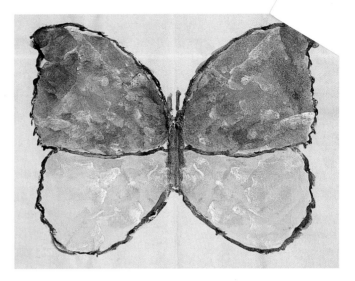

SUPPORT

Acrylic can be painted on any non-greasy surface – plastic, wood, stone, fabric, glass, paper. Use strong paper such as cartridge paper to minimise wrinkling. Paper that is thin will crinkle badly unless it is stretched first (see page 47). Coat the paper with a wash of emulsion paint to prevent the paper soaking up the paint. Card with a slightly shiny surface is an ideal alternative to paper. It does not crinkle and the surface reduces paint absorption.

BRUSH

Use soft brushes for washes and fine details, and bristle brushes and palette knives for applying thick paint. Start with a large brush to encourage children to paint large shapes first.

Wash brushes thoroughly in soap and water after using acrylic, otherwise the paint will harden and ruin the brush. Because of this risk, use inexpensive synthetic brushes. If children are using several brushes, it may be best to allow them to leave the brushes in water. (This is not generally a recommended practice as it distorts brushes, but it is better to risk this than ruin the brush.)

Use fingers for sweeping and swirling movements of colour and to add textures such as scales on a lizard or curls on a head. Use different fingers for different colours. A palette knife is useful for making shapes and adding details that need to be straight; especially useful for buildings and perspective lines.

ORGANISATION

Children will need to learn never to pollute the source colours and never to throw away any leftover paints. Spoon clean paint back into the containers and mix polluted paints together to made a muddy, neutral colour for future use.

Acrylic paints do not wash out easily. The same adhesive quality that makes acrylics so versatile also applies to school clothing so children will need to use waterproof aprons. Keep damp cloths on the table to wipe sticky hands.

Some paint will dry on the palette during the lesson and will not be easy to wash off. Soak the palette in water to soften the paint and scrape it off with the handle of an old brush.

ACTIVITY

PoS 8d
Experiment with tools and develop techniques

1 Add a collage section in an acrylic painting (Y2–Y6). Shells, sand, pebbles and driftwood will stick to a thickly painted area of sea and sand.

2 Use acrylic washes (Y5–Y6).

 • Acrylic washes do not have the subtle colour variations of watercolour washes but they do have the important advantage of being able to overlay colours without getting muddy. Make sure the first wash is completely dry before beginning the second (about ten minutes).

 • Use acrylics to paint a wash background and then overlay with gouache. This is economic and makes the gouache colours more intense.

PRINT-MAKING

Main NC focus

PoS 8d
Children should be taught
to experiment with tools
and techniques for . . .
print-making and develop
control of tools and
techniques (KS2)

Introduction

Printing is a very different techniques from other ways of making art. In printing, children create the surface that will make a picture, rather than working directly on paper and, instead of producing one picture, the printing process results in repeated images. Children enjoy the unpredictable nature of printing; it is an exciting moment when the paper is lifted from a printing block.

Figure 3.1
Cars, made from a cut-shape card print, on a rollered background, in printing inks. Y4

This chapter includes:

■ General printing equipment (page 51)
■ Types of print (page 53)
direct prints (page 53); printing with rollers (page 55); raised-relief prints (page 56); rubbings (page 58); shaped and incised blocks (page 60); monoprinting (page 67); stencil prints (page 71); transfer prints (page 79).

PoS 9d
Respond to and compare
different styles and
traditions

Knowledge and understanding through print-making

The discovery of printing was revolutionary. For the first time, it allowed mass production of the written word and pictures. Printing has a strong association with the reproduction of books and fabric patterns, which means it has often been considered, in Europe, to be more of a craft than a creative tool. Despite this, Dürer in Renaissance Germany and Blake and Hogarth in eighteenth-century Britain used the printing process to make great and enduring works of art.

It was the influence of Japanese prints that revived an interest in printing as an art form during the Art Nouveau and Expressionist periods at the end of the last century (Sekkyo *Eagle*, Shorewood 410; Hiroshige *Full moon*, Goodwill 1(1)). More recent artists such as Picasso and Warhol (*Marilyn*, Goodwill 3(26)) have been happy to use a full range of printing techniques; from traditional wood-block to the more modern screen printing, to make visually stimulating and easily duplicated images.

PoS 4a–d
Learn about visual and
tactile elements

Ages and stages

Printing is a creative process which involves space, shape, line and pattern. Children have to decide how and where multiple images should be placed. They can also vary the amount of ink on the printing block and apply different pressures to produce subtle variations in tone and texture in each print.

Printing allows children to control easily these visual elements. This generates a feeling of control and mastery which is a particular asset at KS2 when many children begin to lose self-confidence in art. Rubbings or trial prints are also easily made so that the work can be reviewed and modified as it progresses.

General printing equipment

PRINTING INK

Traditional printing ink is oil-based, which makes it impractical for primary schools but excellent results can be achieved with water-based printing ink and thickened paint.

WATER-BASED PRINTING INK, FINGER PAINT AND ACRYLIC MIXED WITH A PRINTING GEL

All these resist mixing, retain moisture and are ready for printing over a long time period. They make prints with bright, bold colours. The print adheres to the paper and does not fade or flake off, even if the print is used as a book cover.

WATERCOLOUR, TEMPERA, POSTER AND POWDER PAINT

These paints give more muted hues. The colours dry on the block very quickly and tend to flake off the paper after drying. Mix in a PVA glue, paste, Blockmix or Gelmix medium to keep the paints moist and stable.

If paints are used without this medium, use a sponge (not a roller) to apply colour to the block. The paints need to be worked on the block quickly or they will dry before the print can be taken. Printing inks make prints with stronger colours and higher definition than paints, but they are sticky and less easy to manage. Because of this some teachers, especially at KS1, prefer to use paints.

PRINTING SUPPORT

Prints can be made on stones, bricks, walls and wood but the more usual supports are paper and fabric.

Tip!

Often the best print is the second one. If children roller too much ink on to the printing surface, they could make a first print on newspaper and use the second one for the printing paper.

PAPER

Plain, white cartridge paper provides a strong contrast for dark or bright prints. Different weights and colours of paper can add interest to a print: wallpaper, newsprint, brown paper, wrapping paper, sugar paper, tissue paper. Avoid metallic paper as ink remains sticky on this surface.

FABRIC

Fabric needs thick fabric dyes or acrylic paints mixed with a fabric medium; ordinary paints bleed into the fabric and make an indistinct print. Sponging (not rollering) the colour on the printing block will make a more uniformly coloured print.

Most fabric dyes can be fixed by ironing on the back when the print is dry. Others, such as Berol Fabritint, need to have a fixer painted on afterwards. The fixer stiffens the fabric, so it is better to apply it after displaying the work. The fabric has to be left in a polythene bag for at least two hours and then sent home to be handwashed in warm soapy water.

Thin cotton is an inexpensive and versatile fabric for making prints but it tends to move and crease during the printing process. There is the same problem with stretchy T-shirt fabrics. A piece of card or wad of newspaper pushed inside the T-shirt or stapled to the cloth acts as a stiffener.

Coarse-weave, natural fabric, such as hessian, gives a very interesting texture to a finished print.

ORGANISATION

Lessons that involve sticky printing inks are not easy to manage and need careful organisation. If there are limited washing facilities, use paint, which is easier to deal with.

Printing inks remain sticky for 24 hours where the ink is thick and the prints stick together if allowed to touch. A drying rack is ideal for storage, or prints could be pegged to a washing line.

SETTING UP A PRINTING AREA
This layout helps to keep the printing area neat.

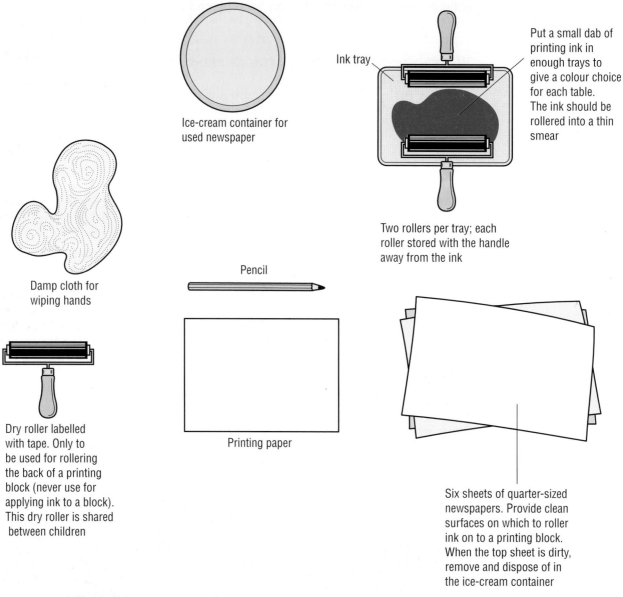

Ice-cream container for used newspaper

Ink tray

Put a small dab of printing ink in enough trays to give a colour choice for each table. The ink should be rollered into a thin smear

Two rollers per tray; each roller stored with the handle away from the ink

Damp cloth for wiping hands

Pencil

Printing paper

Six sheets of quarter-sized newspapers. Provide clean surfaces on which to roller ink on to a printing block. When the top sheet is dirty, remove and dispose of in the ice-cream container

Dry roller labelled with tape. Only to be used for rollering the back of a printing block (never use for applying ink to a block). This dry roller is shared between children

Figure 3.2
Setting up a printing area.

Pad the printing area with several layers of newspapers before placing the printing paper on top to give a softer surface for a better print.

Types of print

PoS 4a
Investigate pattern and texture

Direct prints

Printing with inked or painted objects is called direct printing and children enjoy the immediate and dramatic impact of this type of print. Probably the first printing that most children do is to put dirty hands on a clean surface.

KNOWLEDGE AND UNDERSTANDING

PoS 9c
Relate art to its time and place of origin

Artists as well as children have been intrigued by hand prints. Hand prints appear in pre-historic paintings at Lascaux and also in Picasso's lithography work. Long's *Mud hand circle*, Ginn 12, is a wall mural made exclusively from hand prints. It has been a tradition in Britain to decorate walls with direct prints from crumpled cloth and children may have seen wallpapers that imitate this technique.

AGES AND STAGES

Children at KS1 will find it easier to start printing with rigid objects; they are much easier to handle and can be pushed into an inked pad. Encourage children to make densely patterned areas rather than scatter images across the printing paper. A variety of colours and papers will give interesting variations to prints from the same object.

Direct observation or research will help children at KS2 to match the shape, pattern and texture in a print to that of the real object. At this stage they can discuss the important link between shape, texture and function, for example the strength of the brick pattern in buildings; the streamlining effect of overlapping scales and feather growth; the head, thorax and abdomen of insects.

PRINTING WITH FOUND OBJECTS

EXPERIMENTING

Children need a variety of materials to choose from, so begin to collect objects well ahead of time and keep them in a printing box.

Encourage children to experiment on newspaper or scrap paper to test whether the print is what they anticipated. They will be surprised how some promising materials, such as Lego, prove disappointing and some apparently 'boring' objects, such as crumpled newspaper, provide subtle and interesting prints.

PoS 8d
Experiment with tools and develop techniques

PRINTING WITH RIGID OBJECTS

This technique is for objects that are rigid enough to be pushed into printing ink: screws, sticks, wire mesh, sponges, toothbrushes, tops from containers, washers, straws, small boxes and cylinders, wood, pieces of card – the edge can be curved and shaped – (corrugated card gives an interesting wavy edge to a print); sections of vegetables such as onions, green peppers, okra, leeks; body parts – fingers, hands, feet.

The technique is as follows.

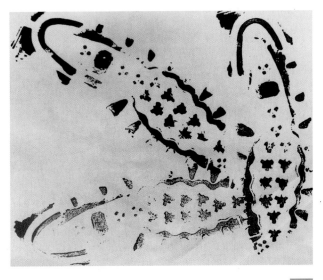

1 Pad the printing area with several layers of newspaper underneath the printing paper. The softer surface produces a better print.

2 Roller out the ink on a printing tray or charge a sponge with ink. Push the end of the object into the printing ink in the tray or sponge and print directly on to the paper. Rid the object of excess ink by making a first print on newspaper.

Figure 3.3
Three-shoe shuffle, direct print of a shoe sole, in printing inks. Y1

PRINTING WITH SOFT OBJECTS

This technique is for objects that are too delicate and pliable to be pressed into ink, for example pieces of fabric (open-weave hessian, lace and net make good prints), paper doilies, leaves, feathers, socks.

You will need: printing ink or paint rolled thinly in a tray, a roller for each colour, metal spoons or small pieces of soft cloth.

Figure 3.4 shows two methods of applying ink to a soft object.

a

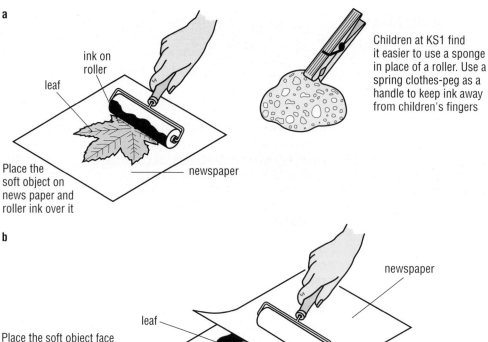

ink on roller

leaf

Children at KS1 find it easier to use a sponge in place of a roller. Use a spring clothes-peg as a handle to keep ink away from children's fingers

newspaper

Place the soft object on news paper and roller ink over it

b

newspaper

leaf

Figure 3.4
Inking a found soft object; two methods.

Place the soft object face down on to an inked surface, cover it with newspaper and roller firmly.

inked surface

There are also two methods of making a print (Figure 3.5).

1

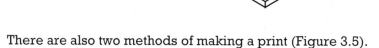

newspaper

Pick up the inked object and place it ink-side down on the printing paper. Cover with a small sheet of newspaper. Rub over the newspaper with a soft cloth or the back of a spoon. The newspaper will stop the ink from spreading around the printing paper. Replace with a clean piece of newspaper for each print

printing paper

2

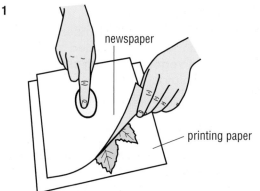

printing paper

Place the object, ink-side up on a sheet of clean newspaper and position the printing paper on top. Apply pressure with a soft cloth or the back of a spoon. This method is less messy, but it is more difficult to position the print accurately

newspaper

Figure 3.5
Making a print with a soft object; two methods.

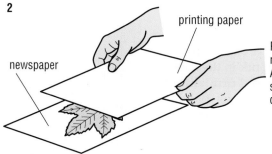

ACTIVITY

PoS 7b
Use resources to stimulate ideas

1 Use a large brush to charge a natural sponge with dye (Y1–Y2). Lightly press it against fabric for a mottled effect. Use several sponges in different colours.

2 Use imaginative ideas sparked by the printing material as a starting point for a picture (Y1–Y6). A natural-sponge print may remind some children of leaves on a tree, others may think of coral or rock formations.

3 Make an invisible plan for a print (Y5–Y6). Heavily outline a drawing in soft pencil or ink and place it under a thin piece of printing paper so the drawing can be seen during printing. Fill in the spaces of a design with closely-worked patterns rather than tracking around the edges. The absence of a heavy outline greatly enhances a print.

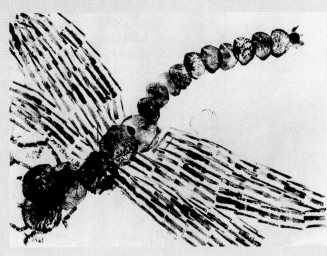

Figure 3.6
Dragonfly, direct print using found objects closely printed, in printing inks. Y6

PoS 4a
Investigate pattern and texture

Prints with rollers

Rollers are usually used for transferring ink to a printing block, but they also make a print with dramatic movement and textures if they are used directly on to the paper. They are made very quickly so roller prints provide excellent backgrounds for other kinds of prints. They can be used for windswept skies, waves of the sea, rolling hills and rays of a setting sun.

EQUIPMENT

The equipment for this technique is relatively simple: rollers, printing trays with printing ink, paper.

A variety of rollers will give different shapes and textures. Rubber printing rollers make interestingly textured prints because they spread ink unevenly. Sponge rollers give a more uniform print which can be varied by altering the pressure. Flock rollers, used in home decorations, are generally too wide for an individual print but they make an interestingly textured background for a large display.

MAKING THE PRINT

Children need to roller the colours on to the paper with vigorous and purposeful strokes. A variety of pressures will create different depths of colour. Children enjoy the action of the rollers, so they tend to prolong the rollering and blanket the paper with colour. They may need reminding that it is the mottled colours and the spaces created between the strokes which make the print attractive.

CARE!

ACTIVITY

1 Make roller prints of different widths, vertically up from the bottom of the paper (Y2–Y6). These look like skyscrapers or blocks of flats. Add details with direct prints.

2 Deliberately load the roller unevenly with ink (Y5–Y6). This makes an interesting repeat pattern. Use lines for bamboo or divided-field landscapes. Use irregular shapes on a sponge roller for tree trunks, clouds or hills.

3 Use the edge of the roller to print linear details on a print (Y5–Y6).

4 Alter the texture of an old sponge roller by cutting away sections of the sponge surface or by gluing small sponge shapes on to the roller (Y6).

Figure 3.7
Blocks of flats, roller-printed, in printing inks. Y2

Raised-relief prints

PoS 4a
Investigate pattern and
texture

Children enjoy the creativity of making their own printing blocks by arranging and gluing string or small objects to card to create a relief surface. Raised surfaces pick up the ink more than the background and make interestingly textured images when they are printed.

AGES AND STAGES

Children at the beginning of KS1 need to see a quick result so they can relate their work to the image it produces. Keep the blocks small and simple; a few lines of string can make a very effective print.

By KS2, children are willing to spend longer making a printing block. They could look through reference books for shapes with interesting outlines and simple internal texture lines, for example: leaves, a fish, a face, a rocket. Alternatively, they could make lines and textures for abstract or repeat patterns.

Too great a variety of objects on the printing block can lead to a confusing mixture of textures on a print. Encourage children to glue similar objects closely together to make tightly-textured shapes and lines.

PoS 8f
Review and adapt the
work

Children at KS2 can review the progress of the printing block by making rubbings (see page 58). If there are any uninteresting areas, children can then make adjustments. At this stage, a whole lesson may be spent making a printing block and a second lesson will be needed to make the prints.

Figure 3.8
Portrait, a) rubbing; b) direct print, from a collaged printing block, in printing inks. Y3

EQUIPMENT

PRINTING PAPER
Use plain paper as a background for a complex print. A more complex background (such as a roller-print background) works if the printing block has a simple design and the background is in muted paints.

ADDITIONAL EQUIPMENT

Strong glue (for example UHU), scissors, printing trays with printing ink, rollers, pads and soft cloth are also required. UHU glue is messy but it allows children to print after waiting 30 minutes. PVA glue is inexpensive and cleaner to use than UHU but will need to dry overnight.

H & S

MAKING A PRINTING BLOCK

PoS 8d
Experiment with tools and develop techniques

PRINTING WHEEL

Children can create raised surfaces on rollers using string or fabric pieces. These prints will cover a large area very quickly so they are particularly useful for printing textured backgrounds in display areas.

1 Wrap string around a card, metal or plastic cylinder. Use toilet-roll centres, drinks cans or shampoo bottles. Secure the string-ends at the sides with tape or elastic bands. If there is time, cover the cylinder in glue, wind the string around and allow to dry overnight. Children in Y1 may find the string too difficult to fix. Substitute elastic bands and wrap them in overlapping patterns around the cylinder.

Alternatively, cut out shapes in felt and glue them on to a can or tube.

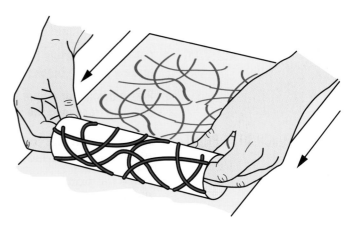

2 Roller the wheel up and down in a tray of printing ink to cover the printing surface. Start at the lower edge of the paper and roller up the paper. Repeat the movement to create a design.

Figure 3.9
Roller print, using string glued to a cylinder. Y1

CARD-RELIEF BLOCK

Cut out card or paper shapes and glue them to a rectangle of card. The shapes can be glued in a single layer or can be layered, although the contrast in relief should not be too great. Narrow gaps between the raised parts will produce a printing block with better definition.

A shallow card-relief printing block gives a halo of white separating the shapes from the background. A high-relief block produces more distinct prints. Cut round the outline of the block to obtain a clearly defined shape.

COLLAGED BLOCK

Collaged blocks are made from a wide variety of objects and materials glued on to card with strong glue. Allow 24 hours for glue to dry thoroughly if it is PVA glue. Impact glue dries in 30 minutes.

H & S

GLUE AND STRING BLOCK

Prints from glue and string blocks have a linear, flowing style especially suited to textures and shapes in the natural environment, for example shells, feathers and tree bark.

There are three ways of making the printing block.

1 Make lines on a rectangle of card with household cement squeezed directly from the tube. The lines of glue make ridges on the card that pick up the printing ink. PVA glue takes longer to dry than impact glue, but the ridges are more pronounced and make clearer prints.

2 Cover a rectangle of card with a thick layer of PVA glue and then create lines in the glue with a stick or a card comb.

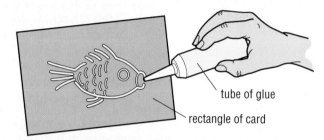

Figure 3.10
Making a relief printing block with glue.

3 Lay string along lines of glue.

tube of glue

rectangle of card

ACTIVITY

1 Cut up card that has been previously textured with glue and allowed to dry, and make a printing block (Y3–Y6).

2 Plan a design for a glue print (Y5–Y6). Sketch the design in pencil on a card block and then trace over the lines with UHU glue from a tube.

MAKING THE PRINT

1 Use a small roller to ink the printing block. Turn the roller in all directions to ensure all the surfaces have been covered.

2 Place the printing paper over the printing block and burnish the surface with the back of a spoon or with a cloth pad. This method applies more localised pressure than using a roller which is very important for a printing block with shallow or uneven relief.

3 Lift up the paper.

Rubbings

PoS 4a–d
Investigate visual and tactile elements

To make a rubbing, place a piece of paper on top of a relief block and then use a wax crayon to rub across the surface of the paper. When artists create their own relief surfaces from which to make rubbings, the technique is called frottage.

Rubbing blocks are inexpensive to produce because they use scrap paper. Once a block has been made, rubbings can be produced very quickly, in limitless numbers, without the need to find adequate drying space. These rubbing blocks can later be used with printing inks to make raised-relief prints.

Figure 3.11
Man, rubbings made from a single block, using rubbing sticks. Y4

KNOWLEDGE AND UNDERSTANDING

PoS 9c
Relate art to its time and place of origin

One of the most important functions of rubbings is to record artists' work from the past. Children may have seen rubbings made from memorial brasses in churches and bas-reliefs on temple walls. A local church may allow children to make rubbings.

Some abstract artists such as Ernst (*Temptation of Saint Anthony*, Goodwill 3(28)) included rubbings in their work.

ACTIVITY

PoS 8f
Review and adapt the work

1 Experiment with rubbings around school (Y1–Y4). Examine different textures and surfaces. Record them by making rubbings, for example manhole covers, decorative plaster work, paving stones, anaglypta wallpaper, sandpaper, floor mats, stippled cement walls, wood with distinct grain, bark, leaves. Use thin paper. Take samples from the most interesting rubbings and record where they were made for future reference.

AGES AND STAGES

Making relief blocks for rubbings (frottage) gives valuable experience in exploring texture, pattern, shape, line and space. Cutting accurate shapes and arranging them precisely also helps children to build-up a good knowledge of the exact composition of the subjects of the print, for example insects, flowers, buildings, figures, shoes.

In general, at KS2 it is better to use the same colour of paper for the main shapes and the details that are overlayed. This makes children more conscious of the build-up of layers without the distraction of colour. However, this does not work well with children at KS1, who tend to draw details on the card rather than cut out shapes. Using coloured paper will satisfy this need to see the detail, while still showing on the rubbing.

Unlike most other media, frottage allows children to go back a stage if they are not happy with a result. Glue from Pritt Stick will hold the shapes in place but will also allow them to be removed and replaced. Children at KS2 who are not very skilled at drawing often produce lively and interesting rubbings.

FROTTAGE – MAKING THE RUBBING BLOCKS

PoS 8d
Experiment with tools and develop techniques

EQUIPMENT
Scissors, smooth cellulose paste or thin PVA glue, sugar paper or thin card, wax crayons or rubbing sticks are required.

METHOD
1 Place a paper or card shape (for example a figure) on a straight-edged completely flat piece of paper.

2 Cut across the shape in several places and spread the pieces apart slightly. When the positioning of the shapes is finished, use small amounts of thin glue to stick them to the paper. These spaces will show as lines on the rubbing.

3 Place cut shapes on top of the first layer. This second layer will register as an additional texture on the rubbing as long as the layers are not made too thick – two layers are ideal. A third layer of thin tissue paper is a possible exception.

ACTIVITY

1 Use a strikingly different colour for the background (Y1–Y6). A black background with a sliced and spread white paper shape will produce a dramatic paper collage design. The collage picture will complement the rubbing in a display.

H & S

2 Use lines of glue on the rubbing block (Y1–Y6).

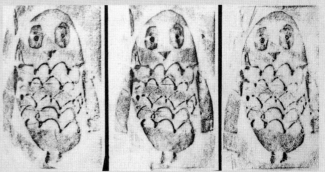

Figure 3.12
Three feathered owls; glue was used to give feather-like texture, in printing inks. Y1

• Add a few lines of impact glue for detail (Y1–Y6). When the glue is almost dry it holds the rubbing paper safely in place while the rubbing is made.

• Make dense patterns of lines on a piece of card (Y3–Y4). Allow the glue to dry and then cut up the card to make an image for a rubbing block.

3 Make folds in the paper (Y3–Y6).

• Cut lines in the sides of a shape and fold back part of the shape for an interesting texture (Y3–Y6).

MAKING THE RUBBING

1 Check the table surface and the rubbing block base are clean. The smallest speck of grit will show on the rubbing.

2 Place a clean piece of paper over the rubbing block and paper-clip them together. Children can concentrate best on the creative aspect of making the rubbing if someone else holds down the paper during the rubbing.

3 Use the whole length of a wax crayon to rub across the block. An alternative is to use the tip of a crayon which gives a harder pressure but often makes the layer of colour uneven. Certain parts of the block can be emphasised by hard rubbing. The direction of a stroke also contributes to the formation of the picture.

4 Move the block to make repeat rubbings, or exchange rubbing blocks to make composite pictures.

ACTIVITY

1 Use a candle on white paper and paint ink over the rubbing (Y1–Y2).

2 Make several contrasting images from the same printing block (Y1–Y6). First rub with black crayon on white paper, and then with white crayon on black paper.

3 Use different base lines and different intensities of rubbing to create a sense of distance (Y5–Y6).

Shaped and incised blocks

PoS 4c and d
Investigate line, shape and space

Shaped printing blocks can be made from card, rolled clay and Plasticine, polystyrene, potato, soft balsa wood or lino cut into shapes. The blocks can be printed as solid areas of colour or they can have linear details incised. Incisions remove areas from a printing block to avoid contact with the ink. The incised details print the colour of the paper; the rest of the shape prints the colour of the ink.

Figure 3.13
Leaves, direct observational prints, using an incised printing block, in printing inks. Y5

Reduction printing (page 65) allows images to be built up in layers of colour.

KNOWLEDGE AND UNDERSTANDING

PoS 5c
Examine styles from a variety of cultures

Carved printing blocks were first used for book illustrations and making playing cards. They have also been used for centuries by artists to reproduce pictures in large quantities for sale to the public. This constant reuse meant they had to be made in a highly durable material, usually hardwood. Block printing has also been used to illustrate books with fine lines and details (Ravilious *Wood engraving of an owl*, Ginn 37; Dürer *Rhinoceros*, ISIS, British Museum Print Room, London).

CARD SILHOUETTE PRINTS

PoS 4d
Investigate shape, form and space

A silhouette has great dramatic impact. Heavily textured backgrounds, such as a monoprint, paper collage or roller prints, overwhelm most other types of prints, but a silhouette print in a contrasting colour looks striking. Silhouette prints on a plain background may look a little stark and need direct prints for added details.

AGES AND STAGES
Encourage children at KS1 to make large silhouette shapes as these are easier to manage. Children at this stage enjoy casting shadows to find silhouettes that

will show an object clearly, for example a jug will look more interesting with the handle to one side. Children at KS2 could make more complex shapes with internal cuts and divisions.

Figure 3.14
Trees made from a card silhouette print, on a tissue paper background, in printing inks. Y6

MAKING THE PRINT
Card is probably the best-suited and least expensive material from which to make a silhouette print. Cut out a card shape, roller ink over the surface and lay the shape ink-side down on a piece of paper. Use a dry roller to apply pressure and then lift the shape to reveal the print.

ACTIVITY

1 Print over a solid printed area to add textures and patterns (Y3–Y6). A hedgehog, for example, could be printed as a solid light-brown shape using a card cut-shape printing block. Allow the block to dry and then cover it with glued matchsticks. Print in dark brown over the original print.

2 Make a night scene by rollering thin white paint on black paper for sky and over-printing with black silhouette card shapes (Y5–Y6).

PLASTICINE OR CLAY PRINTING BLOCKS
PoS 8d
Experiment with tools and develop techniques

Rollered Plasticine or clay is easy to cut and the soft, yielding surfaces make them ideal for texturing. Use old Plasticine (new Plasticine resists water-based paints). Plasticine has the advantage over paper and clay in that it can be used, washed and reused.

AGES AND STAGES
Using Plasticine or clay is an excellent introduction to incised printing for children at KS1. The material is easier to cut and texture than Polyblock (page 62).

MAKING A PRINTING BLOCK

CARE!

Roller out the Plasticine or clay as evenly as possible. Use wooden slats at each side to make sure pressure on the roller is distributed evenly. Draw the outline of the printing block with a pencil and press objects into the Plasticine or clay within the block area to create detail. The end of a pencil, for example, makes good scales for a fish. Cut out the shape using a table knife.

MAKING THE PRINT
Roller with printing ink. Place the printing block ink-side down on printing paper and use a dry roller to apply light, even pressure on the back of the block. Lift off the block and apply more ink for a second print. The textures may need to be re-drawn before a third print.

ACTIVITY
PoS 4a
Investigate pattern and texture

1 Model a large piece of clay or Plasticine into a shape like a rubber stamp (Y1–Y2). Hold the 'handle' and flatten the 'stamp' by pressing it on a table top. Texture the flattened surface and press gently against the table a second time to check it is flat. Press the stamp into ink and print a design.

2 Make a Plasticine or clay wheel on a pencil axle (Y1–Y6). Use a pencil to draw, poke and push textures on to the outside of the wheel. Vary the direction of the print. Make parallel, wavy, interweaving or intersecting lines. Wheel prints can be made to look like tall grass, flames or flowing water.

POLYBLOCK PRINTING BLOCKS

Polyblock, made from dense polystyrene, is supplied by EJ Arnold. The same product is supplied by Berol (Press Print) and by Nottingham Educational Supplies (Easiprint). Polystyrene food trays can be substituted for Polyblock, but they sometimes leave a distinct grid pattern on the print.

Polyblock is expensive and intricate shapes take time to prepare, but the lines are easily incised and remain well-defined, despite frequent use. The blocks can be washed and other colours applied.

AGES AND STAGES

Children at KS1 should draw directly on the block. Older children could plan out their design and then transfer it as mistakes cannot be rectified and the material is too expensive to waste.

PoS 2c
Design and make creative images and artefacts

MAKING THE PRINTING BLOCK

Transfer the design (Y3–Y6) by pencilling a design on a piece of paper exactly the same size as the Polyblock. Clip the paper on to the block and push a pencil or ball-point pen through the paper in quick, short strokes. Throw away the paper or save it for later if you want to mask the background (see page 66).

CARE!

Separate the shape from the rest of the block (Y3–Y6) by cutting straight edges with scissors, but be careful, the material snaps easily if a sharp corner is turned with the scissors. Always cut into the corners rather than turning them. Make sure the whole shape is cut around before pushing the background away.

Avoid thin projections that are easily broken, such as insect legs. It is better to make the body in Polyblock and then add the legs with direct prints.

H & S

Add texture and detail by drawing lines, and press or hammer objects into the surface. Each mark on the block will remain the colour of the printing paper when the print is made. Children at the end of KS2 could use a craft knife for internal cuts.

MAKING THE PRINT

Roller with coloured printing inks or paint sections of colour to produce a multiply coloured print. Place the block ink-side down on the paper and use a dry roller to apply even pressure to the back of the block. Lift off the block and make a second print. A third print may need a further application of ink.

Create an even tone by increasing the pressure with the dry roller for each successive print.

Tip!
Make emergency repairs on snapped Polyblock by taping the back with paper tape. Be careful the tape ends do not overwrap to the front of the block.

ACTIVITY

PoS 4c
Images are made using line and tone

1 Mix paint with washing-up liquid (Y1–Y6). When it is sponged on the printing block it creates a bubbly texture.

2 Use patterned paper as supports for simple prints in black ink (Y1–Y6), for example, marbled paper, painted paper, newspaper or layered tissue paper.

POTATO PRINTS

PoS 4a
Investigate pattern and texture

The cut surface of a potato is easy to carve. The absorbent and slightly broken texture of the potato gives a print a soft quality which is particularly effective on fabric. Unfortunately, a potato block deteriorates rapidly and cannot be used many times. It has to be used the day it is cut, or kept overnight in a fridge.

AGES AND STAGES

Children at KS1 can safely carve out sections of a potato block with a blunt knife or hair-grip.

A potato block allows children at KS2 to carve swirling lines that are difficult to produce with harder carving materials, such as balsa wood and lino.

MAKING THE PRINTING BLOCK

H & S

1 Cut a potato in half. Make sure that the cut surface is perfectly flat by using a sharp knife (an adult will need to do this). Blot the surface with a rag to make it easier to carve.

2 Shape the printing block by slicing off sections from the sides of the potato. Make a square or rectangle for dense, repeated patterns. Alternatively, keep the original and pleasing oval shape.

Figure 3.15
Beetles, using a potato print, on a rollered background, in printing inks. Y1

3 Carve the design directly on to the surface; preliminary drawings usually encourage inappropriate detail. Test and modify the design as it is carved. Avoid cutting away too much or the design will look weak and disjointed.

a) To carve straight lines: use a table knife to make two sloping cuts that meet each other. These V-shaped grooves make the projecting areas stronger. Use lino-cutting tools to remove clean grooves in the block.

H & S

b) To carve curved lines: hold a lino-cutting tool in one hand and press against the potato, while rotating the potato with the other hand. Younger children should use the rounded end of a hair-grip and pull it towards them.

c) To carve spotted or broken areas: jab the tool into the surface and remove small sections of potato.

MAKING THE PRINT

1 At the back of the potato cut a snick near the top edge to mark which way up the potato should be held during printing.

2 Paint the surface with watercolour and make a print, recharging with paint after each print. The transparency of watercolour looks particularly effective with potato prints. Thicker printing inks can also be used, which will not need recharging so frequently.

ACTIVITY

1 Make a square-shaped printing block, and print the block without gaps, to make a solid area of lines and shapes (Y3–Y6). Use the pattern for covering a book or as special wrapping paper.

2 Print on fabric to make scarves, cushion covers, book covers or handkerchiefs (Y5–Y6).

LINO-CUTS

PoS 4a–d
Learn about visual and tactile elements

Lino prints are made from a cut picture and not a drawing, so they have a vigorous quality in texture and line similar to that in woodcuts. Lino has no grain so, unlike wood, it can be cut in any direction. A lino-cut printing block is stronger than Polyblock, Plasticine or clay so it can be used for multiple prints. This makes it a very good choice for Christmas cards, wrapping paper, school programmes and invitations.

Begin by cutting textures with lino tools on small squares of lino, without any pre-planning in pencil.

Figure 3.16
Lino-cut faces.

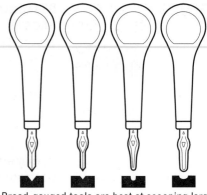

Broad-gauged tools are best at scooping large areas of lino

Figure 3.17
Lino-cutting tools.

MAKING THE LINO PRINTING BLOCK

A range of lino tools (Figure 3.17), pieces of lino from art suppliers, bench presses, paper, printing inks and rollers are required.

HEALTH AND SAFETY

Great care must be taken to ensure children's safety. Misuse of a tool can result in a deep cut to the hand. A bench press allows children to turn a lino block safely. If there are no bench presses, tape a lino block to a larger wooden board to create a wider margin between the hand grip and the block. Figure 3.18 highlights important safety aspects.

Figure 3.18
Cutting lino using a bench press.

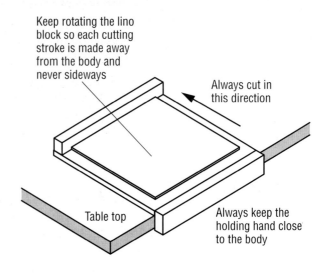

Keep rotating the lino block so each cutting stroke is made away from the body and never sideways

Always cut in this direction

Table top

Always keep the holding hand close to the body

Tip!

On a warm, sunny day leave the lino pieces in the sun to soften. This makes cutting easier.

AGES AND STAGES

Printing with lino-cuts is probably the most difficult of all the incised printing techniques for primary children and should be left until the end of KS2.

A useful introduction to lino-cutting for children in Y3 and Y4 is to use scissors to cut up a lino block into interesting but simple shapes, for example a series of skyscrapers, the wings and body sections of an insect. These can then be glued to the centre of a piece of strong card and a few lines cut in each shape to add texture and detail. The U-shaped tool is easiest to use. This provides a quick and effective way of producing a lino print with a minimum number of cuts and a maximum space between a child's hand and cutter.

MAKING THE PRINT

After the printing block has been carved, draw an arrow on the back to show the upright position of the design. Roller on the printing ink and place the printing paper over the top. Burnish with the back of a spoon before lifting the paper off.

ACTIVITY	
PoS 5c *Review and adapt the work*	1 If there are large areas of white on the print, allow the print to dry and then use delicate paint washes to add colour and texture (Y5–Y6).
	2 Slightly alter the position of an image between prints (Y5–Y6). This produces a print with intriguing lines and textures.

PRINTING IN MORE THAN ONE COLOUR

PoS 4b
Investigate colour

CARE!

Figure 3.19
Lizard, using reduction printing on Polyblock, printing inside a masked area, in printing inks. Y6

Printing blocks are usually rollered in one colour and then printed, but there are ways of producing more than one colour – on the printing block itself, or through the reduction process (see below).

Children often want to make an exciting background for their print, but beware of a strongly coloured background which could swamp a delicate linear design from an incised print.

USING SEVERAL COLOURS ON AN INCISED PRINTING BLOCK

ACTIVITY

1 Make colour blends on the printing block for mottled autumn leaves, rocks, fishes or furry animals (Y1–Y6).

2 Wash and pat dry a printing block and re-roller with a darker colour (Y2–Y6). Make a second series of prints, touching or overlapping the first prints.

3 Make an attractive shadow effect by printing slightly to one side of the first print in a different colour (Y5–Y6).

4 Print additional fine lines on top of a shaped print (Y5–Y6). A tiger, for example, could be printed in orange with internal cuts to leave white areas on the body using Polyblock. This could then be overprinted in black using a string-print block, cut in card to the same shape as the original Polyblock tiger.

REDUCTION PRINTING

Reduction printing is a process of overlaying colours on an image using the same printing block. It can be used with most incised printing blocks.

1 Incise a design into a printing block.

2 Print a first, light colour. Wash and dry Polyblock, wooden and lino blocks to remove colour; wipe off colour on clay and Plasticine blocks.

Figure 3.20
African masks, using reduction printing, in printing inks. Y6

3 Re-carve the block, removing extra lines or areas. The first printed colour will remain visible wherever the design has been re-carved. Extensive areas should be removed during the second carving to prevent the first colour from being overwhelmed by a second, darker layer.

4 Roller the second colour on the block, and carefully place it on top of the original print, which will be wet. Take care that the block is in registration (aligned) with the first print. Use a clean roller to give even pressure.

ACTIVITY

1 Instead of aligning the blocks, try rotating them to make interesting overlap patterns (Y3–Y6) (see page 180).

USING A MASK

Masking an area in the same shape as a printing block will allow the details of an incised print to show clearly.

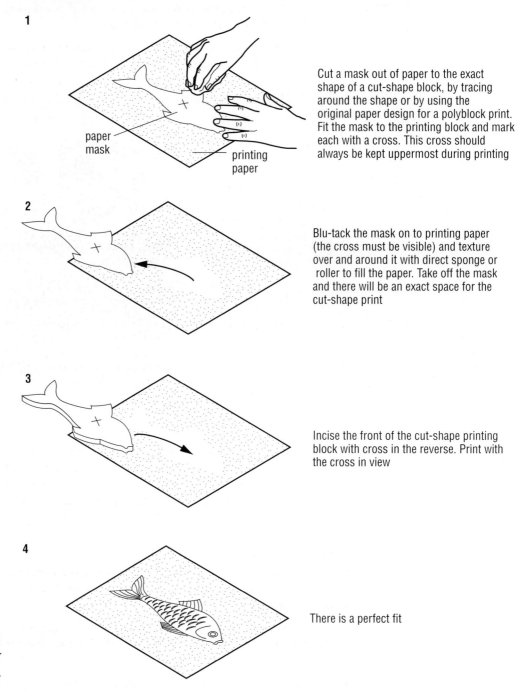

1
Cut a mask out of paper to the exact shape of a cut-shape block, by tracing around the shape or by using the original paper design for a polyblock print. Fit the mask to the printing block and mark each with a cross. This cross should always be kept uppermost during printing

paper mask

printing paper

2
Blu-tack the mask on to printing paper (the cross must be visible) and texture over and around it with direct sponge or roller to fill the paper. Take off the mask and there will be an exact space for the cut-shape print

3
Incise the front of the cut-shape printing block with cross in the reverse. Print with the cross in view

4
There is a perfect fit

Figure 3.21
Making and using a paper mask.

ACTIVITY 1 Use a printing block as a mask (Y1–Y4). Leave the shaped printing block in place, ink-side down on the paper, and print around it. Do this quickly or the printing block will stick to the printing paper. Remove the printing blocks.

2 Mask areas throughout the printing process to achieve interesting areas of different textures and colours (Y6).

PoS 3
Ideas, feelings and meanings are communicated in different visual forms

Monoprinting

Monoprinting is different from most other printing techniques because usually only one print is taken. It involves placing a piece of paper on top of a flat, textured, inked surface, and taking a print. The printing paper absorbs the colour in exciting and unexpected ways.

There are two basic methods. In the subtractive method, colour is rolled evenly on to a surface, lines are incised and a print taken. In the additive method, different colours of paint are applied directly on to a board before a print is taken.

KNOWLEDGE AND UNDERSTANDING

PoS 9c
Relate art to its time and place of origin

The earliest monoprints were a by-product of etching. In the 1630s Venetian artists started taking prints using oil paints on copper plates as a method of adding richness to etchings.

Marbling is a type of monoprint that has always been associated with book binding and was extremely popular in Victorian England.

Figure 3.22
Landscape, using the subtractive monoprint method (see page 68), in printing inks. Y5

EQUIPMENT

INK

Monoprints can be made with paints mixed with paste, finger paints or printing inks. Acrylic paints can also be used. They are expensive but the colours are clear and attractive because they resist being mixed. Flames on a bonfire, a stormy sea or a sunset sky make good subjects. (Protect clothing and wash any brushes in soap and water.) Acrylics keep moist for a lesson if they are applied thickly, and for longer if an acrylic gel is added.

PRINTING BOARD

Board must be smooth, with a flat surface that resists absorption of paint or ink. Pieces of formica, perspex, lino, tin, overhead projector paper or heavy-duty polythene all make good printing boards.

If all the class is making monoprints together, use small, portable boards such as those made for Plasticine. At the end of the lesson they can be stacked in a sink or bucket ready for washing.

Try using a formica table top with small groups. It encourages a more adventurous use of line and movement and the ink can be cleaned very easily with a damp cloth and a bucket of water at the end of a lesson. Printing inks do not stain a table, but red, orange and purple paints do. Using such a large area of colour is not wasteful as the surface can be re-rolled for each new print.

DRAWING TOOLS

Encourage improvisation with fingers, finger nails, sticks, sponges, folded card, rollers, combs, fabric scraps, old rulers, crumpled paper and silver foil to make marks on the inked surface.

COLOUR OF THE PRINTING PAPER

The paper colour affects the impact of the print. Most multi-coloured additive prints need white paper but subtractive monoprints can be printed very successfully on a variety of backgrounds.

SUBTRACTIVE MONOPRINTS

PoS 4a
Investigate pattern and texture

Subtractive monoprinting produces finer textures and lines than additive monoprinting. Masking areas of a printing surface with paper shapes preserves areas from the printing process and creates shapes in the middle of the textures and patterns.

AGES AND STAGES

Designs can vary from abstract patterns of movement and texture, to drawings of trees and landscapes, insects, feathers, shoes and birds. Children in Y5 and Y6 could observe objects such as leaves and feathers under a microscope and try to reproduce the textures and patterns on the inked surface.

MAKING THE PRINT

1 Spoon a small amount of printing ink on to a printing board. Roller the ink over the surface to form an even, thin, sticky surface. You can use more than one colour but the colours blend as the surface is worked and re-worked.

2 Draw a design in the ink by removing areas of colour. Fingers are ideal tools for this. Use different parts of the fingers and different finger spacings. Try a variety of other implements.

3 Place the printing paper over a design and smooth it down gently, using the flat of the hand (not finger-tips). The first print will only need very light pressure.

4 Lift up a corner of the paper to see whether the print is taking. If the print is too faint, return the corner and add more pressure. Take off the paper to reveal the print on the underside.

5 Take another print from the printing board. Second prints are usually more subtle and delicate.

ACTIVITY

PoS 4a–d
Learn about visual and tactile elements

1 Cut the printing paper into any shape (Y1–Y2). A monoprint gives a dramatic texture to an animal cut-out.

2 Take a second print from the first, wet print and display the two mirror images together (Y1–Y2).

3 Use greaseproof paper, tracing paper or heavy-duty foil as printing board (Y1–Y2). Fold or crumple it into an interesting texture or pattern. Smooth it out, roller on the ink and take a monoprint.

4 Use a monoprint as background for other prints (Y3–Y6). Keep the second prints simple, in strong colours and primarily in silhouette so they will not be overwhelmed by the monoprint. Make cut-shape prints of trees on a monoprinted landscape; stencil dolphins, fish or boats on a monoprinted seascape; print flying birds on a ploughed field.

MAKING A MASKED MONOPRINT

Texture an inked printing board but avoid making deep, wide marks. Mask areas of the textured board with paper shapes or flat objects, such as pressed leaves, string and coins. Masked areas appear as spaces on the monoprint. Put additional pressure on the edges of the mask when smoothing down the printing paper to obtain a crisp edge to the shape. String makes a particularly interesting shadow print, with rich tonal variations.

ACTIVITY

1 Link masked monoprints with mathematics (Y1–Y2). Use large, simple geometric paper shapes. The children feel carefully around the shapes as they print and this increases their awareness of shape.

2 Display a masked monoprint alongside the coloured mask (Y1–Y6). They will complement each other in shape, colour and texture.

Figure 3.23
Elephants, the background was masked with paper before printing, in printing inks. Y6

3 Try masking all the background with paper so that only the inside shape is left exposed (Y5–Y6).

ADDITIVE MONOPRINTS

PoS 8e
Experiment with visual elements

Additive monoprints are colourful and highly textured. They do not give fine detail but do encourage children to pay attention to line, colour and shape.

PoS 7c
Work on a variety of scales

AGES AND STAGES

Children at KS1 generally enjoy working on a large scale and are able to complete a picture quickly. If possible, use a table top as a printing board for an additive monoprint. Children who work more cautiously will need a support about the size of a small Plasticine board to avoid the paint drying before a design is complete. Random prints can be made with bubble prints (page 70) and marbling (page 71). At the end of KS2, children can control marbled patterns by floating inks on paste. Roller offset prints (page 71) are exciting but difficult to make and so are best left until the end of KS2.

Figure 3.24
Landscape, with background made from additive monoprinting, and stencilled tree trunks (see page 72) and direct print leaves, in powder paint (powdered gouache) mixed with PVA

MAKING THE PRINT

1 Paint a design in a variety of colours directly on the printing board. Work fairly quickly to avoid the ink drying. The quality of the print depends on the thickness of the printing inks. If the ink is too thick, the print has unsightly blotches of colour; if it is too thin, it is faint and dull.

2 Neaten the edges of the monoprint into the shape of a rectangle or square. Straight-edged pieces of newspaper can be placed around the design before the print is taken.

3 Place a piece of paper on top of the design. Do not use a roller for pressure; instead, rub evenly over the paper with the flat of the hand. Different inks and paints will need different pressures. Use light pressure at first and lift up a corner of the paper to check the print. Half of the paper can be lifted safely in this way. If not enough ink had been printed, smooth down the paper and apply further pressure.

4 After the first print has been taken, apply new areas of pure colour over the blended inks and take another print.

ACTIVITY

PoS 2c
Design and make creative images

1 Make a symmetrical monoprint (Y1–Y3). Fold a piece of paper in half and use one side as a monoprint board. Press the other half over the inked side and take a mirror print. The 'printing board' and the monoprint make the completed picture. Decide whether it is a face, a creature, an object or landscape. Add direct print details to make the image clearer.

Tip!

Place a sketch underneath a perspex printing board to act as a guide for the monoprint.

2 Add textural details to monoprints made with acrylics or printing inks (Y1–Y6). They are strong enough to hold small stones, shells and pieces of bark.

3 Make a print with distinctive brush marks (Y5–Y6). Paint a picture of a vase of flowers in the classroom in acrylics, or finger-paints, in a similar style to Van Gogh. Work quickly and take a monoprint while the paint is wet. The different directions of the brush stokes will be emphasised.

PoS 4a
Investigate pattern and texture

BUBBLE PRINTS

This technique produces a beautiful overlapping pattern of bubbles.

Powder paint or tempera paint, washing-up liquid, a plastic bowl or ice-cream container, straws, paper, water are required.

To make the print use the following method.

H & S

1 Put equal volumes of washing-up liquid and water into an ice-cream container. Mix in powder paint. Put a straw in the liquid and blow until a mass of bubbles appears above the surface of the container. Young children should practise blowing through the straw before putting it into the liquid.

2 Quickly place the paper on top of the bubbles and take a print by gently pushing down until the paper touches the rim of the container. Lift off the paper. There will be a circular print of overlapping bubbles.

3 Blow more bubbles, take another print and repeat until the paper is covered with overlapping prints.

ACTIVITY

1 Put different colours in separate bowls and make overlayered bubble prints (Y1–Y6).

2 Keep the prints separate and cut out the circles when the paint is dry (Y3–Y6). Use them as a background to a story about being trapped in a bubble.

Figure 3.25
Bubble prints, overlapping, in powder paint (powdered gouache). Y1

PoS 4a
Investigate pattern and texture

MARBLING

Marbling makes swirling lines of colour reminiscent of moving water. Children can accentuate the random patterns the inks make with thin lines of glitter glue or glued lengths of yarn.

Marbling inks, a shallow waterproof tray, water, paper that is slightly smaller than the tray, vinegar, a toothpick are required.

To make the print use the following method.

1 Fill a tray with water to a depth of approximately 3 cm. Add a few drops of vinegar to disperse the ink. Using a dropper, place a few drops of marbling ink on the surface of the water. Add a few drops of other colours for a multi-coloured pattern.

2 Stir gently with a toothpick to distribute the droplets.

3 Curve the paper in the centre. Lower it on to the water before releasing the sides. This helps to avoid air pockets forming. The ink pattern will transfer to the paper surface.

4 Lift off the sheet immediately and hang it up to dry for approximately 30 minutes.

5 Add a few more drops of ink before making the next print.

PoS 4d
Investigate shape, form and space

ROLLER OFFSET PRINTS

Prints using this technique produce images of startling detail and clarity with an almost three-dimensional effect. A surprisingly large surface area can be covered with a single roller off-set print, making a good background for displays.

A large amount of control is needed in positioning an object under the roller and in maintaining sufficient, even pressure to make a successful print.

The rollers must be dry (used rollers cannot be washed and immediately re-used). If there is a limited number of sponge rollers, the printing should be carried out over several days, in small groups.

One large soft sponge roller which must be clean and dry, one small soft sponge roller, printing ink rollered out thinly in a printing tray, paper, an object to print (a pair of scissors, a cog wheel, a key, a leaf or a comb) are required.

To make the print use the following method.

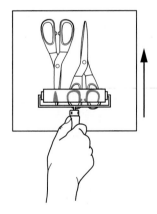

1 Use the small soft sponge to roller ink on to the object to be printed. Roller from all directions.

2 Pass the large soft sponge roller over the inked object. Do this firmly and once only. The image is picked up on the roller. A delicate object, such as a leaf, may stick to the roller and should be peeled off very carefully.

Figure 3.26
Rolling over an inked object.

3 Position the roller so that the lower part of an image prints first. Roller steadily right across the paper and the image will be reproduced many times, becoming softer as the ink decreases.

PoS 2c
Design and make creative images

Stencil prints

Stencil prints are made by pressing colour around a card shape, or through a hole cut in card. The card prevents the printing inks from reaching particular parts of the printing paper and leaves a highly textured shape with well-defined edges.

**KNOWLEDGE AND
UNDERSTANDING**

*PoS 9c
Relate art to its time and
place of origin*

The word stencil comes from the old French estanceler – to cover with small stars. Stencilling has been a folk craft in Europe for many centuries. Traditionally, a decorative pattern of holes is cut in a piece of leather, tin, wood or card. This is then held against the surface that is to be decorated, and paint is stippled through the holes.

Screen printing with stencils has been developed as recently as the twentieth century. It has enjoyed growing popularity over the last 30 years because it allows artists to layer far more colours than with any other printing technique. Warhol's famous portraits of Marilyn Monroe were made with screen printing techniques, Shorewood 1403. Many fabric designs are screen printed. Dorn's *Aircraft* was used on the Orient liner Orcades, and Day's 1951 screen print design *Calyx*, Goodwill 3(30), became one of the fabrics produced by Heals.

Figure 3.27
Dolphin, stencil print on an additive monoprint, in printing ink. Y2

AGES AND STAGES

Although stencilling is simple, it is easier for children at KS1 to work in pairs so that one child can hold the stencil firmly in place, while the other applies colour.

Children at KS1 could start with rubbed and stippled stencil prints (pages 73 and 74). Simple screen prints (pages 77 and 78) could be introduced at the beginning of KS2, but photograms (page 77) should be left to the end of KS2.

Encourage children at KS2 to use specialised vocabulary for these techniques – positive, negative and edge stencils; tabs and bridges; foreground and background. By Y5 and Y6, children should be planning the positions of stencil prints with small pencil marks on the printing paper.

MAKING THE STENCIL

There are three types of stencils: negative, positive and edge stencils.

Negative stencil
This masks a shape and colours the surrounding area. Cut out the shape, starting from the card edge. Add simple internal cuts, such as an eye in a fish stencil. Discard the surrounding card or keep it intact and use it later as a positive stencil. Natural, flat objects, such as pressed leaves, make attractive negative stencils.

Positive stencil

This masks the outside area and leaves a coloured shape. Start by making a small fold and a cut in the centre of the drawn shape. Smooth open the card. Use the cut as an entrance to begin cutting round the edge of the shape. Discard the shape and use the surrounding card as the stencil.

Cut the area around the positive stencil to an approximate 4 cm margin. This helps to place the stencil accurately and minimises smudging.

Edge stencil
Edge stencils leave lines of graded colour. Simply cut an edge in card and use it for making linear stencil prints. Two different edge stencils can be made at the same time by using a long, thin piece of card and cutting a wavy line along the centre of the card, parallel to the longest edge. Both wavy edges can then be used for stencilling repeat patterns, waves, mountain ranges or banks of clouds.

Tip!
Children often make the mistake of cutting from the edge of the card. The cut can be joined successfully with masking tape; although too many mends seriously weaken the stencil.

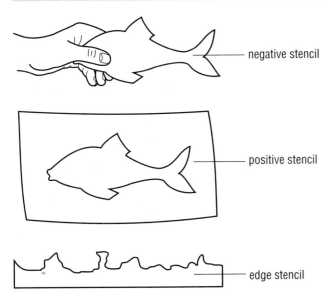

Figure 3.28
Printing with stencils; three methods – negative, positive and edge stencils.

Figure 3.29
Night moths, using a negative stencil for the moths, a positive stencil for the moon, an edge stencil for the grass, in chalk. Y3

MATERIAL FOR A STENCIL SHEET

Slightly waxed card from frozen food packets and milk cartons is ideal for a stencil where paint is being used. Strong paper or card can also be used.

Use acetate for see-through stencils or thin plastic for stencils which need to be waterproof. These materials give a clear, crisp outline and can be used for an almost indefinite period; even with complex designs with many tabs. Because acetate is transparent, it makes it much easier to position the stencil accurately. However, internal cuts in acetate or thin plastic should be made with a craft knife, as folding for an internal scissor cut will ruin the stencil. Therefore, they can be used only in the last years of KS2.

H & S

Scissors, charcoal, crayons, pastels or chalk are also required.

ACTIVITY

Tip!

Use chalks, pastels, charcoal or crayons to discourage unnecessary detail when planning the stencil shape. Too many projections will make the shape difficult to hold in place when colour is applied.

H & S

1 Cut a positive stencil by folding a piece of card in half and cutting the two thicknesses to make a symmetrical shape (Y1–Y2). In using this method the shape and the surrounding stencil are intact so children can then choose either the positive or the negative stencil.

• Carefully cut out a shape in the stencil so that the shape and the background both remain intact (Y3–Y6). Use them as a positive and a negative stencil on the same design.

2 Add details to a large, simple negative stencil print with direct prints, for example scales can be printed on a fish using a curved piece of card (Y1–Y6).

3 Introduce the idea of a tab, or bridge, in a positive stencil (Y3–Y4). Divide an object into closely adjacent shapes joined by thin strips of card. A flower, for example, could have its petals cut very close together.

4 Make a symmetrical stencil with a craft knife (Y5–Y6). Fold a 15 cm square of card in two and pencil in one side of a symmetrical design. Open the card and cut out the design with a craft knife. Fold back the card and use a pencil to trace through to the back of the card. Cut away the other side.

RUBBED STENCIL PRINTS

PoS 4a
Investigate pattern and
texture

AGES AND STAGES

Rubbed stencil prints make a good introduction to stencil printing as they are easy and quick to make. An additional attraction is the unique way in which colour registers on the paper. It softens towards the end of each stroke to contrast with the sharp definition around the edges.

Children at KS1 could start with chalk which makes beautiful, softly coloured stencil prints and graduate on to oil pastels at the end of KS1. Wax crayons need good control over the length and density of the crayon stroke; they are more suitable for the end of KS2.

EQUIPMENT

Soft pastels, oil pastels, chalk or wax crayons, scissors and a craft knife, cotton wool, Blu-tak and printing paper, a stencil are required.

MAKING THE PRINT

1 Cut a negative, positive or edge stencil in paper, card, plastic or acetate. Hold the mask securely in place on the printing paper with one hand, or with very small pieces of Blu-tak.

2 Create reservoirs of colour on scraps of paper with chalk, or round the edges of the stencil with oil pastels. Pick up the colour with a finger, or a piece of cotton wool, and rub from the perimeter of the stencil on to the paper underneath. Rub outwards for negative stencils, inwards for positive stencils and upwards for edge stencils. Gradually work along the entire length of the stencil, making the distribution of colour as even as possible – strong and sharply defined at the stencil edge and gradually losing intensity away from the stencil.

Colours from wax crayons cannot be picked up with a finger, instead rub the colour directly on to the print, over the edges of the stencil, in short, even strokes.

ACTIVITY

1 Encourage children to arrange prints so that they touch and overlap. Children at the end of KS2 could lightly mark the paper with pencil dots to position the shapes (Y1–Y6).

2 Use different colours around the edges to make a multi-coloured print (Y1–Y6).

STIPPLED STENCIL PRINTS

PoS 4d
Investigate shape, form and space

This technique is very similar to a rubbed stencil and uses the more traditional medium of paint. The amount of paint can be controlled to give a stippled effect or a dense covering of colour.

AGES AND STAGES

Children at KS1 and the beginning of KS2 find a sponge much easier to handle than a stipple brush, but they must dab with the sponge (not stroke – this lifts up the stencil edges and spoils the print). It is useful to rehearse the up and down action before using colour. The stippling brush can be introduced once a dabbing action has been firmly established.

Tip!

Strengthen a paper or card stencil for use with paints by wax crayoning around the shape before the stencil is cut out.

MAKING THE PRINT

1 Mix paint to a stiff consistency to prevent colour from seeping underneath a stencil.

2 Use a sponge for large areas and a stipple brush or old bristle brush for edges or small stencils. Dip the sponge or brush in the paint and dry off any excess on a piece of newspaper. Apply the colour in small, dabbing movements to the edges of the stencil. With a positive stencil the entire area can be coloured, using more than one colour.

3 Remove the stencil carefully to avoid smudging and repeat the stencilling until the design is complete. Paper stencils that are only used once should be kept in place for a few minutes until the paint has dried a little.

ACTIVITY

Cut out a positive stencil in card and glue a screen to the back of the card so that it stretches across the stencil (Y3–Y6). Stipple through the screen. The screen can be made of a variety of materials; each gives a different textural finish: surgical gauze, net, butter muslin, plastic netting. The screen also strengthens the card stencil so that it can be used for multiple prints.

SPRAYED STENCIL PRINTS

*PoS 8e
Experiment with pattern,
colour, tone, shape and
space*

Figure 3.30
Air raid, made by splattering
ink around negative
stencils. Y6

Sprayed colours, give an airy, delicate quality to a stencil print which looks extremely sophisticated. Stiff brushes, diffusers or spray-pumps can be used to spray the colour. Splattering from a brush is far easier than blowing through a special diffusing pipe, but diffusers give a finer spray and are cheaper to buy than spray-pumps. The coarser texture effect using a splatter brush can given an interesting grainy look to prints of tree bark, autumn leaves, spray on rough seas or skies at dusk.

AGES AND STAGES

Children at KS1 should use splatter techniques. Diffusing is difficult at first and children do need patience and practice to become proficient; Y4 would perhaps be the earliest time to try. The results are very exciting and introduce a range of advanced stencilling techniques. Children in Y5 or Y6, for example, can control the amount of colour sprayed to make landscapes which fade into paler, more blue colours in the distance.

H & S An air-brush would be an expensive but welcome addition at the end of KS2, as it allows greater control and gives a much finer spray. A cheaper alternative is to buy a plastic garden pump-spray, although the results will be coarser. Rolls of self-adhesive plastic are manufactured for use with air-brush sprays and allow fine definition and intricate shaping with a craft knife.

ORGANISATION

Using stiff brushes, spray-pumps and diffusers is a potentially messy process. It is best done in small groups, with children all wearing aprons and away from other activities. Give each piece of printing paper a wide margin of space. The ink sprays out at wide angles and will colour any nearby objects, as well as the printing paper.

If diffusers are being used, sterilise them in a mixture of TCP and water before allowing children to use them.

EQUIPMENT

A stiff brush such as a scrubbing brush or toothbrush is needed to splatter the ink and a long, stiff object such as a comb, a file or a piece of stiff card is also required.

H & S To spray the ink you will need diffusers or a spray-pump. Diffusers are made from two thin, metal tubes joined with a hinge. One end is put in the ink and the other is bent at right angles and blown through. A pump-spray is best used in pairs; one child pumps while the other one sprays.

Coloured inks, for example, Easibrush, (not printing inks) or paints, printing paper, paper stencils, Blu-tak are also required.

MAKING A SPLATTER PRINT

1 Cut positive, negative or edge stencils to mask areas where ink is not wanted. Natural objects such as leaves can also be used. Keep stencils in place with very small pieces of Blu-tak.

2 Charge a brush with ink. Hold the bristle end of the toothbrush above the paper and tilt the handle away from the body. Pull a card up across the bristles and a spray of colour will be thrown on to the paper.

3 Wait until the ink is dry before removing a stencil. A paper stencil will have an attractive covering of sprayed ink and can be saved for use in another picture.

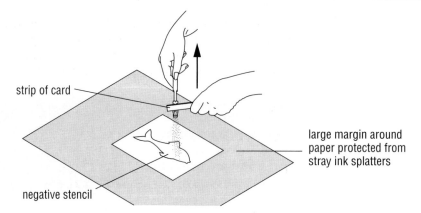

strip of card

large margin around paper protected from stray ink splatters

negative stencil

Figure 3.31
Making a splatter print.

MAKING A PRINT WITH A DIFFUSER

1 Blu-tak stencils in place.

2 Pour a small amount of ink into a waterpot and stand the diffuser in the ink. (Always keep the base of the diffuser submerged in the ink.)

3 Blow into the diffuser approximately 60 cm away from the paper, until a fine spray of ink covers the paper. Several different colours can be sprayed in the same way. If drips occur, the diffuser is too near to the paper. Spraying too long in one place will leave pools of ink as the paper becomes saturated.

4 Leave the stencil in place until the ink is dry. As the ink dries fairly quickly, the stencils can soon be moved around and re-sprayed. This produces overlapping forms with subtle colour changes.

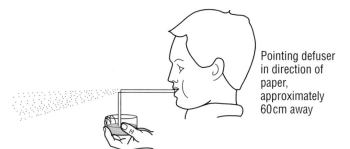

Pointing defuser in direction of paper, approximately 60cm away

Figure 3.32
Diffusing ink.

ACTIVITY

1 Use harmonious, overlapping colours for subtle colour blends: reds, yellows and browns for autumn leaves; yellows and greens for spring flowers; blues, purples and greens for a landscape.

2 Use an edge stencil in a landscape to show hills gradually receding into the distance (Y5–Y6). Position a large stencil near to the top of the page and spray on a fine layer of colour. Lower the stencil to cover more of the paper and slightly realign it. Spray on a denser layer of colour. Repeat until the foreground is reached.

Figure 3.33
Landscape with receding hills using a diffuser and stencil prints. Y6

PHOTOGRAMS

PoS 4d
Investigate shape, form and space

Photograms are produced when an object is used as a stencil on light-sensitive paper. This is a valuable introduction to photographic techniques.

AGES AND STAGES

Using chemicals in a confined space is not safe for children at KS1. They could try out the same printing techniques using specially treated light-sensitive paper. This can be used without a darkroom and without the use of chemicals. The paper is expensive but the results are very good. Working with photograms concentrates children's attention on the form and texture of everyday objects.

EQUIPMENT

Photographic paper, plastic tongues, developer, fixer, water trays, a safe-light and a white light in a dark room, a variety of objects to act as stencils, for example, feathers, leaves, grass, card shapes, metal washers, combs, scissors, are required.

HEALTH AND SAFETY

H & S

Work in small groups, with adult supervision. Children should wear aprons to protect their clothing. Always have spare buckets of clean water available to wash off any accidental chemical splashes.

MAKING THE PRINT

1 Everything has to be done in a darkroom lit by a safe-light. Substitute a powerful torch covered with several layers of orange cellophane if there is no safe-light.

2 Set out the trays in this order: developer, water, fixer, water, and label them.

3 Remove a sheet of photographic paper and carefully seal up the rest in the packet. Place the paper under the white or normal light bulb (switched off) and arrange the objects on top. Thin objects such as feathers and lace can be flattened with a piece of perspex.

4 Switch on the white light and expose the paper for two to three seconds. Switch off the white light and remove the objects.

5 Use the plastic tongs to dip the paper in developer until the image becomes clear against a black background. Dip the paper in the water, then the fixer, and then give it a final rinse in water. If several prints are being made, change the water frequently to make sure the chemicals are rinsed off in a clean bath. The prints can then be taken into daylight.

SCREEN PRINTS

PoS 2c
Design and make creative images

Screen printing forces thickened ink through a mesh of fine fabric after areas have been masked with a positive or a negative stencil. Paper stencils will stick to the mesh after the first printing and this makes it easy to produce multiple copies of the same print.

Figure 3.34
Elephants, sponged through a positive stencil, on a screened background, in screen printing inks. Y5

AGES AND STAGES

Screen printing has the reputation of being very complex, but at the beginning techniques can be kept simple. Children new to screen printing can simply screen a mixture of colours across the paper and then add a sponged stencil print.

Negative stencils could then be introduced; tearing rough shapes where the paper should remain white – clouds, or areas of ice and snow. Then use a positive stencil to print an image on the screened background.

Gradually the processes will become more complex as children learn to use positive stencils, to layer colours and overlap images.

EQUIPMENT

Special screen printing inks can be bought from educational suppliers. If they are not available, thicken paint or dye with cellulose powder glue to a smooth, creamy consistency. If it is too thin it will seep beneath the stencil; if it is too thick it will clog the screen.

Stretch and staple, as tightly as possible, screen printing gauze across a wooden frame to form a screen. An area 50 × 40 cm is large enough for most stencils and yet small enough for most children to manage. Apply insulating tape along the edges of the screen, on the underside. This allows a reservoir of ink to rest along the top of the screen, without coming into contact with the printing paper underneath.

A squeegee (a flat piece of wood with a strip of thick rubber projecting from the lower end), paper for stencils, fabric or paper for printing are also required.

MAKING THE PRINT

a   b

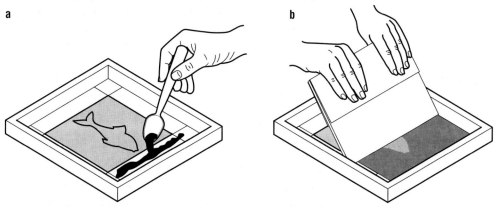

Figure 3.35
Making a screen print.

1 Measure the sides of the exposed screen so that stencils can be cut to the correct size. Negative stencils need to be smaller than the screen. Positive stencils should be approximately the same size as the frame.

2 Place the screen, mesh-side down, on to the printing paper, aligning it carefully with a corner of the paper. Use coloured chalk to mark through the mesh at the corners of the screen. This shows the dimensions of the screen on the printing paper and helps in positioning the stencils.

3 Lift off the screen and rest the stencils on the paper. Replace the screen, carefully re-aligning it with each corner.

4 Spoon the screen printing ink across the top of the screen so that it is lying along the taped area (Figure 3.35a). Make sure there is sufficient ink to complete the journey down the screen. Use one or more colours. Simply pull them down for stripes of colour, or mix them up slightly for interesting blends.

5 Hold the squeegee at 45° and pull the ink down the screen with a single, firm, slow, smooth action (Figure 3.35b). Lift off the squeegee and scrape off the excess ink to use on the next print. Pull the screen off the paper. The stencil will adhere to the screen, making it possible to produce many repeat prints.

ORGANISATION

Screen printing is an ideal medium for working in groups of two or three children. Each member of the group makes a stencil. Then the group co-operates in arranging the stencils on a screen and deciding on the range of colours. Each member of the group can make their own print: one or two children can hold the frame while the other child pulls the ink down in a smooth action. The stencils will stay in the same position but each print will have subtle variations of colour.

The screens do not need to be washed between colours as long as the second colour is darker than the first. However, when the group has finished printing, the whole screen should be washed to remove the colour and the shadow left by the stencil shapes.

ACTIVITY

1 Paint a stencil on an old screen with nail varnish or waterproof glue (Y3–Y6). Use it for a stencil that is complex or going to have extensive use.

2 Introduce internal lines on a negative stencil (Y3–Y4). This can be done quickly and easily by cutting lines across a shape and slightly pulling the pieces apart. The original shape is still recognisable, but now has an interesting pattern of lines.

3 Screen areas of separate colours with positive stencils (Y5–Y6). Start with large areas of light colours and reduce the size of the stencil as the colours become darker.

PoS 4a
Investigate pattern and texture

Transfer prints

Transfer prints transfer an image from one support to another by applying pressure on the back of a piece of printing paper. With inked and wax crayon transfer prints (below and page 81) the pressure is from a pencil; with fabric transfer prints (page 80) the pressure comes from the heat of an iron.

INKED TRANSFER PRINTS

PoS 4c
Images are made using line and tone

Inked transfer prints are made by laying paper lightly over a flat inked surface and drawing a design on the paper with pencil, a stick or the side of a finger. The ink registers strongly on the underside of the paper and the pressure of the pencil makes a fuzzy edged, linear print that is a mirror image of the original pencilled design.

AGES AND STAGES

Inked transfer prints do not allow the drawing-hand to rest on the paper. This creates prints with a refreshing spontaneity of line that is particularly valuable for children at KS2. The speed of the process and the ability to re-roller the ink means children can have several attempts at a single drawing.

The drawings or patterns have to be done quickly at KS1 or the children's drawing-hand will get tired. Try drawing a line across the paper in large swirls and loops, filling in spaces with patterns and textures.

EQUIPMENT

Printing inks, rollers, drawing implements (for example ball-point pen, pencil, wooden spoon, section of a broom handle), paper, Melamine table top or Plasticine boards are required.

MAKING THE PRINT

1 Roller a very thin film of printing ink on to a Melamine table top or Plasticine board. This can be re-rollered and used many times.

2 Press a sheet of newspaper on the printing board to take off any excess ink and discard.

3 To test the effect of different lines and pressures, gently lower a piece of paper on to the ink so that it is resting there very lightly and experiment with different drawing tools. A ball-point pen gives a finer line than a pencil. Print smudgy areas of colour by using light strokes of the thumb.

4 Examine the trial marks and then re-roller the ink. Place a new sheet of paper on the ink. Draw a design on the back of the sheet without touching the paper with the hand. Lift off the paper and the print will be on the under side.

ACTIVITY

1 Before re-rollering the ink, take a print off the inked surface. A 'ghost' outline of the drawing makes this an interesting monoprint.

2 Plan a complex line drawing in pencil on the back of the paper (Y5–Y6). Trace over the lines to make a transfer print.

Figure 3.36
Transfer print, in ink, with 'ghost' image. Y2

FABRIC TRANSFER CRAYONS AND PAINTS

Children can make a transfer print on to fabric using special fabric crayons or fabric paints. The design is made on paper and then transferred to fabric with heat from an iron. The prints do not stiffen the fabric.

AGES AND STAGES

H & S

Children at the end of KS2 can use the iron themselves, under adult supervision. It would be valuable if younger children could watch an adult transferring their design.

EQUIPMENT

Use fabric made from artificial fibres for bright, permanent colours. Fabric crayons and paints leave only a faint outline on cotton and are not colour-fast. This can be an asset if the design is going to be used as a guide for embroidery.

Fabricrayons (Crayola), transfer paints (Colourist) and iron-on transfer paints (Deka) work well.

MAKING THE DESIGN

Use fabric paints on thin paper. The colours appear dull on the paper but brighten when they are transferred to fabric. Allow the paint to dry.

With fabric transfer crayons, press hard to obtain a thick layer of colour when drawing a design. Cut out the drawing to avoid unwanted flakes of crayon transferring to the fabric.

MAKING THE PRINT

1 Place the design on top of the fabric. Make sure no fabric is visible to avoid scorching. Protect the ironing board with newspaper.

H & S

2 Iron at a high temperature (see Ages and Stages above) for at least a minute, keeping the iron moving all the time, to transfer the design to the fabric.

3 The design becomes paler with each print so may need re-colouring after three prints.

ACTIVITY

1 Combine a transfer print with a stencil print (Y1–Y6). Place a positive stencil on top of the cloth. Rub an area of paper with a random mixture of fabric crayon colours and position it, colour-side down, over the stencil hole. Iron to transfer the design.

2 Use fabric crayons to make a rubbing (Y2–Y6). Cut up the rubbing to make an 'exploded' design and glue the pieces on to paper.

WAX CRAYON TRANSFER PRINTS

PoS 4a–d
Learn about visual and tactile elements

Two designs are achieved using this technique. Together they offer exciting tonal and spatial comparisons.

AGES AND STAGES

The initial stages of this technique can be a little tedious for KS1 children, so limit the size of the paper to 10×8 cm. Children will be happy simply to make a print and a negative. By KS2, children can use the two prints together to create one image. Make the colours and patterns of the crayoned layers an integral part of the overall design, for example a river could be in different tones of blues and purples. Encourage solid areas of interesting texture, in addition to more usual linear designs.

EQUIPMENT

White sugar paper about 15×20 cm, wax crayons, white chalk, pencils are required.

MAKING THE PRINT

1 Fold the paper in half and open it out. Label each half A and B lightly in pencil, in a corner.

2 Cover side B completely with white chalk. Hold it up to the light to check that no areas have been missed. Rub the chalk into the grain of the paper and knock off the surplus chalk.

3 Apply a thick layer of crayon on top of the chalk in overlapping patches of colour. Crayon without touching the paper with the crayoning hand to prevent the chalk layer from being rubbed away. (If this happens the transfer will not work.)

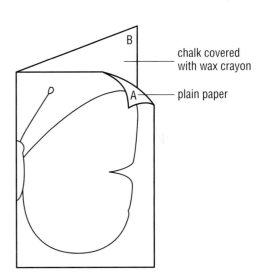

chalk covered with wax crayon

plain paper

Figure 3.37
Arranging paper for a wax crayon transfer print.

4 Re-fold the paper and draw on the back of side A, with firm pressure from a blunt pencil. The chalk rejects the crayon and the design is transferred to the underside of the top paper. Children can look safely between the fold to have a 'sneak preview' and then replace the sheets to continue pencilling. The two designs will form a mirror image of each other.

ACTIVITY

1 **Use the attractive symmetry of a design to direct the choice of subject – a butterfly, the head of an animal, a semi-detached house (Y3–Y4). Draw only half the subject, and work from the fold towards the open edges.**

2 **Make a scene reflected in water (Y5–Y6). The land meets the water at the fold, so a tree or a house that is to be reflected in the water should be drawn upwards from the fold.**

Figure 3.38
Wax crayon transfer of a butterfly. Y3

3 **Experiment with different shapes, sizes and colours of paper (Y5–Y6).**

COLLAGE AND RELIEF

Main NC focus

PoS 8d
Children should be taught
to experiment with (and
develop control of [KS2])
tools and techniques for
. . . collage

PoS 7c
Explore and use 2- and 3-
dimensional media

Introduction

Collage and relief work should be viewed from the front, like a picture, but it also has a worked surface, like a sculpture. Children build up from a flat surface, using layers of material, or carve down from a higher surface. This allows them to gain experience in directly producing texture and form, as in sculptures, in the more manageable form of a flat surface. The height can vary from slight relief with layered paper and fabric, to the high relief of raised paper, quilted fabrics, found objects, plaster of Paris, papier-mâché and clay. The chapter outlines five ways of creating relief:

- Paper collage (page 82)

- Mixed collage (page 90)

- Fabric collage and embroidery (page 91)

- Modelling in relief (clay, Plasticine, dough) (page 97)

- Plaster casts (page 99)

Figure 4.1
Grumpy gran, quilted face in
high relief (see page 96). Y6

PoS 4b and d
Investigate colour, shape
and space

Paper collage

Collage comes from the French verb *coller* – to cut. Paper is one of the cheapest and most available materials because recycled paper can be used. Paper collage allows children to produce large areas of clear, bright colour with crisp edges quickly but without problems of thinning paint and uneven crayoning. These areas of colour can be vibrant or subtle hues from paper off-cuts; strongly patterned areas of colour from old monoprints, rubbings and roller prints; or gradations of colours from paint-washed paper. Paper collage can be easily combined with other media by adding mixed collage sections, or drawing details in ink, crayon, pastels or chalk.

AGES AND STAGES

PoS 7d
Review and modify work

Paper collage gives children at KS1 valuable and enjoyable practice in tearing, folding, cutting and gluing paper – important skills that need to be established during this stage and reinforced at KS2. The shapes are very mobile so children can arrange and rearrange a composition many times to obtain the best possible combination of shapes and spaces. This makes paper collage an ideal medium for discussing elements of line, shape and pattern.

KNOWLEDGE AND UNDERSTANDING

Paper-cuts have been used in traditional crafts for centuries and by many artists, Matisse probably being the most famous. Examining the work of both artists and craftspeople provides an excellent starting point for children's paper collage work.

PoS 9d
Respond to and compare different styles and traditions

MATISSE

Matisse used paper collage in war-time France, initially because of the difficulty of obtaining the more traditional painting equipment. He called the cut-outs *papiers-découpes*. His work has had a profound influence on designers. Children will be able to find many examples of advertisements and posters that use flat, coloured, cut-out shapes in their designs, using the style that Matisse pioneered (*The snail*, Goodwill 3(25)).

ACTIVITY

PoS 7e
Use knowledge of artists' work

Tip!

Sometimes the paper pieces flip over as they fall on to the table making it difficult to place them correctly. Paper that is white on the back makes it obvious when the pieces are the wrong way up. Y1 children should tear the lines while the paper lies flat on the desk. This allows the pieces to stay approximately in position.

Figure 4.2
Head, Egyptian style, an exploded symmetrical shape. Y3

1 Look at Matisse's **Blue nude**, Shorewood 1431, and discuss how he has created lines by cutting a paper shape and then moving the pieces apart (Y1–Y6).

• Take a piece of paper and shape it into the silhouette of a person or an animal. Make an interesting cut through the centre. Move the pieces apart to reveal an attractive internal line. Create more lines with additional cuts (Y1–Y6).

• Draw parallel coloured lines across a white paper shape before making the cuts (Y3–Y6).

• Cut and pull apart a symmetrical shape (Y4–Y6). This makes a symmetrical pattern involving both the shape and the internal lines.

a) Fold a piece of paper in half and cut out a symmetrical shape. Keep the shape folded and cut out details and lines through both thicknesses of paper.
b) Open up the shape. Reassemble the pieces like a jigsaw on a contrasting piece of paper. Gently shift the pieces to reveal internal spaces.

PoS 9c
Relate art to its time and place of origin

PHOTO-MONTAGE

With the introduction of cheaper printing methods in the nineteenth century, magazines and newspapers became disposable items. Young people in Victorian times loved to keep scrapbooks of carefully cut pictures. Some of these were overlapped and layered to make a mass of colourful shapes and colours.

In the early part of this century, Dada artists turned this respectable hobby on its head by using it for work with a biting social message. Picasso also began to incorporate elements of paper collage into his work (*Violin and music score*, Goodwill 1(10)). In the 1960s Pop artists such as Hockney and Rauschenberg used photo-montage in their work. In *Shoes kyoto*, Ginn 27, Hockney made a picture from a large number of photographs taken of the same place but from different viewpoints. In *Retroactive*, Rauschenberg painted on a collage of paper-cuts and photographs (Shorewood 1714).

ACTIVITY
PoS 7e
Use knowledge of artists' work

1 Create heads wearing outrageous hats, using pictures from magazines (Y1–Y4).

2 Cut across a magazine picture of a face and reassemble it in a slightly distorted way (Y2–Y6).

3 Look at Surrealist paintings (Dali *Metamorphosis of Narcissus*, Goodwill 2(15)) (Y3–Y6), or Arcimbaldo's bizarre portraits (*Fire*, Goodwill 3(26)) to obtain ideas for photo-montage pictures. Cut out different body parts from magazine pictures and make a strange figure.

PoS 5c
Examine styles from a variety of cultures

TRADITIONAL PAPER-CUTS

Poland and China have a rich tradition of making paper-cuts for decorating the home during important festivals. The simplest paper-cuts are symmetrical and are based on a single fold, which children at KS1 can manage. Children at KS2 could look closely at internal cuts which give paper-cuts a delicate shape.

ACTIVITY

1 Use paper circles cut from thin paper to make patterns with more than one axis of symmetry and link with work on shape in mathematics (Y2–Y6). Children at KS1 could fold the circle twice; children at KS2 could fold it three times. Cut deep shapes in towards the centre from all the sides. Carefully open the circles to reveal the pattern.

  • Make a paper-cut snowflake (Y5–Y6).

  a) Use a pair of compasses to draw a circle. Keep the same radius measurement and mark off six points on the circumference (circle edge) with the same distance between them.
  b) Join two of the points by folding the circle in half. Join the other points by folding to make a shape one-sixth of the circle.
  c) Make long, decorative cuts into the sides of the shape. Open it out to reveal a beautiful snowflake pattern.

 Try the Acorn program *Snowflakes* (one of the titles in TOPOLOGIKA TOP011).

PoS 9c
Relate art to the time and place of its origin

SILHOUETTES

Monsieur Silhouette was a French Minister of Finance whose unpopular taxes were deemed to have reduced people to paper thinness, and this art form is said to be named after him. Silhouettes made from black paper were very popular in the eighteenth and nineteenth centuries and are still used in some children's book illustrations.

ACTIVITY

1 Make silhouette images.

  • Use an overhead projector, or other strong light, to cast a shadow of an object on to white paper taped to a wall (Y1–Y3). Turn the object round to find the best angle for a clear image of the object and cut the same shape in paper.

EQUIPMENT

Very little equipment – paper, scissors and glue – is required, but it is important to have the correct equipment if children are going to achieve the exciting results possible with this medium.

GLUE

Most children need to be reminded to glue near to the edges of shapes and not in the centre, and to use the minimum amount of glue.

PVA glue is ideal for paper collage but children can waste large amounts if they use it carelessly. Use tiny dabs applied with the tip of a glue spreader.

Figure 4.3
Planet, collage from used paper, with painted washes, sponge prints and roller prints. Y5

PoS 8d
Experiment with tools and

Thick paste is less expensive than PVA glue. It will glue most papers but it stains thin paper and makes some paper dyes bleed.

Impact glue (UHU) is expensive and messy, but it is useful for difficult curves on high-relief paper shapes.

MAKING A PAPER COLLECTION

Collect as many different weights, colours and textures of paper as possible. Use off-cuts of sugar paper, newsprint, cardboard, aluminium foil, cellophane, corrugated card and paper, brown paper, gift wrap, wallpaper, waxed paper, magazines, newspapers, paper napkins and handkerchiefs, sections from abandoned display backgrounds and unwanted paintings. Patterned paper can be made by rollering paint on paper off-cuts, making washes of colour, rubbings and marbled prints.

SCISSORS

Children need to have reasonably sharp scissors and enough left-handed scissors, if they are to cut thicker paper accurately. Children at KS1 particularly need good quality scissors because they can find them difficult to squeeze.

Torn lines are usually more convincing than scissor cuts when children want to make natural shapes such as plants, landscapes or animals. White-backed paper gives a beautiful white edging to torn paper which can be used for foaming waves and snow-capped mountains.

Children at KS1 may feel strange tearing paper after having been asked to treat books carefully. It will be worth assuring them in advance that paper can be torn in some instances while never in others. Children at KS2 may be reluctant to tear paper because they feel it is 'babyish' or because they do not feel fully in control of the process. It is useful for them to see an adult tearing paper with great care and concentration. The shape can be controlled by placing a guiding finger next to the edge of the tear. Children could show the difference between made and natural objects by using cut and torn shapes.

Paper collage techniques

AGES AND STAGES

PoS 2c
Design and make creative images

Encourage children to cut or tear paper without drawing on it first. Preliminary drawings often result in fussy details and shapes which cannot be identified in silhouette. Stray pencil lines also spoil the clarity of colour and shape. Children at KS2 who are reluctant to work in this way could work ideas out on a scrap of paper or use a newspaper template. Use direct observation whenever practical for accurate shapes and details. A few large shapes will have more impact than a scattering of small ones. Children at KS2 should try to use the ridges in corrugated card or textured paper to emphasise a change in the design.

Paper shapes are easily lost in the piles of paper so some children prefer to glue them down as soon as they are cut. If they can find a safe storage place, it is better to assemble all the major collage pieces and then to move them around the paper to find the best arrangement.

MAKING PAPER COLLAGE PICTURES

ACTIVITY

1 Subjects for paper collage.

- Illustrate a character or an incident from a story or poem (Y1–Y6). Sections can be slightly elevated by using Blu-tak to fix them.

- Create pictures of landscapes (Y1–Y6). These can be built-up very quickly with simple overlapping paper shapes. Encourage children at KS2 to work from the background to the foreground. Use torn tissue paper for subtle colour blends.

- Make a paper collage figure (Y1–Y6). Cut or tear paper limbs, making additions where necessary. The joins will show slightly, but the lively, free movements more than compensate for this.

- Make a paper collage mask (Y1–Y6). A face mask can be a rather overwhelmingly large space for Y1 children and they often respond by making tiny features in the centre. Show the exaggerated shapes used in African and Asian masks and decorate the edges of a mask with hair before working with large shapes in the centre.

Figure 4.4
Figure dancing around a bonfire, from torn paper. Y2

Try different ways of shaping paper with KIDCUTS by Bronderbund 165007.

CREATING HIGH RELIEF

PoS 4a
Investigate pattern and texture

Even a small area of higher relief can add interest to a paper collage design.

Children learn by trying out ideas on scraps of paper before they start the collage. They could practise folding, tearing, cutting and scoring scraps of paper of different weights and textures.

MAKING A CURL
Wrap a paper strip tightly around a pencil to make a tight curl. Use a tooth pick for a very tight curl. Make a looser curl by dragging a strip of paper between the thumb and an open pair of blunt scissors. This gives a gentle curve to smaller paper shapes, such as petals and leaves.

MAKING A PROJECTION
Make a series of slits in a piece of paper. Keep the slits open with a strip of paper woven through and turned sideways.

Figure 4.5
Galleon, with relief of curved sails and raised hull. Y4

Fold a piece of paper and make several different cuts into the fold. Open out the paper and fold down the cut shape. This looks best on double-sided paper backed in a contrasting colour.

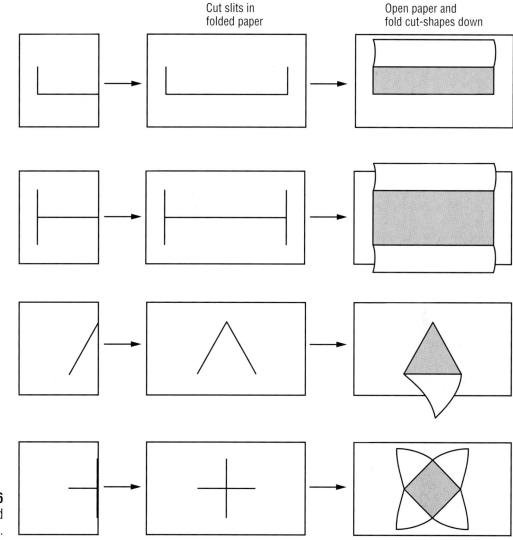

Figure 4.6
Making projections; opened slit shapes.

It helps if children know the difference between valley folds and mountain folds.

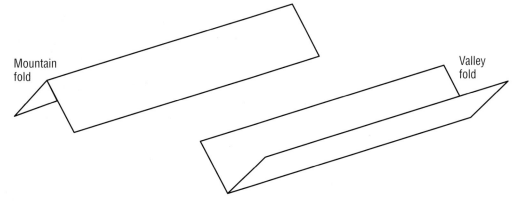

Figure 4.7
Fold types.

CARE! For accurate folding use the pointed edge of a pair of open scissors to draw a line along the edge of a ruler. (KS1 children who find this difficult could try it without a ruler.) This scoring cuts into the surface of the paper but not through it.

ACTIVITY   1   Use the shapes produced in the experiments.

• Glue the shapes close together on to paper to make a highly textured, abstract picture (Y1–Y6).

• Choose a favourite shape and make it the starting point for a paper collage picture. Use long paper curls for hair or for a burst of colour coming from a firework or volcano. Use short paper curls for foliage (Y1–Y6).

• Pick out all the shapes of one colour and glue them to the same coloured background (Y3–Y6). The challenge is to create enough interest in shape, form and texture without the distraction of colour. Children at the end of KS2 could fill spaces with card tubing cut into short lengths with a small saw to make a densely textured collage design.

2   Make paper masks (Y3–Y6). Place a piece of cardboard (28 × 33 cm) so that the long sides are vertical. Cut five slits, 7 cm long, down from the top and up from the bottom edges. Fold the top strips towards the back and staple them together. Do the same with the bottom strips. This makes a curved mask shape which will fit around a child's face. Check staple ends are on the outside of the mask so they do not catch children's hair.

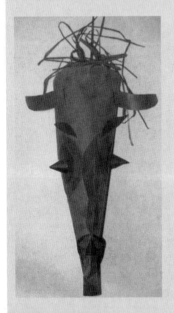

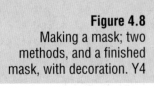

Figure 4.8
Making a mask; two methods, and a finished mask, with decoration. Y4

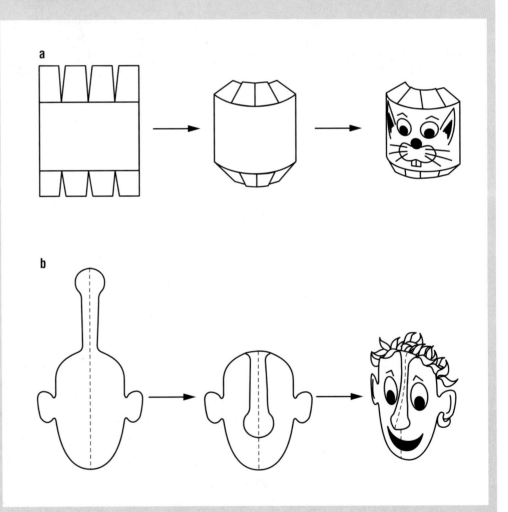

PoS 4a
Investigate pattern

MAKING A PAPER COLLAGE PATTERN

Paper collage is an ideal medium for pattern making. Multiple shapes can be made quickly and easily and then moved around before deciding on the final design.

MAKING IDENTICAL SHAPES

Identical images can be quickly and easily produced by folding and cutting, as long as the paper is coloured on both sides. Tissue paper can be folded four times, thin paper three times and sugar paper once. Turn some of the shapes over to make a mirror image.

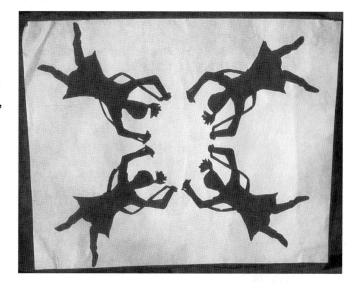

Figure 4.9
Figures, from paper in a circular pattern. Y4

Another method is for children to make their own card templates if they want multiple identical paper shapes. Mark the template on the back with a cross. Place this side uppermost on the back of the paper when drawing round it. Any pencil marks will then be on the reverse side of the paper.

PoS 4d
Investigate shape, form and space

MAKING A REFLECTED IMAGE

1 Cut two rectangles of paper in contrasting colours; make the background piece at least double the size of the piece to be cut.

2 Cut out shapes from the sides of the smaller rectangle and reassemble it jigsaw-fashion on the larger rectangle.

3 When all the shapes have been cut, flip them over piece by piece so that they give a reflected image on the background paper.

4 Glue each shape next to the space it came from.

ACTIVITY

1 Make a reflected face (Y5–Y6).
a) Working from the side of a sheet of black sugar paper, cut half of a face. Flip over the cut shape on to a larger rectangle of contrasting colour (white).
b) Cut out an eye, a pupil, an eyebrow, half the nose and lips and transfer them to the opposite side.

2 Use reflected images cut from long, narrow strips of paper as borders for written work (Y5–Y6).

Figure 4.10
Reflected faces, from black sugar paper and white paper. Y3

PoS 8e
Experiment with visual elements and use texture to make images

Mixed collage

Mixed collage builds up a design using a mixture of found objects, card, paper or fabric. It encourages children to use materials in a creative way because the objects are chosen for their shape, colour or texture and not for their original function. This is a wonderful medium through which to explore texture. Children love to touch the finished picture so a strong glue will be needed to make work for display.

KNOWLEDGE AND UNDERSTANDING

PoS 9d
Respond to and compare different styles and traditions

Using found materials for relief art works was regarded to be a revolutionary departure from the traditional wood and stone. Many examples are found in the work of the Cubists, the Dada movement and the Surrealists: Pablo Picasso's *Still life*, Ginn 2; Dali's *Lobster with telephone*, Goodwill 3(24); Masson's *Two skulls*, Goodwill 3(28); Joseph Cornell's *The Hotel Eden: assemblage with musical box* (1945) Ginn 31.

Figure 4.11
Flying insect, from Brazil nuts and found objects in a park – leaves, seeds. Y5

AGES AND STAGES

PoS 7d
Review and modify work

Children should have time to play with found objects, turning them upside down or grouping them. Those who are a little rigid in the way they approach art may find the jumble of mixed collage objects perplexing rather than liberating. These children could impose their own order by restricting their selection to multiples of, for example, three objects.

PoS 8c
Develop a range of source material

Children at KS1 often search the material until it suggests a subject to them. Metal machinery parts, nuts and bolts, for example, might suggest a robot.

Children at KS2 can usually reverse the process and search for material that will match an image they have already decided to make.

EQUIPMENT

GLUE AND CARD
Glue and card are the basic supports for most mixed collage pictures. PVA glue can be used for light objects and impact glue for heavy objects, such as twigs and pebbles.

PLASTER
Plaster holds bulky and irregular shaped objects such as beans and shells, which are difficult to glue down. Plaster of Paris sets too quickly, but Polyfilla gives the children time to make their arrangements. Mix Polyfilla and water to a ratio of 2:1. Spread it over a card or plastic base to a depth of approximately 1 cm and press in the objects. A varnish helps to fix the objects in place when the plaster has dried.

A COLLECTION OF FOUND OBJECTS
Collect as varied an assortment of collage objects as possible – buttons, beads, fabrics, stone, bark, twigs, small wood off-cuts, string, shells, dried food, nuts, polystyrene shapes, plastic netting, corrugated card, bubble packing paper, paper doilies, drinking straws, paper-clips, old erasers and pencils, pegs, spent matches, nails, buttons, dice, flattened milk bottle tops, old watches and jewellery, feathers, cogs, nails, wire, any small pieces of machinery.

PoS 4a
Investigate pattern and texture

Making a mixed collage design

Choose a subject with a strong, simple outline and interesting textures for a mixed collage picture, for example: hedgehogs, shells, houses and trees have simple but interesting, textured shapes. Alternatively, place the objects in a pleasing, rhythmic design.

Children at KS1 should start with small areas so that the collage can be closely textured. Mixed collage could be used to add textures to a painting or sculpture. In the same way, children at KS2 should try placing similar-shaped collage objects close together to form interesting patterns, textures and shapes. A random and haphazard arrangement is difficult to 'read'.

ACTIVITY

1 Mount a collage pattern on a small piece of pre-cut card.

  • Decorate a small card shape for a brooch (Y1–Y2). Glue it to felt so that it can be sewn to a hair-grip at home, or pinned to clothing with a safety-pin.

  • Design a Saxon brooch (Y3–Y4). Cut a disc, 8 cm in diameter, with a central hole 4 cm in diameter. Push on small paper-clips and glue on small beads, buttons, pulses and curtain hooks. Spray with silver or gold paint. Glue or tape a safety-pin to the back.

  • Take a set of identical objects, such as matchsticks, art straws or paper-clips and see if the design can still be interesting (Y3–Y6).

2 Decorate containers. Glue pressed flowers, string, shells or feathers to the outsides of plastic containers (Y1–Y6).

3 Make a collage with nails and wire (Y5–Y6). This provides good practice in hammering. Children love to hammer and do not seem to mind the high noise level, but teachers generally do. Working outdoors is recommended.

H & S

Lightly sketch out a very simple, linear design in pencil on a block of wood. Hammer nails into the wood along the lines. Use short nails with big heads. Loop thin wire around the nails to complete the shape. Texture the plaque with nails of different sizes.

PoS 8e
Experiment with visual elements

Fabric collage and embroidery

Children take immense visual and tactile pleasure from handling, examining and working with fabrics. Yet fabric collage and embroidery is often neglected in primary schools because it is seen as difficult and time-consuming. Darning, hand-sewing, patching, appliqué and embroidery are now rarely practised at home, so children often lack these foundation skills. This means that a teacher might be faced with the task of teaching sewing to a classroom full of children who cannot begin or end a line of stitches. A good way to begin is to start children with only a very small amount of informal, decorative stitching on fabric that has been glued, rather than sewn, down.

Figure 4.12
Pirate, from fabric collage, with a little decorative stitching. Y4

EQUIPMENT

Scissors

Scissors must cut fabric easily if fabric collage is to be a success. Children find it very frustrating to hack away at fabric with blunt scissors. The younger the children, the less able they are to squeeze scissors to gain pressure on the cutting edge. When any new scissors come into school, test them to see if they cut fabric without squeezing. Once fabric scissors have been selected, it is important to keep them purely for cutting fabric; cutting paper blunts the edges. Label them for use with textiles only.

Glue

Use fabric-glue as glued areas will remain soft enough to pass a needle through when dry. Only give out small quantities of glue as it dries very quickly. Thick PVA glue works well but children will not be able to sew through it when it dries. Suggest to children that they use small dots only of glue.

Needles

Tapestry needles have blunted points for safety and large eyes for easy threading. They pass through coarse fabric and pierce fine cotton easily.

H & S

To sew thick fabrics and layers of fabrics needles with sharp points are needed. Try to buy those with large eyes to minimise threading problems but also have available a few sharp, small-eyed needles for experienced sewers in Y5 and Y6 who need them for quick, small stitches.

Frames

Stiffening a fabric really helps the sewing process. Embroidery hoops are invaluable for beginners. They hold work taut and help to eliminate the problem of puckered stitching. A large design could be taped to a wooden frame.

An inexpensive alternative is to glue fabric to the back of a polystyrene tray and stitch through the tray as well as the fabric. Hessian wallpaper makes a good, stiff background if the stitches are large and uncomplicated.

Threads

Wool covers areas quickly in bright, bold designs and is a good thread for children to start with. Wool will sew easily through hessian but is difficult to pull through finer fabrics.

Raffia is waterproof and colour-fast, but difficult to sew because it is so springy. It works best on a rigid canvas.

Thin braids and ribbons, string and ric-rac can be threaded on large-eyed needles and sewn on open-weave fabrics.

Embroidery threads should be used for sewing fine textures and designs on closely-woven fabrics. Buy a basic range of colours in less expensive balls of thread and then gradually add the more subtle hues from embroidery hanks. Avoid the embroidery threads that can be subdivided; they split as they are threaded.

Embroidery threads are easily tangled. If a holder is made for each of the main colour groups, children will know where to go for any particular hue and be able to see the full range of tones.

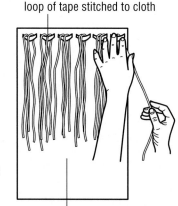

loop of tape stitched to cloth

cloth

1 Cut a piece of cloth approximately 45 × 60 cm. Stitch loops of tape to the top edge. Alternatively, use the same size of paper and large paper-clips.

2 Open up each hank of embroidery thread and cut it at the top end. Push it through a loop.

3 To release a thread, hold the tape loop with one hand and pull a thread with the other.

Tip!

Needles are very easily lost. Try colour-coding the children's tables and pinning the needles into a piece of felt to match each table's colour. Ask a child in each group to count the needles at the beginning and end of every lesson.

Figure 4.13
Embroidery-thread holder.

FABRICS

Fabrics are expensive to buy so it is worth thinking carefully about what they will be used for.

Hessian makes a neutral but interestingly textured background for fabric collage. It is also very easy to embroider.

Felt comes in plain, bright colours and will not fray. It is expensive, so keep it separate from the other fabrics and save the tiniest scrap.

Cotton sheeting is one of the cheapest fabrics and can be dyed or painted before it is worked on.

Some artificial fabric will be needed for crayon transfers.

A little binka (fabric woven into patterns of small squares) is useful for making formal embroidery stitches.

Ask parents who sew and knit to donate scraps of fabrics, braid and odd balls of wool. Cut patches of fabric and buttons from torn clothes before throwing them away. Ask the local theatre group for left-over fabric from costume making – they often have rich velvets and brocades. Cheap textiles can be bought from jumble sales. Plain, textured curtains can be cut up and distributed throughout the school. Collect interesting buttons, scraps of braids, ribbons, feather trimmings, areas of sequins, ric-rac, fringes and lace trims.

PoS 4a–d
Learn about visual and tactile elements

Making a fabric collage picture

Pictures made predominantly with fabric pieces create masses of dense colours and textures; yarn on its own makes a fabric collage with interesting linear structures.

KNOWLEDGE AND UNDERSTANDING

PoS 5a
Examine styles in the locality

Craftspeople who make pictures from fabric often sew a piece on with tiny over-stitches. Children might have seen examples of this appliqué technique on Christmas napkins, tablecloths and baby clothes. North America has a tradition of joining appliqué pictures together to make friendship quilts.

PoS 5b
Examine styles from past and present

Rag-rugging is traditionally used for making rugs. Strips of recycled fabric are pushed into a hessian fabric background to make a dense, raised area. These rugs were made in the last two centuries in Europe as a way of using waste fabrics and were seen as rather homely objects, although they are now a collector's item. It is still a popular craft in West Africa. Children enjoy using this technique to add areas of high relief to fabric collage pictures.

ACTIVITY

PoS 7e
Use knowledge of artists' work

1 Make rag-rugged details (Y3–Y6). Tear fabric into strips about 2 × 10 cm. Use the point of a pencil to push the middle of each strip into the hessian. Pull and wriggle the loop from the underside to give it a good hold. Use rag-rugging for foliage on trees, flower heads or a clown's tufty hair.

2 Make a class friendship quilt by joining small, square, fabric collage pictures (Y5–Y6). The seams of the quilt can be pinned and tacked by children but will need to be sewn with a sewing machine by an adult.

Figure 4.14
Clown, with rag-rugging hair. Y4

AGES AND STAGES

Encourage children to think of subjects for fabric collage that can have an imaginative interpretation or have highly developed textures – a dragon, a landscape, a tree, wood, leaves, a house, a bird, a fish, a fictional character.

Children in the beginning of KS1 find it easier to use small, overlapping pieces of fabric to fill areas rather than trying to cut exact shapes. By the end of KS1, children can start to cut out simple shapes accurately enough to represent an image. Large shapes that overlap look better than lots of small isolated shapes.

Fabrics are expensive so children of all ages should be taught to always cut a shape from a corner and never from the middle. At KS2, children can sketch out the shape in chalk; cutting just inside the lines to avoid chalk marks on the collage.

Children in Y3 and Y4 could start to overlayer fabrics by placing smaller shapes over larger shapes. This leaves attractive margins of colour. Encourage children to use the same colour more than once in the design to give unity to a composition.

Children in Y5 and Y6 can learn to exploit subtle differences in texture and tone by creating fabric collages in limited colours. Look for harmonising colours to reinforce the mood of a picture. Look closely at the texture of the fabrics and relate it to the subject of a collage.

Children in Y6 may be able to make small pictures entirely from fabric and stitches, without any glue.

Encourage children to extend their vocabulary to include smooth, rough, bumpy, furry, fluffy, feathery, silky, threads, wools, fabric (KS1); and cotton, taffeta, nylon, velvet, satin, silk, lace, knitted and crocheted fabric (KS2).

THE BACKGROUND

Keep the size of a collage small, approximately 20 × 30 cm, as it takes a long time to complete a fabric collage picture. Choose a fairly neutral fabric such as hessian, so the background does not attract attention away from the collage and stitching. Cheap, thin cotton sheeting can be used if the background is to be completely covered

Figure 4.15
Elephants, on hessian wallpaper. Y3

with collage pieces, although such extensive work can usually only be expected in Y5 and Y6. If there is not going to be any sewing on the fabric collage, it is more economical to use paper or hessian wallpaper as a background.

ACTIVITY

Paint a background using dyes or fabric paints (Y1–Y6). Add texture by sprinkling salt on the dye. Use tie-dye or batik patterns (see pages 148–159). All these backgrounds will need fabric collage pieces with strong shapes and colours for the foreground.

MAKING A COLLAGE PICTURE FROM FABRIC PIECES

PoS 7d
Review and modify work

Place or pin pieces of fabric to the background first to experiment with different arrangements. Keep assessing and making adjustments as a collage progresses.

ACTIVITY

Create raised areas of fabric (Y1–Y6).

• Pinch and fold fabric before gluing it down to make ripples in the surface (Y1–Y6).

Use this for water or costumes.

• Cut a fabric flower and stitch a circle in the centre (Y3–Y6). Pull the thread to make the petals stand in relief and tie the ends down securely.

• Make a padded section (Y5–Y6).

a) Cut large fabric shapes in felt. Stitch them down securely with backstitch.
b) Turn the picture over. Cut lines at the back of each shape to reveal the felt. Stuff with wadding (cotton wool etc.). Oversew the cuts to keep the wadding in.
c) Finish the picture with added collage and decorative stitching.

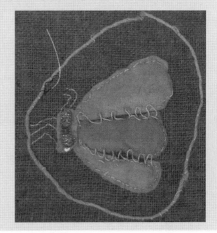

• Make a fabric landscape (Y5–Y6). Cover a laminated paper base with fabrics, or use a paper plate as a base for a fabric garden. Add fabric soaked in paste to twigs, to make trees.

Figure 4.16
Butterfly, padded with wadding. Y5

MAKING A YARN COLLAGE

PoS 4c
Images are made using line and tone

Bark, shells, leaves, flowers, seeds, sections of fruit and vegetables and stylised figures all make good subjects for linear designs. Linear designs can also be filled with textures. String is excellent for making dense areas of linear patterns on bark and shells. Secure any curled string with tape. Glue it and only remove the tape when the glue has dried.

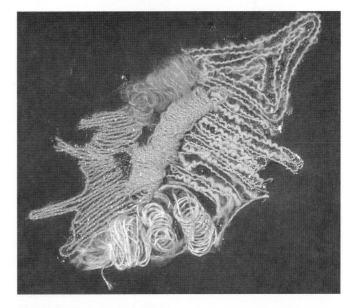

Figure 4.17
Yarn collage picture of a shell. Y5

ACTIVITY

1 Use marbled fabric as a background (Y1–Y6). Dip fabric in marbling inks floating on a tray of water. Follow the streaks and swirls with threads, net, yarn and mixed collage.

2 Stick shells, pebbles, water patterns or pieces of bark on fabric, paper or hessian wallpaper (Y1–Y6). Outline the shapes with linear patterns.

PoS 4a
Investigate pattern and texture

Quilting

Quilting uses tight stitches on padded fabric to create areas of high relief. Children find this highly textured surface very satisfying.

KNOWLEDGE AND UNDERSTANDING

PoS 9c
Relate art to its time and place of origin

Quilting, which originated in the Far East, was introduced to Europe by the Crusaders and became an established traditional craft in South Wales and in the North of England. Modern artists have used quilting techniques to create imaginative soft sculpture plaques.

AGES AND STAGES

Formal quilting involves long lines of small, careful back stitch and should be left to the end of KS2. The more creative quilted faces require much less exacting stitches and could be introduced in Y4 or Y5. Although the stitches are very simple they must be well anchored, so children need to be able to make very secure starting and finishing stitches.

QUILTED FACES

*PoS 3
Ideas, feelings and meanings are communicated in different visual forms*

This is a sewing technique that is guaranteed to cheer up the greyest day. As the work progresses, the faces seem to take on a life of their own and all kinds of eccentric characters emerge (see illustration on page 82). It gives a practical example of how an artist needs to respond to the way the work is evolving and to be adaptable about the end-product.

MAKING A SOFT SCULPTURE FACE

1 Cut a piece of white cotton sheeting and a piece of batting (sheets of cotton fibre) or wadding, both 25 × 30 cm. Pin the pieces together.

2 Turn the edges and corners towards the back to make a face shape. Use very quick, rough stitches to anchor the sides at the back.

3 Pinch a long shape for the nose and stitch the sides together. There will be a lot of tension on these stitches. Use doubled thread and double stitches to start and finish the sewing. Stitch from one side of the nose to the other and make a running stitch under the nose.

4 Make a series of tight running stitches for the eyes. Push the thread right to the back and pull it tight to make the stitches sink into the batting.

5 Nose stitching and eye stitching are the two basic ways of sculpturing the face – raising it up or puckering it down. The lips can disappear into a gummy grimace, or pucker up into a 'kiss-me-quick' pout.

6 Use contrasting thread to add textures and details. Penetrate to the back for additional sculpting, or just stitch on the surface for texture and colour.

> **Tip!**
> Match a thread closely to the fabric so that it 'disappears' into the folds of the cloth. This gives children confidence to try adventurous contour stitching.

ACTIVITY

1 **Make a crowd scene by gluing lots of the faces together.**

2 **Use an old shirt as a basis for the shoulders and stuff with scraps of cloth, crumpled newspaper or batting. Glue the sculpture on a textured background. Add paper hands and make them hold on to the bars of a jail or whatever else suits the character. This could be a rich resource for written work.**

TRADITIONAL QUILTING

H & S

Draw a design in fabric crayon and iron it on to plain cotton fabric. Cut a piece of batting the same size as the cloth and tack the batting and the cloth together with large stitches. Use back stitch to penetrate the fabric and the batting to make a raised image. This takes two or three sessions.

Figure 4.18
Pineapple, in quilting. Y5

Modelling in relief

PoS 3
Ideas, feelings and meanings are communicated in different visual forms

PoS 8e
Experiment with texture and shape

Relief comes from the Italian *relievo*, 'to raise'. With the exception of quilted faces, collage pictures do not allow children to create very deep relief. Modelling introduces a new area of exciting relief work with highly textured surfaces.

Using plastic materials

Children can model with plastic (pliable) materials such as clay, Plasticine and modelling dough. These materials can be rollered and cut into shapes and then further refined by texturing, pulling and pushing the surface. This section describes relief work (see Chapter 5 on sculpture for further techniques with these materials, page 122).

Figure 4.19
Face with plaited hair, in clay. Y2

KNOWLEDGE AND UNDERSTANDING

PoS 5a
Examine styles in the locality

Children will probably have seen decorative clay plaques, brooches and fridge magnets in shops. Pictures of relief work in teachers' packs usually show stone or wood carvings and, despite the differences in technique, they can provide inspiration for relief work in softer modelling materials (*Marsh scene from Sennacherib's Palace at Ninevah*, Ginn 19).

AGES AND STAGES

Children in Y1 may need help in rollering out clay or Plasticine into slabs. They enjoy experimenting with different textures made by pushing objects into the surface of the slab. By Y2 children should build up relief by adding pieces to the surface, as well as creating indentations.

At KS2, introduce the idea of building up the slab in layers – the background first, then the middleground finishing with the foreground. Encourage children to build up patterns in closely-worked areas, rather than using haphazard spacing. Children at the end of KS2 can build up quite steep areas of clay relief by adding card supports. These can be removed when the clay is dry.

MODELLING MATERIALS

CLAY

Clay is malleable and responds to the slightest pressure but thin sections can become very crumbly as it dries. Fire the slab in a kiln if possible. After firing, rub over the clay with polish for an antique look, or glaze (see page 129).

COLD CLAY

Cold clay is made from a mixture of regular clay and fibres. It hardens as it dries, so does not need firing but cannot be glazed. Use paints for colour and varnish for shine.

PLASTICINE

Plasticine needs to be warm before it is really pliable but the surface will make finely-detailed relief areas.

HOME-MADE MODELLING DOUGH

Modelling dough made from flour is malleable for a long time but will not make such fine details as clay or Plasticine. The slab can be dried in a low oven and lasts a long time.

CREATING TEXTURE

PREPARING A SLAB

Use a wooden roller to flatten the material into a slab. Place two wooden slats at the sides and always keep the roller in contact with the slats. This helps children to create an even surface for the relief details.

INCISED DESIGNS

Push a variety of objects into the material in densely-worked patterns to make incised designs: slash the surface with a wire, blunt knife or tooth pick; scrape the surface with a comb or a dry toothbrush; place leaves, string, feathers or cloth on the slab and roller over them to make an impression.

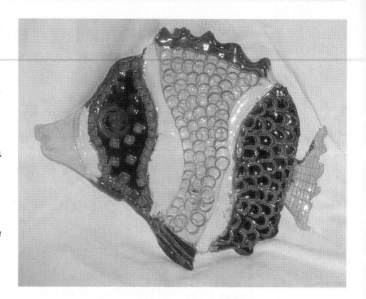

Figure 4.20
Fish, with scales made from the tip of a plastic counting stick, the hollow casing of an old felt-tip pen, and the wire tip of a clay modelling tool. The tail was textured with the edge of a comb. Y5

RAISED-RELIEF DESIGNS

Create raised-relief areas by adding more material: cut out small pieces of flattened material and press them on the surface (water is needed to join the clay); make thin 'worms' and coil them on the slab (keep them raised in high relief, or flatten them slightly with a roller); roller the modelling material very thinly to make gathered clothes or delicate petals.

MOULD THE FORM OF A CLAY SLAB

Lay the soft clay over a rolled magazine to make a rounded slab or crumple newspaper and use it to support the clay.

PoS 7c
Explore and use 2- and 3-dimensional media

Modelling with papier mâché and laminated paper

Papier mâché and laminated paper-relief slabs are light and extremely durable as well as being made from inexpensive and widely available materials.

Use prepared papier mâché (see page 114) or push and pull six pasted layers of newspaper or tissue into ridges, swirls and lines to create a landscape, abstract textural pattern or mask. The newspaper takes about two days to dry out in a warm place. Use white glue and tissue for a hard surface. For higher relief, tape crumpled newspaper on to card and overlay laminated paper.

ACTIVITY

1 Make a landscape (Y1–Y6).

   • Make a strong base for a large model by gluing two pieces of corrugated card together with the ridges going in opposite directions.

   • Make a treasure island with a cave to hide the treasure.

   • Make a moon landscape. Tape shallow card cylinders to the card base for craters.

2 Make animal masks (Y3–Y6). Tape balls of screwed-up newspaper to a card shape to show the raised parts of an animal's face.

3 Make a class wall-plaque (Y5–Y6). Build up texture and patterns on identically sized pieces of card (10 × 10 cm). Obtain ideas from wood grain, scales on reptiles, water ripples, building surfaces. Staple all the squares together to make a large, tactile display.

Figure 4.21
Laminated paper tiger mask. Y4

Modelling with plaster

PoS 4a
Investigate texture

Plaster does not have the same smooth and constant malleability as plastic materials but its grainy texture is interesting to handle and makes a slab closer to stone.

KNOWLEDGE AND UNDERSTANDING

Relief stone carvings can be very complex as in the Roman carving *Sarcophagus front: the return of the body of Meleager to Kalydon*, Shorewood 1785. Children might also be able to see simple carvings in graveyards and on roadside milestones or market crosses.

AGES AND STAGES

Plaster is easy to manipulate but children in KS1 may have problems keeping the classroom reasonably tidy. It is these practical problems and not the skills involved which makes this technique most suitable for the end of KS2.

POLYFILLA

Polyfilla plaster dries slowly so it can be used very successfully to model a relief slab. Use it for making simple, solid forms.

Use Polyfilla in the following way.

1 Mix Polyfilla and water in the ratio 3:1. Add paint and a little sand to make the mixture more like the colour and consistency of stone.

2 Spread the mixture thickly on to a rigid base – an old vinyl tile, an off-cut of hardboard or wood, or a piece of thick card. Create textures and relief areas.

3 Allow to dry overnight.

4 Leave the colour as a pale stone colour or paint and varnish it. Y6 children could try using shoe polish; blend a mixture of colours to obtain the variations you find in wood or stone.

MOD-ROC

Mod-roc is made from bandages impregnated with plaster of Paris. They are sold in different widths and can be cut with scissors. Dip each mod-roc piece in water and use it very quickly as it sets within 30 seconds. Push the mod-roc around on a piece of card to form a relief design such as a mask. Add more mod-roc and pinch and tuck to make features.

ACTIVITY

1 Take a photograph of a local, simple carving and try to reproduce a section (Y4–Y6).

PoS 7e
Use knowledge of artists' work

2 Isolate a Greek or Roman figure by placing a card window frame over the picture of a relief carving (Y5–Y6). Try to build up a similar basic figure in Polyfilla. Use cloth dipped in Polyfilla for draped clothing.

Plaster casts

PoS 8d
Experiment with tools and develop techniques

A cast can be made over a textured surface. The liquid plaster fills in the indentations and yields to the relief areas of the mould so that children achieve an exciting 'reverse record' of their work. Plaster records the slightest change in texture on the mould's surface and yet is also very strong and durable.

KNOWLEDGE AND UNDERSTANDING

PoS 5a
Examine styles in the locality

Children could look at coins and discuss how the surface textures would be made with moulds and then cast in metal. The figures and patterns in the bronze door panel *The journey of the Magi* and *Sanctuary door knocker*, Ginn 13 and 40, would have been made in clay first and then cast in metal, using very similar techniques to those with plaster casts.

Children are usually eager to colour their slab but it is worth reminding them that many artists rely on relief alone to give impact to their work.

Damp sand is a popular modelling material for children at KS1 and casting enables them to make a permanent record of their work. When children make their first casts they will be surprised to discover that the plaster indents where the mould projected. This will continue to intrigue children at KS2, but they should start to anticipate this result in the planning of their plaques.

Although the usual precautions have to be taken with using plaster, because the creative process is in making the mould, the children need not be directly involved with making the cast. This makes it much easier for the teacher to organise and means that children as young as Y1 can use these techniques.

Making a plaster cast

MAKING A MOULD

1 Roll out a piece of old clay or soft Plasticine 2 to 4 cm in depth. (Never reuse this clay for models which will be fired. A tiny amount of plaster can cause an explosion in the kiln.)

2 Dust talcum powder over the clay to stop impressed objects from sticking to the clay. Brush a Plasticine mould with soapy water. These techniques also help the plaster to separate from the mould.

3 Make imprints with fingers and objects from a texture box: pencils, string, pegs, sticks, small boxes, shells, tools, fabrics, feathers, rocks, bark.

MAKING THE CAST

BUILDING A WALL
Walls can be built entirely of clay but it is more economical to use card off-cuts. Push card strips around the edges of the slab, overlapping at the corners. Hold the strips together with paper-clips. Seal any small gaps on the outside with clay or Plasticine. Use a pencil to mark the limit to which the plaster should rise.

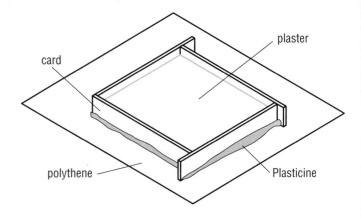

Figure 4.22
Making a plaster cast.

Meat trays or shoebox lids make ready-made walled containers but do not provide much depth for indentations on the slab.

MIXING THE PLASTER
Half-fill a container with plaster of Paris. Use a disposable container as plaster sets solid and cannot be removed. Add enough water to reach the top of the plaster. Add paint to the water if you want the plaster to be tinted.

Mix with a stick to make a liquid like thin cream, but do not stir too much as air bubbles spoil a cast.

POURING THE PLASTER
Pour the plaster quickly into a mould. Start at the deepest part to avoid air bubbles. Spoon the plaster into sand casts to avoid disturbing the sand. Reinforce large casts by pushing chicken wire just below the surface of the plaster. Push a loop of wire into the back to act as a hook if the plaque is going to be hung on a wall.

NAMING THE PLAQUE
Name each cast immediately by pushing a named piece of paper into the back of the plaster. It will be impossible to recognise work from the back of the cast and it is important that children should remove their own casts from the mould. The exact relationship between the textures they made and the relief that is produced is an important and exciting learning experience.

REMOVING THE CAST

Plaster sets very quickly and children enjoy feeling the warmth generated by the process. Simple relief casts can be removed after approximately 20 minutes. A complex relief should be left overnight to ensure it is completely set.

Figure 4.23
Malaysian-style house, made from a painted plaster cast. Y5

Pull away the plaster from the base. Remove any clay that is still clinging to the cast using water. Ask the children to compare the mirror images of the cast with the mould. Notice how the indentations have become projections.

File any rough edges after waiting a day to allow the plaster to completely dry out.

ACTIVITY

1 Use ready-made forms to make relief patterns (Y1–Y6).

• Use natural objects, such as a piece of bark, cabbage or rhubarb leaf. Support the edges of the leaf with rolls of clay or press it into a bed of sand.

• Press toy animals and soldiers into clay. The cast makes a relief scene similar to those of a carved relief Greek or Roman procession.

• Grease an old dessert spoon and support the handle to make it level. Pour in plaster and leave overnight. Turn it out of the mould and use it to make a badge, a mouse, a tortoise or a fish. Glue two smooth moulds together to make an Easter egg.

• Use crumpled tin foil, bubble-pack plastic, or cellophane for a shallow but interesting texture.

2 Use damp sand to hold small objects (Y1–Y6).

• Make indentations and place shells or other disposable, small objects in the sand, face down. The sand textures the surface of the plaster cast and the objects come out fixed to the plaster. Varnish the plaque to stop the sand from wearing.

• Use a dustbin lid filled with sand and wedge each side of the handle with a brick to keep the mould stable.

3 Make imitation beadwork when studying Native American culture (Y3–Y4). Poke a blunt pencil into a small piece of clay in a dense pattern. The plaster cast will look like a beaded medallion or headband.

SCULPTURE

Main NC focus

PoS 8d
*Children should be taught
to experiment with (and
develop control of [KS2])
tools and techniques for
. . . sculpture*

Introduction

Children particularly enjoy working in three dimensions (3D) because they can see, hold, feel, weigh and turn the material. The sculptures reflect, in a satisfying way, the solidity of objects around them. In this chapter sculpture techniques are divided into construction, carving and modelling.

- Construction (page 103)
  card and paper (page 104); found material (page 107); wire (page 109); plaster of Paris (page 112); laminated paper (page 114); soft sculpture (page 116)

- Carved sculptures (page 119)
  soft materials (page 119); wood (page 121)

- Modelling (page 121)
  materials (page 122); techniques (page 123); slab-pots (page 124); thumb pots (page 126); coil pots (page 127); using a kiln (page 128); glazing (page 128)

Figure 5.1
Galleon, made from boxes, card, dowelling and string. Y4, in pairs

PoS 3
*Ideas, feelings and
meanings are
communicated in different
visual forms*

Knowledge and understanding through sculpture

Artists create sculptures to be walked around and examined from all angles. Ideally children should visit art galleries with sculptures on display but this is not usually possible. Instead, small 3D art works can be brought into school. If possible they should be in the same material or made with similar techniques to those that the children are going to use. They do not always have to be professional artists' or craftspeople's work; they can be sculptures that the children have made before, or work from other classes. The important thing is to examine the sculpture from all angles to encourage children to do the same during construction of their own sculptures.

PoS 7d
Review and modify work

Ages and stages

At the beginning of KS1, children need time to explore thoroughly the different materials used in sculptures. This is important because they need to discover for themselves the strengths and limitations of materials, and also because they need the freedom to communicate their own ideas in symbolic form. Children at this stage often 'talk' to their model and make it part of their fantasy play. This spontaneous element is central to children's work at this stage but teachers have an important role in extending ideas and teaching new skills. In Y2, a child could be taught to make a thumb-pot, for example, but then use his or her imagination to transform it into whatever he or she chooses.

While children at KS1 are usually content to develop their own images independently, children at KS2 often need stimulation from the teacher. Poems and stories provide ideas for imaginative work while history and geography can generate ideas for more realistic sculptures. References from magazines and books are useful in providing guidance for shape, form, colour and textural detail.

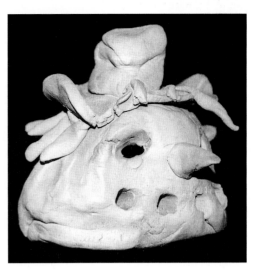

PoS 2c
Design and make creative images and artefacts

Figure 5.2
Hallowe'en candle lamp, made from a thumb-pot. Y2

Children at KS2 can begin to make decisions about the most appropriate medium and technique for the image they wish to produce. Clay would not be appropriate for a delicate-legged deer but wire and mod-roc, or wire and foil would. Children at this stage are capable of assessing and modifying a design as work progresses.

PoS 7f
Respond to and evaluate art

Talking about sculptures

At KS1, children respond best to sculptures with an easily recognisable form. Sculptures of people are an interesting focal point: Michelangelo's *Pieta* (1499) St Peter's Rome, Shorewood 1790; Auguste Rodin's *The thinker* (1880); Henry Moore's *Reclining figure*, The Tate Gallery. With a little guidance from their teacher, children at KS1 can enjoy the more abstract sculptures if they talk primarily about their emotional and personal reactions – what they notice first, how they feel when they look at the sculpture, how the shape, textures and material add to this feeling.

At the beginning of KS2, children could discuss whether the sculpture has been made for a particular place – a civic square, a church, a graveyard, a garden, a private house – and how this has affected the scale and material used. Is the piece useful or is it mainly expressive? Is it pleasing to look at or is it disturbing?

[IT] An example of computer software sculpture packages is Acorn's *Art in the National Curriculum Key Stage Two* AVP COM5002 for sculptures by Michelangelo, Epstein and Giacometti.

Construction

In construction, children make sculptures by joining various materials. Although primary children cannot weld metal or make joints for timber, they can find other ways of joining materials using tape, glue, staples, stitches and pins.

Figure 5.3
Victorian-style doll's house, made by the whole class, taking several sessions. Y6

While carving and modelling have a long artistic tradition, construction dominates modern sculptures (Nash's *Ladders*, Ginn 30). Many crafts are also based on construction. Children could discuss the skilled trades of a carpenter, cabinet-maker, pattern-maker, cooper and wood-turner and examine the way that wood is joined in tables and chairs. Perhaps a local craftsperson could be asked to talk to the children about his or her work.

Building with bricks and Lego is an ideal introduction to construction. These materials can easily be added to and taken away, so they give valuable experience in assessing and adapting a structure as it is constructed. Children at KS1 also learn about balance and stability when they build high structures using boxes. If there is room to keep the structure for a while, use touches of impact glue to make it more permanent.

Construction with card and paper

Card and paper have many advantages as construction materials. They are relatively cheap, easily available, have few storage problems and come in a wide range of colours. Paper is ideal for experimenting with structures because off-cuts can be used and shaped very easily by folding. Card is light but reasonably rigid, so it is more suitable for a standing form. The completed works are also light enough to be suspended from the ceiling or a branch supported in a vase, which helps with a problem of storage.

Children are so used to seeing card and paper as flat objects, they feel a particular sense of achievement when they transform them into sculptures. Adding just a few paper relief details can transform a very simple form. A folded triangle can become a mouse by the simple addition of a curled tail and ears.

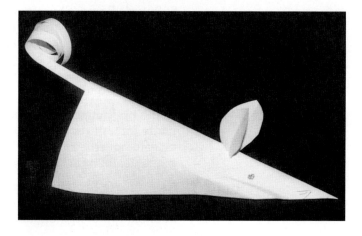

Figure 5.4
Mouse, evolved from a triangle by a simple fold and the addition of two eyes, a pair of cut ears and a curled tail. Y2

Joining card and paper can be a problem for children at KS1. Children in Y1 will usually be happy to use tape but older children in Y2 often dislike the rough finish this gives to a model. Paste takes time to dry and temporarily weakens paper and card, because it makes them wet. Contact glue is messy and must only be used in a well-ventilated room, but it is very useful for difficult areas that need to be quickly joined. PVA glue is a good compromise for most joins as it does not weaken the structure and there is no problem with fumes. Spread thinly, the glue dries in under a minute. Thickly spread glue will take about five minutes to dry.

Children at KS2 can experiment with joining card shapes with slots, paper-clips, staples and split pins as well as glue. Corrugated card shapes can be joined with short lengths of kebab sticks pushed into the raised ridges. Children at the end of KS2 could make constructions using the geometric nets they have learned about in mathematics.

The simple techniques that follow transform flat shapes into 3D objects. They provide a useful introduction to working in 3D because, although there are only two sides to work on, children become used to turning the model around to view it from both sides.

ACTIVITY 1 Use stuffing to inflate a sculpture (Y1–Y2). Cut identical shapes from strong paper. Glue the edges together, leaving a large opening. Children in Y1 could use a paper bag to make a head. Colour and decorate the shape. Stuff a small form with tissue paper and a large form with newspaper. Close the opening with tape or glue.

2 Inflate a tissue paper fish (Y5–Y6).
a) Cut out two pieces of tissue in a fish shape. Make sure there is a generous space where the body narrows at the tail fin. Add details in black pen.
b) Glue along the outline leaving a gap for the mouth. Use the minimum of glue to prevent the tissue from sticking to the table. Allow it to dry.
c) Insert a straw into the mouth and blow into the fish to inflate it gently. Seal the mouth with glue.

MAKING SIMPLE CARD CUT-OUTS STAND UP

Making a flat shape stand independently can transform it into a sculpture.

ACTIVITY 1 Use pegs for stand-up card animals (Y1–Y2). Cut out the side view of an animal. Paint, crayon or cover it with fuzzy felt. Clip on wooden spring clothes pegs as legs.

wooden spring clothes-pegs

Figure 5.5
Making a peg animal.

2 Separate two card shapes (Y2–Y4).

• Cut out two side views of an animal or bird and use a small box to separate the shapes (Y2–Y3).

• Cut the front and back view of an animal and use a cotton reel to separate the shapes (Y3–Y4).

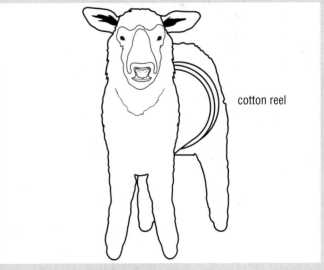

cotton reel

Figure 5.6
Separating card shapes.

3 Slot card shapes together to make a stand up animal (Y3–Y4). Use the thickest card that can be comfortably cut. Glue will fix wobbly connections.

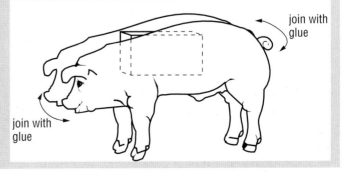

join with glue

join with glue

Figure 5.7
Making a slotted-card animal.

MAKING GEOMETRIC SHAPES

CYLINDERS

Cylinders are very simple to make. Just curve a rectangle and glue or staple the edges together. These provide an excellent base for masks, lanterns and puppets.

ACTIVITY

1 Make a simple cylinder mask from card large enough to put over a child's head, approximately 62 × 42 cm (Y1–Y6). Mark where the child's eyes are and cut the mouth there. This means the mask's eyes can be in proportion, half way up the cylinder, while still allowing the child inside to see.

2 Make a lantern (Y3–Y6). Make mountain folds along the length of a rectangle of paper and cut diagonally into the folds. Flatten the paper and pull the cuts up or down to make triangular holes. Curve and glue the sheet into a cylinder. Place several of the sculptures in a dark corner and shine a lamp on the surfaces.

CONES

Make a paper cone from a circle or semicircle. This provides a stable base for figures. Use a variety of papers; paper doilies folded in half are strong enough for a body.

ACTIVITY

1 Make a cone figure (Y2–Y3).

• Make a cone. Cut a card head with a long neck and push the neck into the top of the cone. Glue on arms. Add wings made from paper doilies to make an angel or fairy.

• Cut a doughnut shape in card and push it over the cone to make a witch's hat.

• Add a ruff of slashed paper for a seated lion's mane. Glue legs to the front and a tail at the back.

2 Make a cone figure with moving arms (Y3–Y4).
a) Make a cone base. Use a pencil to drill two arm holes directly opposite to each other.
b) Push an art straw through the holes. Inside the cone, hook another shorter art straw over the arm straw. Glue down the hook.
c) Pull and push the inside straw to make the arms wave up and down.

Figure 5.8
Witch, with moving arms.
Y3

PYRAMIDS

Make a three-sided pyramid from a square of paper. Fold across the diagonals of the square, to make four mountain folds radiating from the centre. Place the two bottom edges together and make a valley fold to the centre. Glue the two surfaces together to form a pyramid.

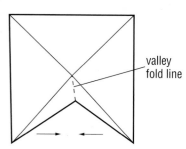

valley fold line

Figure 5.9
Making a pyramid.

ACTIVITY

1 Use pyramids to make roofs, relief details and abstract sculptures (Y3–Y4).

2 Join two pyramids together to make a prism. Use it for a Christmas decoration (Y5–Y6).

CUBOIDS

Pull small boxes apart and use the shapes as a net for making similar 3D shapes.

ACTIVITY

1 Make cuboids into gift boxes or use them as a basis for a model of a house (Y3–Y6).

2 Build a futuristic city or an abstract sculpture with cylinders, cones, pyramids and cuboids (Y3–Y6).

PoS 8c
Develop a range of source material

Construction with found material

Found materials are very difficult to construct into completely realistic images, so it is better to choose subjects that reflect the forms of the materials. Wood, seeds and other natural found objects would be useful for imaginary forest creatures. Boxes are more suitable for made objects such as buildings, furniture, robots or vehicles but corners can be softened with card surrounds, laminated paper or collage. Children's imaginative skills often transform the most unsympathetic materials into convincing sculptures.

KNOWLEDGE AND UNDERSTANDING

PoS 9d
Respond to and compare different styles and traditions

Simple sculptures have been made from an arrangement of bricks (Tate Gallery, London), old vacuum flasks (National Museum, Singapore) or plastic shapes (Royal Marks Gallery, New York). Picasso created a head of a bull using a bicycle seat and handlebars and a head of a baboon using a toy car as the muzzle. Nash used fallen tree trunks to make the sculpture *Ladders*, Ginn 30.

AGES AND STAGES

PoS 8c
Develop a range of source material

The wide variety of materials provided can act as a distraction. A clear aim helps children to focus and be positive. The aim can be as wide as 'Find something with a shape that reminds you of an object, animal or person and add details to make a sculpture.' This will focus children's attention away from the function of the object to its form and texture. For example, a date-box lid might suggest a toboggan or the hull of a cargo ship instead of reminding them of the food they ate on Christmas Day.

H & S

Children at KS1 will need quick results as they build constructions. Tape that can be torn with fingers is very useful. Impact glue could be introduced in Y2.

PoS 8d
Experiment with tools and develop techniques

Children at KS2 will have much more control over the form their sculpture takes if they are allowed to use the tools from the woodwork box. They could make holes with a centre punch, a hand drill, a hole punch or by hammering a nail into plastic. They could join surfaces by gluing with thick PVA glue and clamp the pieces with a spring clamp until the glue sets. Children in Y5 and Y6 could cut thin balsa wood and plastic with a craft knife, minisnips or a saw under close supervision.

H & S

CARDBOARD BOXES

PoS 7b
Use resources to stimulate ideas

Cardboard boxes will probably make up the bulk of the materials available – they are clean, light and comparatively easy to store. Collect mostly small boxes, especially those with unusual shapes such as Toblerone packets. They can be glued together to make larger, more complex shapes. A few large boxes could be collapsed and stored flat. Washed small cream or milk cartons make good basic shapes for houses – the slope of the containers makes a convincing roof.

Join boxes with tape and glue and reinforce weak corners with card triangles. Card shapes can be glued to the surfaces to refine the shape of a structure.

ACTIVITY

1 Colour the sculpture (Y1–Y6). The sculpture may look best left uncoloured to show how it was constructed, but if labels on the boxes act as a distraction then colouring will unify the structure's form. Use powder paint mixed with water and PVA glue.

• Overlay paper to make narrow margins of colour (Y3–Y6).

• For a very durable finish, cover the surface of the model with Polyfilla mixed with paint and water in a ratio of 2 : 1 (Y5–Y6). Press in wooden spills to add details to a building or draw in lines and patterns.

CYLINDERS

PoS 7b
Use resources to stimulate ideas

Cylinders are a useful shape because they suggest an animal or human form. Save card tubes from inside rolls of paper or foil, cleaned tin cans that have not been opened with a tin opener and plastic bottles.

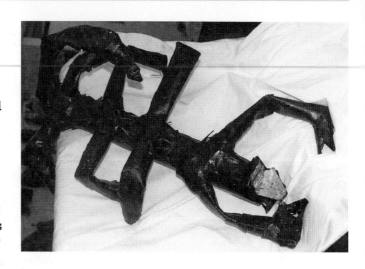

Figure 5.10
Scorpion, made from joined cylinders, standing over 1 m high. Y4

Join squeezy bottles together to make a long shape by cutting a cross in the base and pushing the next container up into the hole. Tape them together.

ACTIVITY

1 Make a pencil holder by decorating a card cylinder with collage or paper patterns (Y1–Y2). Glue braid along the top and the bottom. Glue the cylinder to a card base 1 cm wider than the cylinder to give it stability.

2 Make a simple figure by adding collage details to a cardboard cylinder (Y1–Y4). Include the head in the cylinder shape or push back the front of the cylinder and glue on a ball of paper or a ping-pong ball for a head. Slit up the middle of the cylinder to create a trouser divide and add card feet.

3 Use a card cylinder for an animal's body (Y1–Y4).

 • Cut a slit at the front and push in a card profile of the head (Y1–Y2). Cut out side-views of the legs and join them to the side of the cylinder using tape.

 • Make a sit-up mouse or kangaroo (Y3–Y4). Cut two slits, 1 cm long, down from the top of the cylinder and wedge in the ears made from card.

4 Use cans with plastic lids – a ground-coffee or powdered-milk tin to make a money box (Y4–Y6). Cut a section out of the plastic lid for the money. Paint and decorate the tin as a post box, a funny face, a sitting bird or a robot.

5 Make abstract sculptures by building high with the same type of boxes (Y5–Y6). Long cylinders massed together can make a complex and elegant structure.

PLASTIC CONTAINERS AND PACKAGING

Plastic yoghurt pots, ice-cream containers, transparent soft drinks bottles provide useful shapes. They can also be cut up for curved surfaces.

ACTIVITY

1 Make a shaker from two yoghurt pots (Y1–Y2). Put rice into a yoghurt pot. Place another identically sized pot on top and tape it securely to the other. Cover with foil and add more decorative tape. Shake, rattle and roll.

2 Use moulded plastic packaging to create Space City (Y1–Y3). Glue on details using buttons, lids, tops and tiny boxes.

H & S

3 Colour the sculpture using acrylic paint mixed with PVA glue or metallic spray paints (spray paint will melt some plastics). Crush sheets of kitchen foil around a sculpture to give it a shiny, interesting texture.

NATURAL FOUND OBJECTS

PoS 7b
Use resources to stimulate ideas

Shells, driftwood, bark, dried pods, nuts, seeds, cones, leaves and pebbles make interesting sculptures and are useful for adding final detail to sculptures made from other materials.

ACTIVITY

1 Make a support for a branch sculpture (Y1–Y6).

• Glue half a plastic cup (cut vertically) on to a piece of card to form a vase. Glue twigs on to tissue paper leaves and flowers, and arrange them in the vase (Y1–Y2).

• Mix Polyfilla to a thin cream consistency and pour it into an empty margarine container (Y5–Y6). Leave for one and a half hours to harden a little. Stand twigs or other shapes in it to make a sculpture. Leave for another two hours before taking it out of the mould. Spray with silver.

2 Use half a walnut shell to make a fridge magnet (Y2–Y4). Glue a lump of Plasticine inside the walnut so that it sticks out from the shell slightly. Push in a small magnet and let the children use their imagination to transform it into a mouse, a hedgehog, a tortoise, a beetle or a mask.

WOOD

Balsa wood off-cuts and craft sticks (1 cm wide wooden lollipop sticks that can be purchased in large numbers) provide a good opportunity for sawing, sandpapering, drilling and joining. Parents and carpenters may also be able to provide off-cuts. Packing firms often give away dismantled boxes but the wood is usually too hard for children to saw. See if there are any parents who will use their power-saws to cut the wood into interesting small shapes. These can be used to make abstract sculptures or to add details to card structures. Wood shavings look wonderful as hair.

ACTIVITY

1 Cut the wood into shapes (Y3–Y6). Children at KS2 should have learned to use basic wood-cutting tools in their design and technology lessons and this knowledge can be used to shape softwood into pieces for art. Work in small groups with adult supervision and support the wood in a clamp or a bench press. (A bench press is a sawing board. Push the wood against the upper lip to keep it firm during sawing.) Children in Y5 and Y6 could use a craft knife or minisnip scissors (strong scissors for cutting balsa wood) to cut thin balsa wood under adult supervision.

H & S

2 Join wood pieces (Y3–Y6). Use a hammer to drive in nails and pins. If possible, drill a pilot hole with a bradawl (boring tool) to avoid splitting the wood along the grain. Sandwich the wood between a clamp and a spare piece of board before drilling. A hole punch can be used for punching holes in thin softwood which can then be joined with wire ties. Glue light woods together clamping until the glue dries. Use balsa cement with balsa wood.

3 Glue card triangles over joins on squared wood to keep them rigid. If the triangles intrude on the finished design, snip away the excess card when the glue has dried.

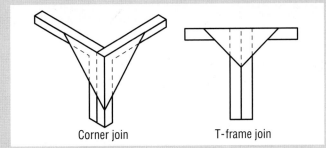

Corner join   T-frame join

Figure 5.11
Joining wood.

PoS 4c
Images are made using
line and tone

Construction with wire

Children enjoy the malleability of wire and its light, airy quality. Wire also is very useful as an armature or support for other material such as foil and mod-roc.

KNOWLEDGE AND
UNDERSTANDING

PoS 5b
Examine styles from past
and present

Bronze and steel are very popular materials for public sculptures and using wire for sculptures allows children to feel they are, in some ways, part of the same tradition. If possible bring in small metal sculptures or artefacts or look at photographs of metal sculpture: *Elephant and castle candlestick*, Ginn 28; Lalique's *Peacock brooch*, Ginn 22; *Viking armlet*, Ginn 21; Yoruba Peoples' *Herbalist's staff*, Shorewood 1801. Some sculptors, such as Giacometti, used wire as an armature. His elongated, almost skeletal figures use wire giving height and delicacy to the forms.

Tip!

If your classroom has ceiling tiles, open a paper-clip to act as a hook for the mobile. Thread the string from the mobile through the lower loop of the paper-clip and wedge the other loop between the metal grid and the ceiling tile.

Mobiles are based on wire structures that move (Calder *Fishbones*, Goodwill 3(22)). When Alexander Calder, an American artist, was in Holland in the early 1930s, he visited the painter Mondrian's studio. Mondrian had arranged yellow, red and blue rectangles on plain white walls and Calder was struck by the way the white of the wall isolated and intensified the colours. He arranged simple, coloured shapes on a white background in a sculpture called *Things ranged on a plank against a wall*. He also decided that the red, yellow and blue would look fascinating if they moved, so in 1932 he made a series of shapes in primary colours, balanced them on thin wires and used an engine to propel them around. The French artist, Marcel Duchamp, gave them the name mobiles. Calder's static sculptures were called stabiles, to contrast with his mobiles. Stabiles are sculptures that suggest movement while being solidly on the ground and are usually made from wire and paper.

Figure 5.12
Tree, in wire. Y5

ACTIVITY

H & S

*PoS 7e
Use knowledge of artists'
work*

1 Make a very simple mobile (Y1–Y3).

• Hang objects with transparent fishing line (Y1–Y2). Find objects that make interesting sounds as they touch each other. Hang metal chains with drinks can rings, plastic spoons and cotton reels, threads of pasta and beans softened in water (warn children not to eat them).

• Cut a spiral from a coloured-card circle with the centre removed (Y2–Y3). Use paper with different colours on each side. Hang the spiral up from the outer edge of the spiral and it will twirl in the breeze.

• Use two wire coat-hangers and cross them at 90° (Y3–Y4). Tape the handles together. Cut and decorate card shapes, staple them to threads and hang them on the wire cross pieces.

2 Create a stabile (Y3–Y6).

• Glue flags of coloured paper to wire shapes pushed into a polystyrene block. Use card and flexible wire, and shake to make a mobile stable (Y3–Y6).

• Connect thick pieces of straight wire to polystyrene balls of different sizes (Y5–Y6).

AGES AND STAGES

*PoS 6
Use materials, tools and
techniques safely*

H & S

Wire is dangerously sharp at the ends so pipe cleaners are a safer alternative for children at KS1 and early KS2. The fabric covering also provides an easier surface on which to attach other materials. The wire inside is light and easy to bend, yet will support the form of a standing figure. Plastic-covered wire ties for plastic bags can also be used for small sculptures. Plastic covered coat-hangers are difficult to bend but could be used by children at the end of KS2, with the help of pliers.

Older children could be given pre-cut pieces of wire, less than 50 cm in length. Ask them to handle the wire very cautiously, keeping it well away from eyes, always bending it towards the centre of the table and holding fingers over the ends whenever possible during the construction of the sculpture.

At the end of KS2, children should be able to use wire cutters to cut a wire to the desired length. This is best done from lengths already cut by the teacher – unwinding wire from the main coil can cause the end to wave dangerously in the air.

MODELLING WITH WIRE

PoS 8d
Experiment with tools and develop techniques

SHAPING

Soft wire, such as standard gauge 20, can easily be bent by hand. Wire is very difficult to straighten once it has been twisted so making a wire sculpture needs careful thought and deliberate shaping. Experiment with small constructions. Use a variety of lengths and thicknesses of wires to learn how they handle. Use old scissors and pliers to bend, twist, loop, curl, wrap and join the wire. Children in Y6 could try straightening bent wire by holding on to one end with pliers and pulling along the length of the wire.

JOINING

Joining wire securely can present quite a challenge and pipe cleaners are much easier to handle than bare wire. If a limb is too long, bend it back on itself rather than cutting the wire.

Join thin wire by twisting it tightly together making a long, widely-spaced, twisted join. Join thicker wire by overlapping the pieces and twisting a thin piece of wire along the join.

MAKING A STABLE BASE

If the sculpture has a wide enough base, bend the wires at the bottom to an L-shape and secure the sculpture to a wooden base with a staple gun or masking tape. Twist the feet of a figure so that they are at right angles to each other and staple them down. If the base is made of balsa wood or Plasticine, push the wire in. Y6 children could drill a hole in a piece of wood with a bradawl twice as wide as the wire then push in epoxy resin along with the wire supporting the sculpture until the fixture dries.

H & S

ACTIVITY

1 Make moving figures using wire ties from plastic bags (Y1–Y2). You will need four ties for each figure. Loop one over for the head. Twist two more round the bottom of the head for the legs and one across for the arms. Glue them in groups on black paper or staple them to a wood off-cut.

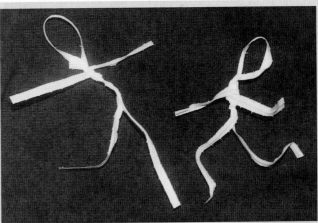

Figure 5.13
Moving figures, made from wire twists. Y2

2 Shape wire into geometric shapes (Y3–Y6). Wrap wire around cylinders to make coils and over the corner of the table to make sharp angles. Use pliers to pinch wire into precise shapes.

3 Interweave fuse wire or florists' wire through the lines of a wire sculpture to add extra line and texture (Y5–Y6).

USING WIRE TO BUILD AN ARMATURE

PoS 4d
Investigate shape, form and space

Standard wire gauge 20 and pipe cleaners are very flexible and easy to cut and will support light materials such as foil.

Standard wire gauge 18 supports heavier material while still being pliable enough to bend. Use it for laminated paper and plaster of Paris models. It is also useful for an armature for large foil models.

.1 Make figures with pipe cleaners (Y3–Y4). Tear pieces of foil about 10 × 10 cm and crumple them around a wire armature. Two figures standing together and touching provide a wider, more stable base than a single figure.

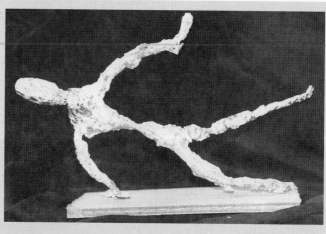

Figure 5.14
Gymnast, made from wire and foil, has a hand and a foot stapled to the base. Because they are at 90° to each other the figure stays standing. Y3

2 Cover wire gauge 20 with foil (Y5–Y6). Criss-cross thin wire over the foil body for added texture and strength. This looks particularly good for reptiles.

3 Make a wire armature for figures in mod-roc (Y5–Y6). Cut two pieces of wire, 50 cm and 30 cm in length. Bend the longer wire in half. Twist a loop in the bend to form a head and continue twisting to form the body. Be careful not to twist the wire too far or the legs will be too short. Twist two loops for feet. Take the shorter wire and twist it around the neck to form the shoulders and arms. Bend back the wire for hands.

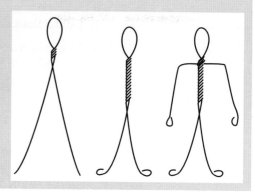

Figure 5.15
Making wire armatures for figures.

PoS 8d
*Experiment with tools and
develop techniques*

Construction using plaster of Paris

Children are fascinated by the process of changing a powder into a liquid and then watching it turn into a solid closely resembling stone (see Health and Safety Appendix for handling plaster of Paris). The easiest way of sculpting with plaster of Paris is to use gauze impregnated with plaster of Paris powder. This material is supplied ready-made as mod-roc. Alternatively, use cloth dipped in a Polyfilla water mix.

AGES AND STAGES

Because a wire armature needs to be made of strong, stiff wire to support heavy plaster, children generally need to be at the middle or end of KS2 to use this technique.

SCULPTURES MADE FROM MOD-ROC

Mod-roc adds bulk to wire models. It is supplied in different width bandages and can be cut with scissors. The lengths are dipped in water and have to be used very quickly as they set within 30 seconds. Wet mod-roc is very heavy and may need support as it dries. Use wooden blocks to support a whole body weight. Flying cloaks and swirling skirts only need cardboard box supports. Once the sculpture has dried it is very light.

MAKING A MOD-ROC MODEL

1 Make a sturdy wire armature. This will act as a skeleton for the muscle of the mod-roc. Uncoated wire will rust and stain the plaster if it is near the surface, so try to spread an even coat of plaster on the armature.

2 Place an ice-cream container of water in front of each pair of children. Cut the bandages to size.

3 Dip the first bandage in the water and squeeze it round the wire near the base. Build upwards.

Keep the figures lean if you wish to accentuate movement. Mod-roc can also build up bulk to create massive-looking animals.

ACTIVITY

PoS 7c
Work on a variety
of scales

1 Use chicken wire as an armature for large sculptures (Y5–Y6). The wire is tedious to cut but creates massive bulk. Roll and tape the chicken wire into a rough shape. Tape on pads of newspaper for extra padding.

2 Add fabric to a mod-roc figure (Y5–Y6). Dip fabric in wallpaper paste and drape it around a figure. The cloth dries into stiff folds.

Figure 5.16
Victorian beggar, a good subject for using frayed fabric scraps. Y6

CLOTH AND POLYFILLA SCULPTURES

Polyfilla is a type of plaster of Paris. It is more expensive but is excellent for this technique. Polyfilla takes longer to set than plaster of Paris, allowing children to take their time and drape the cloth carefully. These sculptures are full of dramatic movement and are especially suitable for ghosts, nuns and monks, medieval lepers and beggars.

MAKING A FIGURE

1 Make a strong, stable wire armature figure. Staple the figure to a wooden block, making sure the feet are at right angles to each other for stability.

2 Mix the Polyfilla with water in a ratio 1:1, to the consistency of thin cream.

3 Cut three pieces of thin cotton into squares, large enough to make many folds – one for the front, one for the back and one for the cowl or shawl.

Figure 5.17
Dickens' Ghost of Christmas Future made from cloth dipped in Polyfilla over a wire armature.

4 Dip the back cloth in the Polyfilla and drape it round the back, pinching it to the neck of the armature. Do the same for the front and then drape on the top piece over the head.

5 Add any accessories such as a rope girdle, also dipped in Polyfilla. Use up the remaining Polyfilla to texture the base.

Construction with laminated paper and papier mâché

A laminated-paper sculpture is made by overlayering strips of glued paper on an armature or support. Papier mâché has to be prepared a few days in advance using torn paper and paste, but finer details can be made with this method. A disposable armature can be left inside the sculpture or removed if the sculpture is to be hollow.

Figure 5.18
Young zebra, in laminated paper, on a box base. Y5

H & S

Paste is the cheapest glue to use with the paper strips, but diluted PVA glue gives a much harder finish. Newspaper is an ideal weight of paper for most models. Tissue paper dipped in diluted white glue is quicker to prepare and can be modelled into fine details, although it is too expensive to use over large areas.

Papier mâché models can be sanded smooth when thoroughly dried and painted in acrylic for a tough finish.

KNOWLEDGE AND UNDERSTANDING

India has a long tradition of making laminated paper trays, containers and even light furniture. Masks and masquerade heads are also often made out of laminated paper. If children look carefully at the back of a traditional Guy Fawkes mask they will be able to see the paper-pulp pieces. Try to find pictures of Chinese lion and dragon heads, and laminated paper sculptures used in carnivals and parades (*West Indian carnival costumes*, Ginn 21).

AGES AND STAGES

PoS 4d
The use of shape, form and space in images and artefacts

Children at KS1 will often use laminated paper in their found object sculpture as a strengthening technique. At KS2, children can make more radical changes and adjustments to the original form. Taping down wads of newspaper and padding out the sides of a sculpture teaches children to assess the form without any distractions of colour or texture. Smoothing over a slippery surface encourages them to become aware of subtle variations in form and texture. The last layer of white paper clarifies and transforms a sculpture and it is really only once this has been laid that children learn whether the mass of newspaper and glue they have assembled has created the exact form they envisaged.

LAMINATING WITH PAPER AND GLUE

1 Use a paper-cutter to cut newspaper into strips 2–3 cm in width. Give each pair of children an ice-cream container of paste and put a tray of newspaper strips in the middle of each table.

2 Layer the strips over the base, pasting between layers. Use an old paint brush for small models. For large models, dip the strips directly in to the paste and use hands to smooth and round a form. If the base is made of plastic, use PVA glue for the first layer to help it stick. Tear the strips into smaller pieces for hollows and detailed surfaces.

3 Use small pieces of thin, white paper for the last layer. This gives a smooth finish that absorbs colour easily. Alternatively, paste on coloured tissue paper as a final layer. This smooths the surface in addition to giving colour.

Papier mâché is a more traditional material for working with paper and glue. It takes time and labour to prepare but it makes a soft pulp which makes possible finer detail than with laminated paper. Tear up newspaper and soak in water with a little disinfectant added until the paper disintegrates. This takes at least three days. Put on rubber gloves and squeeze out excess water. Mix with fungicide-free wallpaper paste and a little PVA glue to make a pliant material.

MAKING ARMATURES WITH FOUND OBJECTS

Encourage children to be versatile and use many different sources of shapes. Tape the boxes or containers into a rough shape and soften any hard corners with crushed, taped newspaper.

ACTIVITY

1 Make the base of a head with a card cylinder (Y3–Y4). Form a ball of newspaper and tape it to a cardboard roll for the neck and head of a puppet. Tape on smaller balls of paper for the cheekbones, ears and nose and add glue and paper.

2 Small plastic containers, such as yoghurt pots, are useful for stumpy legs and animals' snouts (Y1–Y6).

3 Plastic bottles. The sloping 'shoulders' of bottles make them a perfect base for figures, snowmen, penguins and owls. Small, plastic cream jars are a good size for Y1 and Y2, small plastic milk and orange bottles for Y3 and Y4. Weight them with a little sand or water to make them stable.

PoS 7c
Work on a variety of scales

- Make Russian doll shapes in a variety of sizes, using a ball of crushed newspaper for the head (Y2–Y6).

- Dip fabric in paste and drape it around a laminated-paper bottle figure (Y5–Y6). Old cotton sheets are ideal; use large pieces of fabric so that they can have rich pleats and folds. Cut squares of cloth for sleeves, measuring the diagonal of the square against the length of the arm. Add details with braid and string. The folds set hard like a sculpture, yet keep the colour and texture of cloth. Make Indian, Greek, Roman, African, Arab or nativity figures where the clothes are draped in folds. Try spraying the figures with a metallic spray.

MAKING AN ARMATURE WITH PAPER SPILLS

Roll newspaper from corner to corner as tightly as possible. Spread a light glue across the last roll to hold the curve and to strengthen the shape. Bend the spills to shape and leave to dry. Paper spills are strong and light. Tape them together to make large shapes. Make a quantity of glued paper spills and hang them up to dry.

A quicker method that makes cruder but useable spills, is to roll up sheets of newspaper and tape the ends down.

ACTIVITY

1 Make a giant insect or spider and use paper spills for legs (Y1–Y4).

2 Use thin spills for details on 3D landscapes – flag poles, fencing, log cabins and rafts (Y5–Y6). Use them for the walls of a model log cabin or to make large trees in a landscape. Twist and untwist the spill to create the rough texture of bark and cover each spill with glued, brown tissue paper.

REMOVABLE ARMATURE

A removable armature is useful for making money boxes, containers, puppets and masks when the form needs to be light and hollow.

ACTIVITY

1 Use a balloon (Y4–Y6). Cover a balloon with paper strips and glue, leaving a small opening at the tie. After the paper strips have dried and hardened undo the tie or burst the balloon. Use a greased inflatable beach-ball for an extra large sphere. Leave a small hole over the inflater to draw out the deflated ball.

- Use the balloon as a base for a head, a pig, an elephant or a portly monster. Tape on cylinders and card pieces for legs and facial features.

- Make a model of a hot-air balloon with a margarine tub suspended underneath.

- Cut the form in half and cover the cut half with strong tracing paper to make a drum. Tape the sides of the tracing paper down and cover the join with laminated paper.

- Cut the form in half and use it as a base for a hat or *Feathered war cap*, Shorewood 1786.

Soft sculptures

Soft sculptures can be made from fabrics supported on an armature or they can be entirely made of fabric with stuffing inside. The soft, interesting texture of the fabric makes them particularly attractive to children.

PoS 3
Ideas, feelings and meanings are communicated in different visual forms

KNOWLEDGE AND UNDERSTANDING

PoS 9c
Relate art to its time and place in origin

Figure 5.19
Owl, a simple stuffed shape. Y6

Fabric has been regarded by recent sculptors as just another interesting medium to use alongside more conventional plaster, stone, wood and metal. Clothes are part of Degas' sculpture *The little fourteen-year-old dancer* (1880), The Tate, London and Davies' *Young man* (1971), The Tate Gallery, Liverpool. Christo is a sculptor who is famous for wrapping public buildings or structures in fabric (*The Pont Neuf wrapped* (1984), Goodwill 2(19)).

ACTIVITY

PoS 7e
Use knowledge of artists' work

1 **Make a Native American doll (Y1–Y3). They are very simple dolls traditionally made by Native Americans from scraps of fabric. They can also be made with handkerchiefs.**
   a) Roll up a ball of fabric and put it in the centre of a 16 cm square of plain fabric.
   b) Hold the ball inside the cloth and tie an elastic band around the neck. Drape a piece of dark cloth over the head and use another elastic band to tie it at the neck.
   c) Wrap around more fabric for a long dress and a shawl. They could be Native American women or Lancashire mill workers from the last century.

2 **Make a very simple rag-doll (Y1–Y4).**
   a) Cut two identical rectangles of felt. Use scissors to round off the corners and glue two sides together using impact glue.
   b) Push fabric scraps or cotton wool inside the shape and glue the other side.
   c) Add felt shapes for legs and arms and make fabric-collage faces.

Figure 5.20
Adapting an arched shape.

   • **Add legs and arms that can bend (Y5–Y6). Sew long tubes for the arms and legs, stuff and stitch across the elbows and knees. Push the limbs into the body and stitch securely.**

AGES AND STAGES

PoS 2a
Express ideas and feelings

Children at KS1 can use very simple joining techniques to make soft sculptures. Large soft sculptures, for example, can be made in the dressing-up corner. If Velcro tabs are sewn on to large pieces of fabric, children can join them to make a costume. Small soft sculptures can be made using glue. Sculpting with fabrics is made easier if children can work on an armature (support) which has already established the form of a sculpture. At KS2, children can practise their skills of gathering and sewing on small areas of fabric but can glue on the remainder. As children's sewing skills progress, stitching becomes increasingly important. Clothing a figure is quite a challenge. Children at KS2 could cut newspaper to experiment with different shapes and sizes. They will be surprised how much fabric is needed for a full, long skirt or long sleeves.

USING FOUND OBJECT ARMATURES

PoS 7b
Use resources to stimulate ideas

Plastic bottles, cones and wooden spoons are useful armatures for children to make figures with long, high-waisted dresses or long, loose robes. Children at KS1 should use small cones or bottles that allow them to use pipe cleaners for arms.

Figure 5.21
Victorian figure, largely clothed in pieces from an old velvet curtain, with added lace trim. Y6

ACTIVITY

1 **Make a spoon figure (Y1–Y2). Draw a face on an old wooden spoon. Tie a square of fabric to the neck by twisting a pipe cleaner tightly around the top. Use two more pipe cleaners twisted around the neck for arms. Add hair and a hat.**

2 **Make a waisted figure (Y5–Y6). Make a wire frame for the upper body. Pad it with cotton wool bound with thread. Push the body into a card cone and tape it in place. Make a long skirt and 'top' from fabric.**

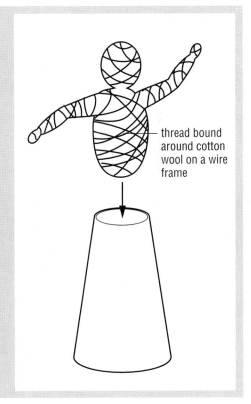

thread bound around cotton wool on a wire frame

Figure 5.22
Making a cone figure.

MAKING STUFFED SHAPES

PoS 7c
Explore and use 2- and 3-dimensional media

Stuffing gives soft sculptures a solidity that children find very appealing. Simply sew or glue two shapes together, leaving an opening for the stuffing which is then closed. If there are several narrow places in the shape of the sculpture, leave more than one gap. Use scraps of fabric for stuffing unless the soft sculpture needs to be washed, in which case use shredded old net curtains, batting or foam pieces.

ACTIVITY 1 Using ready-made shapes (Y1–Y6).

• Make a glove figure (Y2–Y4). Turn an old knitted glove inside out. Sew across the middle finger where it joins the glove and cut it off below the line of stitches. Children who cannot sew could close the gap with impact glue. Turn the glove the right way out and push in the stuffing. Sew up the entrance to the glove. Make a neck by tying wool around the entrance to the glove and pulling tightly. Add fabric-collage clothes and hair.

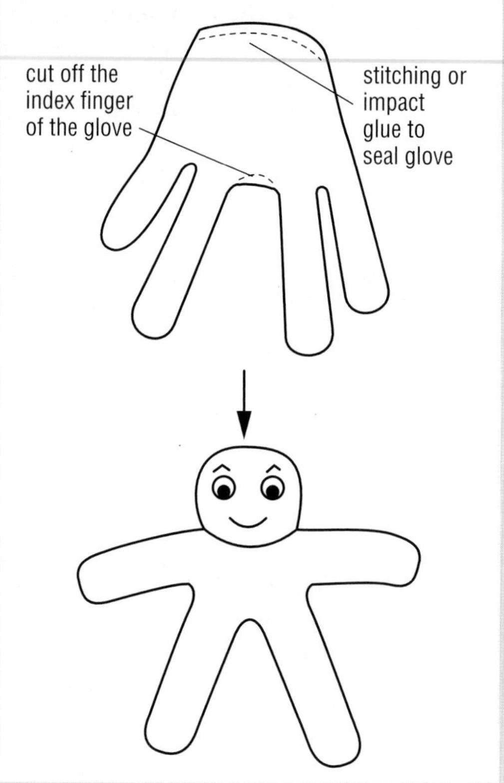

2 Sew or glue the sides of the two identical shapes together but leave the base open. Felt is an ideal fabric as it does not fray. Other fabrics will need turning inside-out. The opening can be filled with an object when it is used (egg-cosy or finger-puppet) or permanently filled with stuffing. Children at KS1 could simply glue the edges together.

Figure 5.23
Making a glove figure.

• Make a quilted head in profile (Y5–Y6). Cut out an exaggerated profile in two pieces of cloth. Sew the edges together with back stitch, leaving the neck open. Turn the right way out and push in the stuffing. Add stitching to contour the face.

• Use a gusset (Y5–Y6). A gusset is a piece of fabric that is sewn into the structure to make a base or a side. Adding a single gusset gives a soft sculpture enough of a base to stand up. Use ready-made templates as examples but ask children to try out their own simple shapes. Try making a seated cat, a nesting hen or duck, a perching owl or a baby's shoe.

Figure 5.24
Mouse, made by sewing two identical halves together, with a gusset at the base. Y5

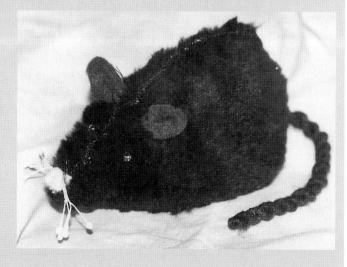

3 Make a padded ball (Y3–Y6). Cut a circle in felt. Make a running stitch along the edge of the circle and draw the thread in a little. Stuff the felt with scraps of fabric or batting. Push in a small card circle to hold in the scraps. Pull the thread tight to close the felt as much as possible and tie the threads tight.

Vary the amount of stuffing and use it as a base for a head, a pin-cushion, a pebble with lichen growing on it, an iced bun, a fat spider, a ladybird or a tortoise.

In the top illustration, labels read:

cut off the index finger of the glove

stitching or impact glue to seal glove

PoS 3
Ideas, feelings and meanings are communicated in different visual forms

Carved sculptures

Most art involves adding materials to build up colour and form. Carving is radically different because it removes materials permanently. Sculptors start with a solid block and remove parts of the surface to reveal a sculpture inside. Michelangelo (1475–1564), the Italian sculptor, described his task as 'the freeing of the statue from the marble'.

KNOWLEDGE AND UNDERSTANDING

PoS 5a
Examine styles in the locality

Marble is a favourite material for sculptors to carve because of its yielding, luminous qualities. Local art galleries and churchyards will probably have examples of marble statues. There may be local examples of carvings in rough stone (*Stone crosses* in Goodwill's *Celtic to Medieval art* 52). Look at pictures of wooden sculptures (Chinese *Woman's figure in dancing position*, Goodwill 2(17); *Oceanic art* and *African art*, Goodwill 57 and 58)). If possible, bring in examples of bold wood carvings so children can run their hands over the surface and turn the piece to follow the grain. It is interesting to contrast a smooth wood carving with the rough texture but elegant shape of a wooden cooking spoon. Pictures of unpolished wood carvings from Africa and Asia and stone carvings from Mexico sometimes show the strokes of the carver (Yoruba Peoples of Nigeria *Eshu figure* and *Gelede mask*, Shorewood 1798 and 1803). Ask a retired woodworker to discuss the different qualities of wood, how to plan a piece and how carvers go with the grain.

Children with Asian backgrounds may have seen butter, ice or vegetables carved and used as centre-pieces in restaurants. Discussing these can be a useful introduction to carving unconventional materials.

AGES AND STAGES

At KS1, children should only carve very soft materials – fruit, vegetables or new, soft plaster. These need a minimum pressure applied with a blunt tool such as a table knife, paper-clip or teaspoon. Start with simple indentations in Y1. In Y2, some children will be able to carve away surrounding areas forming an elevated shape.

Figure 5.25
Plaster of Paris carved heads. Y6

Children at KS2 can progress to harder materials such as soap, balsa wood and set plaster. Encourage them to make shapes that are simple and unhampered by detail, aiming for a broad effect and only adding textures and details at the end. Children should cut away a little at a time, working over the entire surface instead of concentrating on only one area.

Files are the easiest and safest tools to start with and bench presses provide a resistant surface to work against (see page 64).

Carving soft materials

FRUIT AND VEGETABLES

PoS 8d
Experiment with tools and develop techniques

Choose fruit and vegetables that are fairly solid – apples, potatoes, turnips, large carrots, pumpkins. These sculptures shrink after a few days although painting using acrylic will prolong their life.

ACTIVITY 1 Make a dried apple head (Y3–Y6). This is a traditional Native American craft for making dolls for children. A more macabre craft would be the head-hunters' skull-shrinking techniques of Indonesia and Papua New Guinea.
a) Peel an apple and use a table knife or a paper-clip to carve out eyes, mouth and cheeks either side of the nose. Carve out a hole at the base.
b) Put the apple head in a low oven for three hours to begin the drying process. It will then be shrunken, wrinkled and orange. Push a stick into the neck hole and stand the head near to an open window to dry completely. (Make these during the summer term.) Children are fascinated to see the gradual increase in the wrinkles as the head shrinks to a third of its former size.
c) The head will continue to shrink for several weeks, but meanwhile it can be dressed. Push cloves in for eyes and draw a mouth. Wrap the doll in shawls, one over the head and one over the shoulders.

Figure 5.26
Figure, with a head made from a dried apple carving.
Y3

PLASTER OF PARIS

Plaster of Paris is soft enough to carve and can be cast in a wide variety of shapes and sizes. Young children should use plaster fresh from the mould when it is soft enough to carve with a spoon or old table knife.

CONTAINERS
Moulds should be prepared before mixing the plaster of Paris. Yoghurt containers, plastic cups and toilet-roll centres provide a good size for beginners. Avoid tins unless they can be greased. They quickly rust and the plaster picks up the colour. Line non-disposable moulds with polythene sheeting.

MIXING THE PLASTER

H & S

Mix plaster of Paris and water to the consistency of thin cream. Mix just a small amount as the plaster sets very quickly. A rough guide is to put some powder into a plastic icecream container and pour in enough water to cover the powder. Mix quickly to prevent lumps from forming. Pour the mixture into the moulds immediately. Use it straight away for easy carving or leave it overnight to harden to make sculptures with finer detail.

CARVING TOOLS
For soft plaster, teaspoons, hair grips, metal nailfiles and blunt table knives are required. For hard plaster lino-cutters, chisels, saws and coarse sandpaper are required.

ACTIVITY 1 Vary the textures and colour of the plaster (Y1–Y6).

- Add a proportion of sand to make a rougher surface for carving.

- Mix powder paint with the plaster before adding water for an even colour.

- Add thick liquid paint as soon as the plaster has been mixed. Fold in the colour to add streaks for a marbled effect.

2 Use a washing-up liquid bottle as a mould and carve a totem pole (Y3–Y4).

3 Saw a mould into sections and glue the pieces together in a new arrangement with impact glue (Y5–Y6).

Carving wood

Balsa wood is soft and easy to carve, although it lacks the beauty of a grained wood. Clamp the wood firmly in a vice or use a bench press (see page 64). Start with round files to carve lines of different widths and depths. Make them criss-cross in an interesting design. Drill decorative holes.

CARVING TECHNIQUES

PoS 8d
Experiment with tools and develop techniques

Plan the areas to be reduced and shade them in with a ball-point pen. Always file in the direction of the grain. Use a vice or G-cramp to grip the wood, leaving two hands free to work on the wood. Keep removing the wood from the vice to check the shape. Start by filing down areas and rounding off corners with flat files and old steel nailfiles. Round files are ideal for making concave sections and children find them easier to grip than a flat file. Use them in one place to make decorative grooves.

Children in Y5 and Y6 could use a hacksaw blade to make V-shaped cuts to remove sections. Avoid deep cuts, working gradually to reduce an area rather than attempting to remove it all at once. Make holes with bradawls and old screwdrivers. Use lino-cutting tools for fine detail.

PoS 3
Ideas, feelings and meanings are communicated in different visual forms

Modelling

Modelling is almost the reverse process of carving. Instead of starting with a block of hard plaster or wood, modelling materials are soft and malleable. Dough, Plasticine and clay can all be pushed and pulled into shapes and extra pieces can be added.

KNOWLEDGE AND UNDERSTANDING

PoS 5a
Examine styles in the locality

Figure 5.27
Iguana, made from kiln-fired clay. Y5

Traditionally doughs have been used in the home to model into edible decorations – pastry and icing rosettes, marzipan leaves, bread plaits and harvest loaves. Bread sculptures, or *pan de muertos*, are made every November in Mexico to celebrate the festival of the dead. Parents in Britain may have allowed children to make small models in the kitchen using scraps of pastry or icing. Saltdough is also used for making Christmas decorations, but the dough is inedible.

Plasticine is comparatively new to the art world, although it has gained great popularity in schools. Some film animators use it for models that need to be moved slightly between each frame and children will probably have seen these models on television. Clay has been used for modelling by craftspeople and artists all over the world for many millennia. If possible, look at pictures of Stone Age clay goddesses and vases from Susa made in 2000 BC. Coiled clay is used all over Asia and Africa to make beautifully formed pots.

AGES AND STAGES

PoS 4a–d
Learn about visual and tactile elements

When children are introduced to a new modelling medium they often manipulate it without trying to make anything. This experimental stage is important because it allows children to explore the strengths and limitations of the material without the pressure of making any specific form. Once children have built up their knowledge, they should discuss what they know about the modelling material before they start to manipulate it. This is especially important with clay which dries out and loses its plasticity if it is over-handled.

Children at KS1 begin by squeezing the material into forms to make solid shapes. Wire can help to support some thin structures (but not clay that will be fired). Mould the body parts of long insects to a pipe cleaner or add legs to insects and spiders by pushing in small pieces of florists' wire.

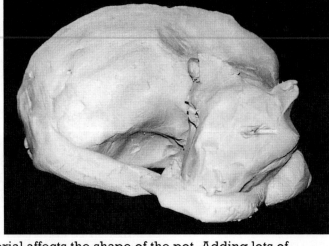

Figure 5.28
Sitting leopard, made from clay. Y3

Children at KS2 need to think carefully about how the quality of the material affects the shape of the pot. Adding lots of projections is a risky procedure with clay because they are easily knocked off while drying. Generally it is better to pull shapes out of modelling materials rather than adding them on, keeping the shapes as chunky as possible. A sturdy elephant is much easier to make than a delicate-legged horse. Seated animals solve the problem of supporting legs.

Modelling materials

EDIBLE DOUGHS

As long as the work surface and the children's hands are kept clean, children can use edible doughs such as marzipan and fondant icing as modelling materials. Being eventually able to eat what they have modelled seems to have a magnetic attraction for children of all ages. Pastry and gingerbread doughs that are malleable enough to model make tough biscuits. Fortunately, children are generally so pleased with their models they feel this is a minor drawback. Bread dough actually benefits from handling, as long as it does not dry out, but the models puff out as the yeast works and details are obscured

PLAYDOUGHS

Playdough is available commercially and can also be made in school, as long as there is a pan and cooker available. The dough will not harden and should only be used for temporary models. Saltdough is a traditional modelling material which can be hardened in the oven and made very durable. The recipe for saltdough is one cup salt, one cup flour, 1.5 cups water. Mix and knead the ingredients for about five minutes. Make the models and then bake on foil for two hours at 300°F or 150°C.

PLASTICINE

Plasticine is a synthetic clay, invented in 1899 by an art teacher from Bath called William Harbutt. It is oil based rather than water based, so it reacts to cold by becoming hard and is pliable only when it is warm. Children may need to warm it up by kneading it in the warmth of their hands or placing it in a bowl of warm water or in the sun.

CLAY AND COLD CLAY

Clay comes in various shades of grey and brown, depending on the earth from which it was extracted. Grey clay turns white or beige when it is fired; brown clay turns a terracotta red. Purchase non-specialist clay suitable for all types of processes. Clay should be left to dry for two days before firing in a kiln. Firing makes the clay durable and glazing adds an attractive, strengthening, deep gloss to the model. (For details on firing and glazing see pages 128–129.) Clay can be left to air-dry in schools that do not have access to a kiln but the models will need to be chunky and firm as any thin, delicate areas will crumble and break. Cold clay is available commercially as a response to this problem.

Cold clay or Newclay is a natural clay with added fibres. The fibres bind the clay when it dries so there is no need for firing. It cannot be glazed but it can be painted and then varnished or coated with diluted PVA glue for a shiny finish. Cold clay does not quite have the consistency of natural clay but it is a very good substitute. It also has the advantage that it can be modelled around a wire armature. True clay would shrink and crack.

H & S

CUTTING UP CLAY

A large pack of clay is very difficult to split into manageable pieces unless wire is used. Tie a small piece of wood to each end of a length of wire. The wood provides handles for the wire which cuts through the clay. In general this wire should only be used for cutting individual pieces of clay from the large pack, but Y6 children sometimes enjoy using it for sculpturing their clay.

STORAGE

Use large plastic containers with air-tight lids to store open bags of clay. Plastic dustbins are ideal. Sprinkle the clay with water and close the bag surrounding the clay as much as possible before closing the lid. A cheaper alternative is to put unused clay inside a large, black plastic rubbish bag and tie it with a wire tie. Dry clay and cold clay can be recycled by soaking in water, but once clay has been fired it cannot be reused.

At the end of the lesson, stand unfinished models on damp newspaper placed in a tray and slide the tray inside a plastic bin liner. Cover with more damp newspaper and close the bag with a wire tie. This will keep the clay moist and malleable for at least two weeks.

Slip is an essential ingredient in clay modelling. Two clay pieces joined without slip may stick initially, but fall apart as they dry.

Slip is simply clay mixed with water. It can be pre-mixed in small pots but it is much less trouble for children to make slip every time it is needed.

Wet a toothbrush in water and rub both surfaces of the clay vigorously. This produces the slip with an added bonus of a rough surface to promote sticking. Press the two surfaces together firmly and smooth over the join on the outside.

Modelling techniques

TEXTURING THE SURFACE OF A MODEL

PoS 8d
Experiment with tools and develop techniques

AGES AND STAGES

Modelling materials are particularly responsive to pressure and will make clear prints and patterns. Children at the beginning of KS1 will make fairly random marks but these should gradually be replaced by closely-worked patterns or textures. Use direct observation or reference books for ideas.

EQUIPMENT

A texture box containing objects that make interesting impressions will encourage children to experiment with different textures: plastic modelling tools; small lengths of wire; flat lollipop sticks; blunt knives; combs; toothbrushes; paper doilies; nails; screws; small geometric shapes; twigs; pencil stubs; string; bits of lace; fresh leaves; netting and sacking.

A clay press is a very useful tool for adding textures to models. It pushes out soft modelling material in long, shaped ridges like an icing syringe. Different discs allow children to change the texture. Keep the clay syringes in water during the lesson so that the modelling material inside does not harden and block the tube.

ACTIVITY

Experiment with a variety of textures (Y1–Y6). Push with objects from the texture box. Slash and scrape with a wire, dry toothbrush or knife to make texture like fur. Add shapes or coils and press them on to the surface.

• Make a leaf (Y1–Y3). Place a leaf, vein-side down, on rollered modelling material and roller over the leaf. With the leaf still in place, cut around the edges and then remove the leaf.

• Make a bark print (Y3–Y4). Press rollered modelling material very firmly against the bark of a tree. Remove and use crushed newspaper as a support to make a hollow log.

• Place textured fabric (hessian, lace, net) over a slab of modelling material and roller until it is very thin (Y4–Y6). Use this for folds of fabric on figures.

SUPPORTING THE MODEL

A model made from Plasticine or playdough will never harden so it must support itself. Use wire for internal support. Saltdough hardens with heat and can be supported in the oven with ceramic stilts bought from craft shops. Projections on clay and cold clay models need supports until the material hardens. The legs of a standing animal can be modelled while the belly rests on a narrow cardboard box. Carefully judge the length of the legs so they will all reach the ground when the support is removed. Pull rigid supports away from the clay once it is leather-hard. Clay shrinks as it dries and if there is no flexibility in the support the clay will crack and break away from the main piece. Pliable, small card boxes and crushed newspaper make ideal supports.

Figure 5.29
Water-buffalo. The legs were modelled while the belly was supported on a box. Y5

Slab-pots

Slab-pots are built-up from flat slabs of modelling material.

AGES AND STAGES

PoS 7c
Explore and use 2- and 3-dimensional media

A cylinder makes a good basic slab-pot shape for children at KS1. It is easy to make, stands up without problems and does not require elaborate measuring. Children at KS2 could cut out a rectangle in newspaper to test the approximate length and breadth that will be needed for their cylinder. This provides valuable experience in relating flat shapes to 3D forms.

Cuboids are very difficult to make and should be left until the end of KS2. They need to be accurately measured and the material has to be leather-hard or the box might collapse. This rules out Plasticine and the doughs, but clay and cold clay become leather-hard if they are rollered out and left overnight. Softer clays can be supported inside the box with crushed newspaper.

ORGANISATION

Set each child's place with a piece of discarded sugar paper to stop clay from sticking to the table (Plasticine and dough roller best on formica); two slats to act as thickness gauges; a roller to flatten the clay; a toothbrush to wet and rough up joined surfaces and a palette for water (for clay).

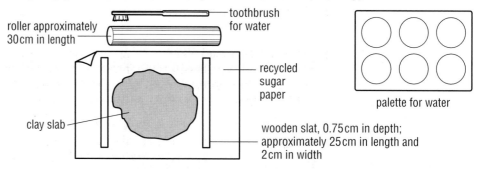

roller approximately 30cm in length

toothbrush for water

recycled sugar paper

clay slab

wooden slat, 0.75cm in depth; approximately 25cm in length and 2cm in width

palette for water

Figure 5.30
Setting out equipment at each child's place – 'as if for a feast'.

MAKING A SLAB-POT

1 Stand up so the weight of the body is over the modelling material. Press down with the heel of the hand to flatten it as much as possible.

2 Use a roller to flatten but always keep at least one side of the roller in contact with a slat. This stops the modelling material from becoming too thin.

3 Test the thickness by pushing down hard with the roller in several places, all the time keeping in contact with the slats. If there is a large dent in the slab, it is not even.

4 Lightly trace out the shape with a wire – any errors can easily be rollered out.

Children at KS2 could make a template for a symmetrical shape by folding and cutting a piece of paper. The rollering is hard work with clay and cold clay, so encourage the children to make large shapes and use as much of the slab as possible.

MAKING A CYLINDRICAL SLAB-POT

1 Roller out the material and cut round a newspaper template (made by the children at KS2). Use a wire as a cutter and a slat as a straight edge.

2 Roller or press on any textures. Do not press too hard or the slab will become thin and difficult to handle.

3 Lift the slab on to its edge and form a cylinder. Place a slat inside the cylinder and press against it when smoothing down the join (clay and cold clay need water at a join).

4 Roller out any spare material and use it for the base. Place the cylinder on the base and cut round the bottom of the container with a short section wire. Always smooth over joins to strengthen them.

ACTIVITY

1 **Add textures and details.**

- **Cut out shapes in the sides with a pastry cutter to make a candle-pot (Y1–Y3).**

- **Make an owl-pot, a dustbin, a toadstool house or a Toby-jug (Y2–Y6).**

- **Close both ends of the cylinder with circles of modelling material. Lay the cylinder on its side, slit along the top and add handles to make a sports bag (Y5–Y6).**

2 **Thin out sections of the clay to make a bark-like structure (Y4–Y6).**

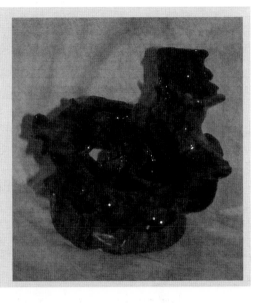

Figure 5.31
Bark pot. Y5

USING A MOULD

Moulds help to support the softness of thin, rollered clay. Newspaper provides a cheap and versatile support. It can be simply crushed into a rough shape to support a model shell or piece of bark, or it can be taped into specific forms such as a cone for a wigwam.

ACTIVITY

1 Use a paper- or fabric-lined bowl as a mould (Y1–Y6). Y1 children find it difficult to roller cold clay very thinly so use shallow bowls to prevent the clay from creasing in thick folds.

2 Support the inside of the cylinder with crushed newspaper and bang it into a cuboid using the flat of a ruler (Y3–Y6). Use this as the base for a building.

3 Make a slab-pot of a training shoe (Y4–Y6). Use strong scissors to cut up an old training shoe. Cut card templates of the flattened upper pieces and sole and use them to cut out the sides and base of a clay shoe.

4 Cut out a semicircle of card and make a cone, supported inside with crushed newspaper (Y4–Y6). Use it as a base for a simple Christmas angel or princess.

5 Mould shell shapes around crushed newspaper (Y5–Y6).

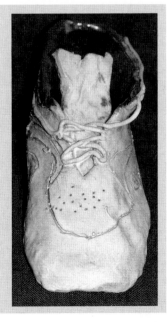

Figure 5.32
Training shoe. Y4

PoS 2c
Design and make creative
images

Thumb-pots

Thumb-pots are rounded pots formed in the hand by turning and pressing with the fingers.

AGES AND STAGES

A thumb-pot is easy to make and is a very versatile base for model-making. A joined thumb-pot makes an elongated egg shape that is even more versatile because the newspaper inside is flexible enough to allow major reconstruction, and firm enough to prevent the model from collapsing. This technique can be introduced at the beginning of KS2 once children have become skilled in making a thumb-pot. Children at KS1 could simply mould the modelling material around a ball of crushed newspaper to form a similar basic shape from which to begin modelling. This method produces uneven walls which might make the model unsuitable for firing.

MAKING A THUMB-POT

1 Take a ball of modelling material and push the thumb into the centre, nearly through to the other side.

2 Remove the thumb and practise the 'pinching' action. (Another name for a thumb-pot is a pinch-pot.) Children usually pinch by closing the tips of their fingers but they need to use the flat of their fingers like a crocodile's mouth opening and closing to make the walls smooth and even.

3 Replace the thumb in the pot and make a closing action with the fingers deep inside the pot. Keep the fingers away from the entrance so that the clay here remains thick and strong. Keep turning the pot and closing the fingers to make the walls an even thickness. Aim for an even thickness of approximately 1 cm.

4 Hold the pot in the palm of one hand and stuff pieces of newspaper into the cavity. This will support the walls for any reshaping and further modelling.

ACTIVITY

1 Invert the pot and add details and textures.

- Make holes in the side for a candle-pot (Y1–Y3).

- Flatten the sides by slapping with a ruler to make a house (Y2–Y3).

- Turn the pot on its side and use the opening as a mouth of a dragon or monster (Y3–Y4).

- Add a body and create a Victorian lady in a crinoline (Y3–Y6).

- Press down the centre of the open edge, invert it and make a pair of clown's baggy trousers. Add a clown's head and arms (Y4–Y6).

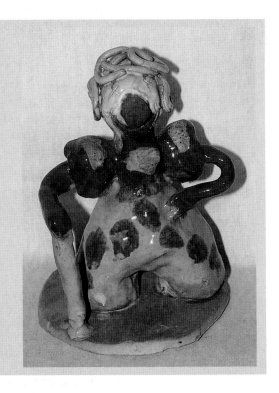

Figure 5.33
Clown, modelled from a thumb-pot. Y4

MAKING A JOINED THUMB-POT

1 Make two thumb-pots from similar sized balls of modelling material.

2 Cradle one of the pots in the palm of the hand to stop it from flattening and stuff it so full of newspaper it is bulging out of the entrance. Do the same with the other pot.

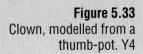

3 Rub each of the entrances with a wet toothbrush if the pots are made of clay, and push the two pots together. Use fingers or a tool to smooth the join. At this stage it looks like a giant peanut.

4 Push and pull the modelling material down into the dip in the middle of the peanut shape – from the mountains to the valley – to make a smooth, elongated egg shape.

edges of each clay thumb-pot rubbed with wet toothbrush to aid joining

Two thumb-pots pushed together

5 If clay is being used and it will be fired, push a wire into the centre to allow the trapped air to escape once the model has been completed.

Figure 5.34
Making a joined thumb-pot.

Smoothing the join

ACTIVITY
PoS 2a
Express ideas and feelings

Ask children to use their imaginations to transform a joined thumb-pot into many different models.

1 Lay the joined thumb-pot on its side.

- **Add fins for a fish (Y3–Y6).**

- **Pull one end to make the head of a mouse (Y3–Y6).**

2 Stand the joined thumb-pot upright.

- **Open up the top by pressing in a metal bottle top to make a vase. Open the bottom and make a long-robed figure (Y3–Y6).**

- **Squeeze the base to make a neck for a bust (Y3–Y6).**

3 Use combinations of thumb-pots and joined thumb-pots.

- **The head of a penguin can be made by joining a small thumb-pot to a large joined thumb-pot (Y4–Y6).**

- **Seat clay figures on a small thumb-pot (Y5–Y6). Use a tiny joined thumb-pot for the torso and another thumb-pot for the head. Roller clay sausages for limbs.**

PoS 8d
Experiment with tools and develop techniques

Coil-pots

A coil-pot is built-up using thin 'sausages' of modelling material.

AGES AND STAGES

Rollering out coils and building up a wall makes this a very time consuming technique. If the shape goes out from the base it quickly collapses when soft doughs are used. Plasticine is easier to use because it is stiffer. Clay coil-pots can be built-up in several stages but this technique is only suitable for the end of KS2. For most primary children, coiling is probably best kept for adding small sections to a slab or thumb-pot.

MAKING A COIL-POT

1 Cut a base from rollered modelling material. The base could be any shape but keep it fairly regular when making a first coil-pot. A circle is easiest.

2 Roll out a thin sausage of modelling material. Start to build-up the pot by laying the coil on the outside of the base and circling it round to form the beginning of a wall.

3 Keep adding coils, one on top of another until the wall starts to wobble, then finish the pot. Clay can be left to become leather-hard and then built higher. Keep the top coil moist by covering it with a wet cloth, otherwise there will be a problem joining the new wet clay with the semi-dry clay.

4 To seal the inside of the pot, use a blunt modelling tool to smooth out the coils. This can also be done on the outside, although the coils make an attractive pattern if they are left as they are.

1 **Practise making even coils and then make a nest of worms or snakes (Y1–Y2).**

2 **Twist two long coils together and curve it round to make a bracelet (*Viking armlet*, Ginn 21; *Jewellery*, Goodwill 61) (Y5–Y6).**

Using a kiln

Firing clay was a technological innovation that revolutionised people's way of life allowing them to cook liquids, store food and collect water. It turned dry, crumbly earth into a hard, durable material that will outlast metal and wood. Children love to know that they have made something that will last for centuries.

A kiln is an expensive piece of equipment, but it gives children the opportunity to make strong models with permanent, subtle colour blends.

RELEASING THE AIR BEFORE FIRING CLAY

There must be no air in clay to be fired. The air expands in the heat of the kiln and, if there is no exit, the model will explode.

WEDGING

The traditional way to rid clay of air is to wedge it. To wedge clay throw a block of clay down hard on the table to force out air, cut it with a wire, slap the pieces together and throw it down again. Repeat many times. Wedging is noisy and great fun for the children, but they often end up with more air bubbles than they began with. The clay also dries with over-handling.

ALTERNATIVES TO WEDGING

Newly-bought clay is free of air bubbles. Use a new batch of clay for thumb-pots and keep the walls of a pot as thin as possible. The act of rollering clay eliminates bubbles in a slab- or coil-pot.

RELEASING AIR IN MODELS

Small pockets of air are trapped when hollow clay sections are added to a main piece of clay. At the end of a lesson, use a small piece of wire to push a hole through to the air pocket. Choose a discreet place that will not spoil the model. The hole needs only to be very tiny in diameter but it must be deep enough to reach the air pocket.

FIRING CLAY

PoS 9c
Relate art to its time and place of origin

BISCUIT FIRING

After the clay has dried for two days it is biscuit fired. Increase the temperature in the kiln by 100° every hour until it reaches 850°C. Allow the clay to cool in the kiln. This will take about 36 hours.

Pots should be stacked on special kiln shelves to prevent them crushing pots underneath.

PoS 4b
Investigate colour

Glazing

Glazes are a kind of liquid glass which, when they harden, strengthen fragile shapes and details and give a wonderful, glossy, smooth finish with exciting colour blends and deepened textures.

KNOWLEDGE AND UNDERSTANDING

PoS 5c
Examine styles from a variety of cultures

Different times and cultures have favoured different glazes – the jade green, crackled glaze of Thai Celedon pottery, the green and orange streaked glazes of the Tang Dynasty, the blue and white delicate patterns of the Ming and Qing dynasties. These blue and white designs became particularly popular in Europe during the eighteenth century.

CHOOSING GLAZES

Powder glazes are cheap but the dust is hazardous if it disperses in the air. Mix it when the children are not in the classroom and use a gauze mask. These glazes can only be used for dip glazing which involves dipping all or part of a pot in a container of glaze. It is a very quick method but children usually prefer to have greater variety and greater control over the colours.

Paint-on glazes are more expensive but the results are much more predictable and they add to children's painting skills. They are also much safer to use because they create less dust.

Figure 5.35
Dustbin, glazed. Y5

Most glazes are glossy but there is a matt velvet glaze. Reds are the most difficult colours to achieve. They need a thick layer of colour and still may come out matt or mottled. Crystal glazes give exciting variation of colour. The crystals look like small pieces of gravel in the glaze. When they are heated in the kiln there is a tiny 'explosion' of colour on the background.

ORGANISING GLAZING

Keep the glazes on trays with their own paint brushes and ask children to move around to the colour they want to use. This gives every child a choice of colour and keeps the glazes safely in one place. Remind children to look behind them before they move out of the glazing seat in case someone is waiting behind, holding a piece of pottery.

HEALTH AND SAFETY
Some of the more exciting colours in paint-on glazes contain lead. Anything with red in usually has a high lead content. Make sure children wear aprons and do not put their hands near their mouths when they glaze. Wash hands and any splashes thoroughly after glazing. Discard any newspaper with glaze splashes on it, folding the paper carefully to contain the dust. Use lead-free glazes at KS1 and in Y3 and for all model dishes that may come into contact with food.

USING GLAZES

The colour of a glaze does not usually bear much resemblance to the colour it will be when the firing is completed. Making a chart of tiny glazed tiles will help with this problem. Paint the glaze on to a model with a dabbing motion using a brush until there is a thick coverage. Use two or three layers for a good deep colour and shine. (Dry clay absorbs moisture very quickly so there is no need to wait between layers.) Paint red particularly in a thick layer.

Stripes and small areas of colour can be painted on the pot but in general a well textured pot looks better in a single colour or tones of the colour. Interesting mottled effects can be obtained by overlayering colours with highly contrasting colours, and subtle colour blends are obtained by overlayering harmonious colours.

FIRING GLAZED POTS

Stack pots in the kiln on small stilts so they do not touch the shelves or each other. Take the temperature up to 1000°C, increasing by approximately 150° each hour and then allow the pots to cool in the kiln.

TEXTILES

CHAPTER 6

Introduction

Main NC focus

PoS 8d
Children should be taught to experiment with (and develop control of [KS2]) tools and techniques . . . exploring a range of materials, including textiles

Children take interest in all the visual and tactile elements of texture, pattern, colour, line and form present in textile work. They enjoy its three-dimensional (3D) aspect, constantly picking up their textile work, weighing it in their hands, turning it and examining the back. Perhaps the idea that they are making something useful as well as decorative helps to explain children's fascination with dyeing and creating textiles. This chapter examines the ways in which textiles can be made by:

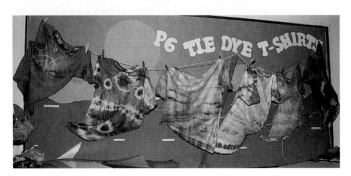

■ Yarn wrapping (page 131)

■ Knotting and knitting (page 138)

■ Weaving (page 141)

■ Dyeing textiles (page 146)

Figure 6.1
Tie-dye T-shirt display. Y6

■ Batik (page 154)

PoS 5b
Examine styles from past and present

Knowledge and understanding through textiles

Artists in the past have tended to consider textile-making a craft rather than an art. William Morris (1834–1896) and the Arts and Crafts Movement of the nineteenth century did much to increase artistic interest in textiles. Some famous painters have produced textile designs – Matisse, Delauney, Dufy, Ken Done and many contemporary artists use textiles in their work.

In the past spinning played a major part in local economies and it has featured prominently in many folk tales and legends. There is the story of Rumpelstiltskin who saved the life of a spinner by spinning straw into gold thread, and the Greek myth about Clotha, Lachesis and Atropos, sisters who spun the thread of each person's life, wound it on a spindle and eventually cut it with shears. These stories make a good introduction for work involving yarns.

ACTIVITY

PoS 5a
Examine styles in the locality

Examine textiles in the immediate environment (Y1–Y6).

- **Look at towels, sheets, blankets, curtains, cushion covers, carpets and rugs and discuss how designers have tried to make them decorative as well as functional.**

- **Examine clothes. Clothes have to be designed so that they are easy to put on and take off, protect from the weather and also look attractive (Maria Likarz, *Number 557*, Goodwill 2(16)). Uniforms have the additional function of identifying people's roles. Examine the difference in fabrics for day and night, for hot and cold weather, for formal and informal occasions. Look at the way the cloth has been joined using seams, rivets, studs, buttons or glue.**

 There are examples of traditional costumes in Acorn's *Art in the National Curriculum Key Stage One* AVP COM5001; *Art in the National Curriculum Key Stage Two* has a special section on how artists portray textiles.

Working with yarns

Yarns form the basis of all textiles and the more children know about the structure of the yarns, the more they will be able to control this medium.

Collect a wide variety of yarns. Ask parents who embroider or knit to donate leftover threads or balls of wool.

When buying yarns, choose several tones of the same colour in a wide variety of thicknesses and textures of yarn – fine wool, silky embroidery thread, hairy yarn, fluffy Angora, tightly-textured string. Hanks of wool are cheaper to buy than balls of wool.

Learning about the composition of different yarns makes an interesting link with science and is also important for understanding how yarns react in textile work.

KNOWLEDGE AND UNDERSTANDING

PoS 9c
Relate art to its time and place of origin

NATURAL FIBRES

Archaeologists in Egypt have found preserved pieces of linen thousands of years old. The same basic techniques for making natural yarns are used today because these yarns insulate well and absorb moisture.

Cotton and linen are made from plant materials. Cotton is made from the fibres covering the seeds of a cotton plant and linen is made from the fibres in the pith of a flax plant.

Wool and silk are from animal by-products. Wool is made from the fine undercoat of sheep, goats and llamas. Silk is made from silk-worm threads. If they are fed on mulberry leaves silk-worms produce soft silk and if they are fed on oak leaves they produce a coarser silk.

Felt is made from wool fibres that have been soaked in soapy water to open the fibres, and then rubbed to cause the fibres to hook on to each other.

ARTIFICIAL FIBRES

Artificial fibres make strong, durable and easy to clean yarns.

Rayon is made from chemically treated wood pulp. The original idea was put forward in 1664, but it was not actually produced until 1886.

Nylon was invented in 1928 and is made from coal and wood.

Fibreglass is made from finely spun glass.

Tip!

Teachers can test whether a fabric is natural or artificial by carrying out the following experiment (with the children at a safe distance). Pull out a thread from the sample, place it in a saucer and light the end with a match. Natural fibres burn readily; artificial fibres smoulder.

Ages and stages

PoS 4a–d
Learn about visual and tactile elements

Children at KS1 need time to experiment with yarns. Sorting lengths of yarn into different textures, thicknesses as well as colour groups helps them to become familiar with their characteristics. Untwist yarns and cords to see how they are made.

Children at KS2 should refer to a colour wheel to make a considered selection of colours. Which colours are harmonious and which provide contrasts? They could consider the texture of a yarn to enhance their work.

Yarn wrapping

PoS 7c
Explore and use 2- and 3-dimensional media

Creating textiles can be a very lengthy procedure. Knitting, crocheting, macramé and weaving take time and patience. Yarn wrapping allows children to produce quickly densely textured areas in the form of yarn wrap pictures (page 132), and God's eyes (page 132) and stick-weaving (page 136). They can also use yarn wrapping to make long cords (page 133), fluffy tassels (page 134) and pom-poms (page 135). This not only increases children's confidence in their textile-making skills, it also acquaints them with all the different thicknesses, textures and colours of yarn.

Yarn-wrap pictures

Yarn-wraps use wool to build-up a design in strips of dense colour (see photograph on the book cover).

AGES AND STAGES

PoS 8e
Experiment with visual elements

Children at KS1 should be encouraged to concentrate on wrapping the yarn closely in a slow, methodical action to cover the card support completely. Y1 children could wrap earth-coloured yarns around a small section of a branch, so that any gaps would complement the design instead of detracting from it. Landscapes make an ideal subject for a yarn-wrap around card. At first the layers will be flat areas of colour, but by the beginning of KS2, children could be wrapping some of the layers at an angle to create interesting overlayers. Starting with the background, then making the middleground and finally the foreground, will be valuable reinforcement for ideas of perspective at the end of KS2.

EQUIPMENT

A rich variety of yarns with subtle colour differences and changes in texture; thick card cut into rectangles about 13 × 20 cm; paper masking tape are required.

MAKING A YARN-WRAP

1 Start at the top of a piece of card. Anchor the end of a ball of wool to the back with a little tape.

2 Wrap the wool around the card slowly and carefully so that the threads are very close together and no card shows between the strands. Gradually progress down the card until very close to the lower edge.

3 Change colours by taping the old and new ends down at the back. Change angles by starting half way up the last section on one side and going down to the bottom edge of the last section on the other side.

ACTIVITY

1 Use a window frame to add interest to a plain yarn-wrap (Y1–Y2). Cut out the shape of a fish, a butterfly, a balloon or a Christmas tree from the centre of a piece of card and place it over the yarn-wrap.

2 Wrap yarn around card cylinders and use imagination to create forms (Y2–Y3).

Figure 6.2
Card-wrap on a cylinder. Y2

PoS 4a
Learn about pattern and texture in natural and made forms

God's eyes

God's eyes are similar to yarn-wraps except that the yarn is wrapped around two crossed sticks.

KNOWLEDGE AND UNDERSTANDING

Traditional God's eyes are made in Mexico as brightly coloured good-luck charms to hang on the wall. In England they are woven in straw at harvest time and are called Bridget crosses.

AGES AND STAGES

Although yarn wrapping is not complicated, the dexterity needed to start and turn a cross means the technique is probably most appropriate for children at KS2.

WRAPPING THE YARN

1 Tape together two sticks (approximately 20 cm in length) to form a cross. Use wooden meat skewers with the ends blunted. Older children could use art straws if they wind the wool gently.

Figure 6.3
God's eye yarn-wrap. Y4

yarn wound over
and around each stick

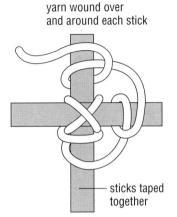

— sticks taped
together

Figure 6.4
Wrapping yarn to make a
God's eye.

2 Wind wool around the centre to hide the tape, trapping the end of the wool underneath. Keep the wool taut and hold the cross rigid. Wrap the wool round the back of one of the spokes and under and over the next one. Keep turning the cross and wrapping under and over when a spoke is passed.

3 To change colours, tie the new thread to the end of the old one. The joins can be pushed out of sight at the end of the wrapping.

4 As the yarn wrapping proceeds, children will discover that the sides differ. One side will have the wood showing as a raised cross, the other side will be flat. They should choose which one they prefer for the front, and then push any knots through to the back.

ACTIVITY

1 Decorate a God's eye (Y3–Y6).

- Make a cord to hang it up, using threads related to those in the God's eye.

- Add a plait, beads and a tassel to the base. In Mexico it is traditional to add tassels to the sides as well.

2 Make a star-shaped God's eye (Y5–Y6).

- Use three crossed twigs, art straws or dried straws to form a star shape and wrap the yarn around in the same way.

- Use a plastic bracelet and wind tape around the edges. Sew a star design in the centre by anchoring the stitches to the tape. Use a needle to wrap fine wool around the spokes.

Cords

AGES AND STAGES

PoS 4a
Learn about pattern and
form in natural and made
forms

The technique is not complicated as long as children can tie a knot. Children at KS1 often let go of cords just as they are getting tight enough to finish. Most children will just try again but it is worth checking that no one is becoming too discouraged. Children at KS2 can experiment with using more than four threads and varying the thread thickness.

MAKING A CORD

Start making cords by working in pairs.

a   b   c

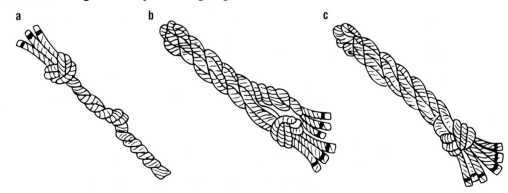

Figure 6.5
Making a cord.

1 Knot three or four strands of wool together, each one measuring about an arm's length. One child should be at each end of the stretched yarn, twisting the yarn in opposite directions.

2 When the cord has become very tightly twisted, one child reaches out and holds the centre, then walks up to his or her partner to get hold of both the other ends in the other hand. The centre is then released and the strands will twist around themselves to make a cord.

3 Tie the ends together to prevent the cord from unravelling.

ACTIVITY

1 Use cords as hair-ties, necklaces, bracelets and sashes on model figures (Y1–Y3).

2 Incorporate cords into weavings and fabric collage pictures or coil them into mats (Y3–Y6).

3 Find a door handle and try making a cord without a partner (Y3–Y6). Loop the middle of the yarn threads over the handle and twist. Cut the loop before joining the ends. Use the back of a chair or a table leg as alternatives to a door handle.

4 Create a thick cord by twisting three thin cords together (Y5–Y6).

Tassels

AGES AND STAGES Tassels require a tight knot so children at KS1 need help with the final stages.

MAKING A BASIC TASSEL

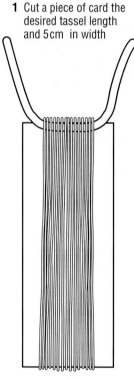

1 Cut a piece of card the desired tassel length and 5 cm in width

2 Place a strand of wool 15 cm in length across the top of the card to be tied later. Using a ball of wool wrap yarn from top to bottom around the card, trapping the tie

3 When the tassel is of the desired fullness, pull the tie ends together and tie a knot

4 Cut the yarn at the bottom of the card

5 Wrap a thread 2 cm from the tassel top around the tassel body and tie tightly

Figure 6.6
Making a tassel.

ACTIVITY   **1   Make a simple tassel doll (Y3–Y4).**

1 Make a very full tassel on card approximately 15 cm in length (see Figure 6.6)

3 Pull up strands of wool from the sides to make arms. Trim them to the doll's thigh level. Tie at the wrists

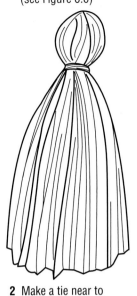

4 Make ties at the waist and at the ankles if the doll is to have gathered trousers

2 Make a tie near to the top for the neck

5 Add fabric collage details

Figure 6.7
Making a simple tassel doll.

2   Use tassels as decorative ends to cords and plaits (Y5–Y6). Use tiny tassels as textures on fabric collage or add them to the warp threads of weaving looms.

Pom-poms and candlewick

MAKING A POM-POM

Pom-poms are satisfyingly fluffy and three dimensional. A pom-pom is made in the same way as a tassel except that it is wrapped from the centre of two card discs. They can be used as decorative ends to cords and plaits or made into models of small birds and animals.

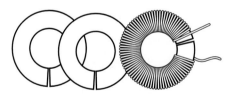

1 Place two card discs together and wrap wool around until there is no centre hole

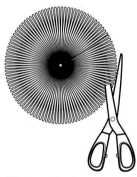

2 Slip the ends of a pair of scissors between the outer edges of the discs. Cut the wool.

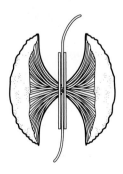

3 Pull a length of wool between the discs and loop it around the centre. Tie a tight knot

Figure 6.8
Making a pom-pom

4 Pull off the card discs. fluff out the pom-pom

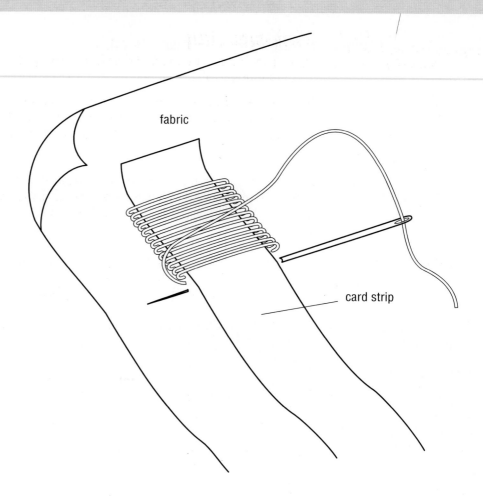

Figure 6.9
Making candlewick.

MAKING CANDLEWICK Candlewick stitching is based on the same techniques used for making pom-poms, but instead of working around a circle, children work on a long narrow piece of card tacked to a fabric background.

AGES AND STAGES Wrapping wool around a pom-pom card can become tedious for young children and a thin pom-pom makes a very unsatisfying form for a model. In general it is better to leave pom-poms until KS2 when children can work throughout the time it takes to fill the discs with wool.

Candlewick sewing could be introduced near the end of KS2.

ACTIVITY 1 Once children have learned how to make pom-poms, they can be used for imaginative work in constructing birds and animals. Teachers could make one or two suggestions but then encourage children to use their own ideas and adaptations.

• Make a spider (Y3–Y4). Thread four pipe cleaners through a single pom-pom.

• Make a bird. Use a pom-pom 5 cm in diameter for a body and a pom-pom 4 cm in diameter for a head (Y3–Y4). Sew the pom-poms together and add eyes, a beak and other details. Use yellow wool for a chick and glue it inside half an egg shell or stand it on felt feet stiffened with paste.

2 Use candlewick as part of a fabric collage picture for trees, fluffy animals, hairy caterpillars or ploughed fields.

PoS 7c
Explore and use 2- and 3-dimensional media

Stick-weaving

Stick-weaving is a method of wrapping yarn around sticks to create lines of highly textured fabric.

Use specially-made weaving sticks or make weaving sticks from dowelling or long pieces of thin wood. Cut the wood to a length of 12 cm and a width not exceeding 2 cm. Drill a hole 1 cm from the end of each stick.

AGES AND STAGES

The wrapped yarns used in stick-weaving can be removed from the sticks, so this technique provides a quick and easy introduction to actually creating new fabrics. If children at KS1 can be given assistance at the beginning, they usually manage the wrapping quite easily. Problems mainly arise when children wind the wool too tightly and cannot remove it from the sticks.

WRAPPING THE YARN

1 Place two sticks alongside each other with the holes at the bottom. Thread a piece of wool, 1 m in length, through each of the holes pulling it through so the strands are equal. Join all four ends in one knot. Children at KS1 will need to have the knot tied for them.

2 Start in the middle of the sticks, wrap wool around them both in a figure of eight. Keep the yarn close together but loosely wrapped. Push up the end of the wool and trap it in the yarn wrap. Continue to wind the wool loosely around to the top.

3 Push down the wrapped yarn to create more space at the top and continue the yarn wrap. Eventually the yarn will reach the tails on the end of the sticks. Push it down on to the dangling threads but always keep some yarn wrap on the sticks.

4 To change colours, cut the wool in use and join it with a knot to a new colour. Push the knots to the back at the end.

5 Continue wrapping around the sticks until a desired length has been reached. Cut the hanging yarns and tie a knot.

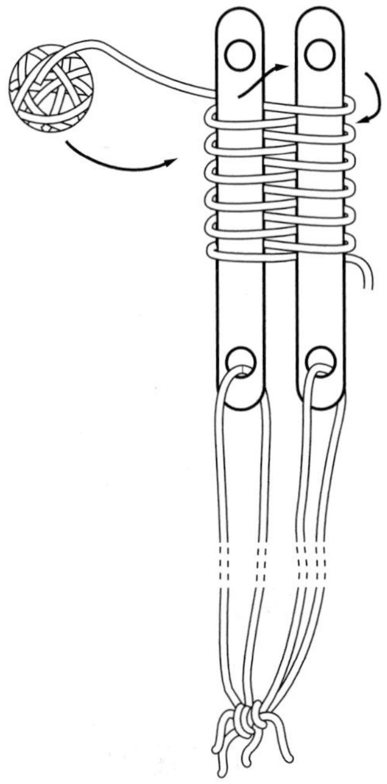

Tip!

If the yarn comes completely off the sticks and the wrapping has not finished, cut the thread and start the wrapping again on the sticks. The two sections will join up later and any loose threads can be pushed through to the back.

Figure 6.10
Weaving sticks and threads.

ACTIVITY
PoS 2c
Design and make creative images and artefacts

Once children have learned how to make a stick-weaving, they can use their imagination to create collage pictures or 3D objects.

1 **Create mini-beasts (Y2–Y3).** Make snakes, worms, slugs, snails or caterpillars and glue them to a fabric collage picture or push pipe cleaners into the yarn so that a caterpillar or snake can bend, twist and stand up.

Figure 6.11
Caterpillar, made flexible with a pipe cleaner. Y2

2 **Make a dancing figure (Y4–Y5).** Make several stick-weavings and arrange them into a dancing figure. Plan the relative length of the arms, legs and torso.

3 **Make a mat (Y5–Y6).** Roll a long, thin strip up to make a mat. Sew the edges together or glue it to a piece of card.

H & S

4 Use thin wire instead of yarn at the end of the weaving sticks. Bend and shape the stick-weaving into a 3D model (Y5–Y6).

French knitting

In French knitting, wool is wrapped around four nails hammered into a cotton reel and a growing tube of fabric snakes out of the bottom of the central hole.

It is traditional to use a wooden cotton reel, but as these are now mostly made from plastic, a cylinder of wood with a hole 1 cm in diameter drilled down the centre might be needed. A parent who likes woodwork may make a few. Hammer in four 0.5" small-headed nails around the top edge.

AGES AND STAGES

Introduce French knitting at the beginning of KS2, after children have had some experience with stick-weaving.

WRAPPING THE YARN

1 Push wool up through the central hole and wind it around the outside of the nails until it comes back to the first nail.

2 Use a crochet hook or needle to hook the bottom strand over the top strand. Loop it over the nail. Continue with this procedure around the nails. Eventually the French knitting appears from the bottom of the cotton reel.

3 To change colours, cut the wool and tie the new colour to the old. Use a crochet hook to push the knot inside the fabric at the end.

4 To finish, take the last loops off the nails, thread the wool through each loop and pull.

a b  c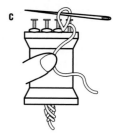

Figure 6.12
French knitting.

ACTIVITY

1 Use French knitting for bracelets, necklaces and dolls' scarves (Y3–Y6). Incorporate short pieces into fabric-collage for tree trunks, snakes, caterpillars and worms; use long pieces for weaving.

H & S

2 Push thin wire inside short pieces of French knitting to make wriggly mini-beasts or roll a long piece up to make a mat and over-sew the edges together (Y5–Y6).

Knotting and knitting

Macramé (below), plaiting (page 139) and knitting (page 140) are all ways of twisting, twining, knotting and binding yarn to make fabrics.

Macramé

Macramé is a method of making fabrics through joining yarns in a series of knots.

In the past, sailors' lives would depend on a knowledge of knotting and they would spend long hours practising what they called 'marlinespike seamanship' skills. As well as learning useful knots, they also experimented with ornamental knots. This kind of decorative knotting, or macramé, reached its peak in the eighteenth and nineteenth centuries and it is still used to make wall-hangings, pot plant-holders, room dividers and mats.

ACTIVITY
PoS 7e
Use knowledge of artists' work

Link macramé knots to expressive writing (Y3–Y4). Sailors used knots for magic. They could buy knots that were supposed to release a wind during a calm. Ask the children to make as complicated a knot as possible but keep it loose enough to undo. Write a piece about what would happen if the knot were released and hang the knot by the writing.

AGES AND STAGES

Primary children will not be able to learn complicated macramé knots, but very interesting textures can be created with the simple thumb knot and a few experimental knots.

MAKING MACRAMÉ KNOTS

PoS 8d
Experiment with tools and develop techniques

SETTING UP THE YARN

Tie a piece of string between two chairs or stools. Fold six strands of thick yarn or string 70 cm in length in half. Take the folded end of each one and fold it over the anchored string from the back. Thread the rest of the doubled string through the loop. This very simple knot has the satisfyingly complex name of a 'reversed lark's head' knot. Suspend all the strands of wool in the same way next to each other.

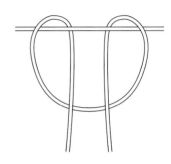

Figure 6.13
Tying a 'reversed lark's head' knot.

Children who cannot manage this beginning could hold the yarn down with a bulldog clip.

MAKING THE KNOTS

Make loops, tie thumb knots and tie invented knots in rows vertically and horizontally, tie the yarn in twos and threes, plait three strands together.

ENDING THE MACRAMÉ

Sometimes one thread is used up more quickly than the others. Just make a firm knot and end the strand there. Tie any remaining ends in groups of two to make small tassels.

Trim the ends for a neat edging or leave them uneven for branches on a tree trunk.

PoS 7c
Explore and use 2- and 3-dimensional media

Plaits and braids

Technically speaking, plaits and braids use a simple weaving technique. Children, however, usually feel that plaiting is more like tying a long, continuous knot. Anything that is long, flexible and fairly fine can be plaited. Try using thick knitting yarns, coloured string left over from tie-dyeing, dried grass, art straws, strips of fabric, strips of plastic carrier bags.

KNOWLEDGE AND UNDERSTANDING

PoS 5c
Examine styles from a variety of cultures

Children often have practical experience of plaiting and braiding using hair. If possible, find pictures of West African women who use elaborate plaiting patterns in their hair.

Barbara Chase-Riboud has made an impressive sculpture *The cape* (1973) with a bronze and hemp plait on an aluminium and steel support (The Lannan Foundation, Los Angeles).

Figure 6.14
Tree, made from a plait of string used in tie-dyeing. The ends of the plait form the roots, the branches were made by fraying the free ends. Y4

AGES AND STAGES

There will be a marked difference in children's abilities to plait depending on their experiences and interests rather than their ages. Children who cannot plait need to be helped at the beginning of a plait and reminded to continually pull the threads tightly. Mistakes are not disastrous and can add textural interest.

TYING A PLAIT

PoS 8d
Experiment with tools and develop techniques

1 Tie three strands 40 cm in length together with a knot. Tape down the knot on a table or pull a thread through the knot and tie it to something solid.

2 Bring the outside strand over into the centre of the other two. Work from the left and then the right. Keep the threads taut to make an even plait.

3 Repeat the same action from left to right until the strands have been used up. Tie a knot in the end.

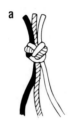

Figure 6.15
Tying a plait.

TYING A BRAID

Braids are plaits which use more than three strands.

1 Tie four thick yarns together. Tape the knot to a table.

2 Take the centre left strand and plait to the right.

3 Take the new centre left strand and place it over the far left strand and then plait to the right. Keep repeating this action.

Figure 6.16
Tying a braid.

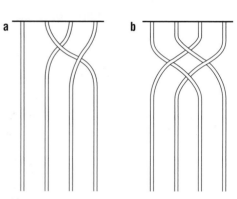

ACTIVITY

1 Using plaits and braids (Y2–Y6).

• Finish off warp threads on a weaving by knotting them into plaits or braids.

• Make friendship bracelets.

• Use braids to add details to a fabric collage.

2 Make a sculpture (Y5–Y6). Dip cotton string plaits in PVA glue and drape them over a greased mould such as a balloon. They will take on the form of the mould as they dry.

3 Over-sew thick plaits made from strips of fabric and make a mat (Y5–Y6).

4 Make a headband (Y5–Y6). Make two fabric strip plaits of the same length, press them with an iron and sew them together to make a headband.

Knitting

KNOWLEDGE AND UNDERSTANDING

PoS 5a
Examine styles in the locality

Knitting tends to be associated with making woolly pullovers, but in the past it was used to make very finely textured fabrics that are now made by machine. Knitting has undergone an artistic revival recently and hand-knitted pullovers are now sold in adventurous textures and colours. Artists sometimes incorporate knitted sections into wall-hangings.

AGES AND STAGES

Children usually have enough textile skills by the middle of KS2 to start knitting. Once they have learned the basic skills of casting on and off and they have learned plain knitting, they become very independent.

MAKING THE BASIC STITCHES

Instructions for knitting are difficult to show with diagrams. This is one of those occasions when a parent who can demonstrate the basic rules is far more helpful. Ask him or her to show you how to cast on, knit a plain stitch and cast off. Once this is established learn how to purl to produce an interesting variety of textures.

VARYING THE TEXTURES

STOCKING STITCH

Knit one plain row and then one purl row.

RIBBING

Alternate a plain stitch with a purl stitch on the same row. Bring the yarn backwards for each plain stitch and forwards for each purl stitch. Start each row with the opposite stitch from the one at the end of the last row.

MOSS STITCH

Moss stitch is the same as ribbing except each new row begins with the same stitch as the one at the end of the previous row.

INCREASING STITCHES

Make a loop at the end of a row and knit it as though it were a stitch.

DECREASING STITCHES

Knit the first two stitches together. Do the same with the last two stitches. Do this on all the rows until the desired width is reached.

ACTIVITY

1 Use small, irregular shapes with dropped stitches for foliage in a fabric-collage picture (Y4–Y5).

2 Make knitted rectangles (Y4–Y6). Use one for a knitted blanket for a doll's bed or a doll's scarf.

  • Knit a thin rectangle so that it is double the length of the index finger. Fold it over and sew up the sides to make a finger puppet. Add fabric-collage details.

  • Overlap rectangles knitted in the colours of earth, sky and water to make a landscape.

Weaving

Like knitting and crocheting, weaving allows children to create a fabric from different yarns. Most children's clothes are woven on machines, so they enjoy creating fabric using basically the same techniques.

KNOWLEDGE AND UNDERSTANDING

PoS 5b
Examine styles from past and present

Weaving is an ancient craft. Egyptian weaving from 1400 BC has been found in tombs on the shores of the Black Sea and in Egypt. Children enjoy looking at tapestries where pictures are woven on a loom (*Peasants hunting rabbits with ferrets*, fifteenth-century French tapestry, Ginn 20).

Paper weaving provides a good opportunity for children to explore patterns used in handwoven cloth because the warp and weft are equally balanced and the patterns are clear. With card looms the weft dominates, which distorts the pattern. Only looms with a heddle and shuttle (see page 142) will show patterns as clearly as paper weaving.

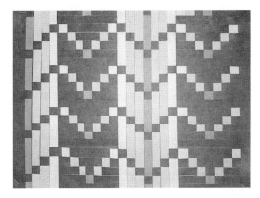

Figure 6.17
Paper weaving, using the sateen pattern worked from the back and the front. Y6

1 Look at weaving made on a large scale (Y1–Y6). Examine baskets, woven mats, lattice fencing and hedge laying. Some sculptures use weaving techniques.

2 Take scrap pieces of loose and tightly woven cloth and compare how they fray, fringe and unravel (Y3–Y6).

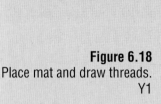

Figure 6.18
Place mat and draw threads. Y1

3 Pull threads on hessian to examine the structure of the weaving (Y1–Y6).
Use a very small piece of hessian (10 × 10 cm) at KS1. Pull threads from the outside edges to create a fringe. This makes it easier to grip the ends of the threads. Make a regular pattern by drawing warp and weft threads and counting the intervals.

AGES AND STAGES

PoS 4a
Investigate pattern and texture

Sometimes children, particularly at KS2, feel overwhelmed by the choices involved in art media, such as painting. With weaving, the warp and weft (see below) impose a structure on the work that many find very reassuring. This leaves them free to be adventurous in their choice of weft threads and patterns.

Children in Y1 will not be able to make closely woven fabrics but they can make very attractive wall-hangings. A disposable loom such as a polystyrene tray will hold in place any loosely woven weft threads such as twigs or ribbons. New vocabulary could include: weave, sequins, beads, ribbon, hessian, fine, rough, smooth, loom, wall-hanging.

Weaving patterns

Weaving patterns are based on the spacing and colours of the warp and the weft.

The *warp* is the set of threads which are laid across the loom at the beginning of the weaving.

The *weft* is the pattern of threads woven in and out of the warp.

THREE TRADITIONAL WEAVING VARIATIONS

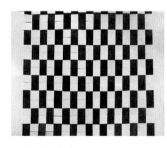

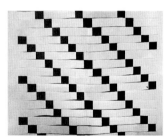

Figure 6.19
Three traditional weaving patterns.

 Use *Weaving* in the *Art Machine Pack* by Acorn to explore different weaving patterns.

MAKING A PAPER WEAVING

Make the paper warp by folding a rectangle of paper in half. Draw a margin along the open side. Cut straight lines at regular intervals from the fold to the margin. Open up the paper.

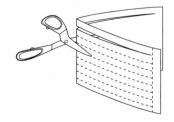

Figure 6.20
Cutting the warp in paper weaving.

Cut the strips of paper (the weft) on a paper cutter. They can be in a variety of widths but make them all slightly longer than the width of the rectangle weaving frame.

When the weaving is complete and all the strips have been pushed closely together, trim the edges with a paper cutter.

ACTIVITY

1 Use a variety of papers for the weft (Y1–Y6). Tie-dyed paper, rubbed and painted paper, sugar paper off-cuts, metal foils, crêpe paper, cellophane, and coloured pages from magazines cut into strips are all suitable.

2 Layer colours on the weft (Y3–Y6). Push a thin strip over one or two of the weft strips to add layers of colour.

3 Use a combination of weaving pattern (Y4–Y6).

Equipment and techniques for weaving with yarn

KNOWLEDGE AND UNDERSTANDING

Before the Industrial Revolution in Europe all fabrics were woven on handlooms. When machines were invented to spin yarn in the eighteenth century, the handloom weavers became prosperous because of the demands for their work, until their skills also were superseded by machine technology. If children look at pictures of handloom weaving from as many different countries as possible, they will see that the differences are surprisingly small.

If the school has a wooden loom, show it to the children so they can relate their simple looms to a more complex one.

AGES AND STAGES

PoS 8d
Experiment with tools and develop techniques

The loom is the frame that supports the weaving. It can be made from card or a frame of wood or wire. Card looms are ideal for beginners. It is very important to start small. Weaving is very time consuming and it is better for children to finish one small weaving with enthusiasm than leave an over-ambitious project unfinished. Small looms also have the added advantage that they are easy to turn around after each row.

THE WARP

The warp is the thread laid across the loom. Use fine, smooth strong yarn. Avoid yarns that will catch the weft as it is threaded in and out. String coloured during tie-dye is ideal.

Children in Y1 usually make an irregular warp as they wrap yarn around a card-loom; this can be integrated into the design, especially if the subject is the sky or an underwater scene. Weave cut shapes and pieces of fabric loosely across the uneven warp.

After the warp has been laid, children at KS2 should use thick yarn to weave a row at the top of the loom and a row at the bottom of the loom, going under and over at the same threads. This separates the warp threads and makes weaving easier.

The simple looms mostly used in primary schools need widely spaced warp threads so that children can weave the weft threads under and over the warp. This means that the more densely packed weft dominates the weaving and every change in colour makes a stripe.

THE WEFT

The weft is the thread woven through the warp. Check that children do not pass the weft thread behind the loom when they start a new row, as this can waste a vast amount of yarn.

Tip!

Most beginners make an hour-glass shaped weaving because the warp threads are pulled too vigorously. Weave the weft in an arch on the loom and then push the yarn down. This gives a much looser tension.

The shuttle moves in and out of the warp. With simple looms where the warp threads are far apart, KS1 children often prefer to use their fingers.

Shuttles can be made by taping the weft thread to a pencil or smooth stick, using a narrow piece of stiff card with a hole punched in the end as a weaving needle or using a tapestry needle with a blunt point (a sharp point constantly catches at the warp).

Push down, or tamp, the weft thread with a blunt needle, a fork or a wide-toothed comb. This packs down the yarn and makes a stronger weave and a pattern with better definition.

Change colours by weaving the old and the new warp threads side by side. Any stray threads can be pushed to the back at the end.

Release the weaving from the loom by cutting the warp threads at the back of the loom. Tie the ends together in pairs to stop the weaving from unravelling. The warp ends can be plaited, twisted into cords or decorated by threading beads or bells.

ACTIVITY

Tip!
To keep a wide, loose weft section in place sandwich it between two tightly woven wool sections.

1 Vary the texture and pattern of the warp (Y3–Y6). Thread beads or sequins on warp threads; vary the thickness, the colour and the gaps between the threads.

2 Use a variety of weft threads to add interesting textures (Y1–Y6). Knitting yarns, rolled sheep's wool, dried rushes, raffia, strips of lace, pipe cleaners, dyed and knotted string, Christmas tinsel, cords, plaits, ribbons, and ready-cut polythene bags are all suitable. Add decorative objects that will thread through the warp such as feathers, dried leaves, thin roots and pieces of bark.

3 Use fabric strips (Y1–Y6). Push fabric strips close together to make a highly textured, dense weaving. If flat fabric strips are required, stiffen them with paste and dry them before starting to weave.

Figure 6.21
Fabric weaving. Y4

4 Create a lacy texture (Y5–Y6). Use the weft thread to pull small groups of warp threads together.

5 Objects to make with a rectangular woven piece.

• Weave a long, narrow strip in fine wool to make a bookmark (Y3–Y4).

• Flatten a wool weaving by leaving it overnight under a weight. Then use it as a decorative mat (Y3–Y6).

• Make a wall-hanging. Tie the warp threads to dowelling and then trim the excess. Add collage detail to create a picture (Y5–Y6).

• Make a pouch by sewing two pieces together at the sides and the bottom (Y5–Y6).

LOOMS

CARD LOOMS

Card looms are probably the best looms to begin with for all ages. Cut a piece of strong card into a rectangle approximately 15 × 20 cm. Starting from the centre, cut slits every half a centimetre along the top and bottom edges. Use slightly wider gaps for KS1. Card looms can be bought in different sizes from educational suppliers.

To wind on the warp, tape the end of the wool down at the back of the card so that children can concentrate on obtaining a tight warp. When the warp has been wound around the card from one side to the other, cut the wool from the ball and tie a knot with the taped end. Bend the card slightly as the warp is wound around. This helps children to weave more easily across the warp. Children in Y1 might need the card close to the warp to hold any loose pieces of weaving. In this case, do not bend the card.

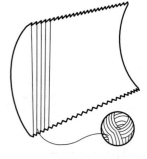

Figure 6.22
Curved card loom.

OTHER KINDS OF LOOM

ACTIVITY

1 Try a polystyrene tray loom (Y1–Y4). Glue fabric around the outside to reinforce the rim and wrap the warp around. Use the concave side of the tray for a traditional wool weaving. Use the convex side for a weaving with loose warps, such as twigs and thick ribbons.

2 Use a hanging loom (Y1–Y6). Tape the ends of the warp between two pieces of stiff card. Staple the top card to a notice board. Pull the loom slightly out from the wall and start weaving.

3 Make a cardboard box loom (Y4–Y6). Cut notches at each end of an open shoebox and wrap the warp around the box.

4 Set a forked branch in a pot of plaster of Paris to make it stable and use it for a loom (Y5–Y6). Wind the warp threads across the fork and fix them in place with glue. The weaving could be made to look like a spider's web.

Figure 6.23
Pin loom.

5 Use two facing lines of bobble-headed pins stuck in corrugated card and wind the warp between them to make a pin loom (Y5–Y6). Stick the pins in at an angle across the line of the corrugation. Use a pin loom on a polystyrene wig block to make a headband.

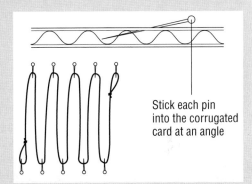

Stick each pin into the corrugated card at an angle

H & S

6 Use a wire circle to make a weaving frame (Y5–Y6). Cut a length of stiff wire or cane and tape the ends together forming a circle. Wind string tightly around the outside of the frame. Use the string to anchor the warp threads. Include the loom in the final design. The weaving can be confined to the centre or extended to the edge.

Figure 6.24
Weaving on a wire circular loom to show the shapes, texture and colours of the sky. Y5

PoS 4d
Investigate shape, form and space

Picture weaving

By turning the weft thread before it reaches the other side children can introduce shapes into their weaving.

AGES AND STAGES

It is very important to leave the weaving loose to prevent the shape from becoming distorted. It is best to try picture weaving with children who have had some weaving experience. Abstract patterns and irregular shapes give children the freedom to explore the strengths and limitations of the technique. Starting with a representational design often puts unrealistic demands on a weaver.

PLANNING A DESIGN

Push a very simple linear drawing under the loom as a guide – landscapes are suitable. Weave up to the lines, then turn around and weave back to the edge. Weave from the edge to the line until the area of colour is complete. Dovetail all the colours to finish the weaving.

ACTIVITY

PoS 1
Work individually, in
groups or as a class

1 Make a class weaving (Y1–Y6). A large frame is needed. The back of a wooden table top (without legs) or a shallow packing case is ideal. Alternatively, make a large hanging loom and staple it to a notice board.
   a) Tape a design to the back of the frame. Wind wool around the frame or tape across medium sized wire mesh.
   b) Use fabric strips to fill areas of colour. Work in small groups and change around so each child makes a contribution.
   c) Add fabric-collage details. Finer areas of weaving can be added later by weaving separate shapes.

2 Create weavings that can be removed from the loom as a shape (Y5–Y6). Use them as decorative patches on woollen pullovers, glue them on to card for badges or stitch them on to a woven background.
   a) Place a simple shape behind the centre of the loom. Stitch around the shape, using the colours that will be used in the weaving.
   b) Fill in the area with straight rows of weaving, packing the weaving very tightly to make the threads secure.
   c) When the shape has been filled, cut the warp threads approximately 4 cm from the shape edge. Turn them to the back and glue with impact glue.

3 Try needle weaving (Y6). Needle weaving uses the warp and weft in loose woven fabric as a loom or a fine warp of threads sewn across supporting fabric. Darning a sock is a form of needle weaving.

For the loom use loose woven cloth (hessian, binka, dish-cloths, lace curtains or fabric mesh). Pull out threads from hessian in a regular pattern; stitch a closely worked series of warp threads across a shape, pencilled on cloth; use sequin waste or net from a vegetable bag (hold the net taut in an embroidery hoop).

For the weft thread a blunt-pointed tapestry needle with wool, thin ribbon or strips of fabric and weave in and out of the warp threads.

PoS 4a and b
Investigate colour, pattern
and texture

Dyeing textiles

Dyeing is a dramatic process. As soon as the textile touches the dye it absorbs the colour and is transformed. The dye does not penetrate protected areas so they remain the original cloth colour. Contrasts between the newly dyed areas and the protected areas create a dramatic design.

Cotton sheeting is invaluable for dyeing work. It is one of the least expensive fabrics and yet is thick enough to hold colour.

KNOWLEDGE AND
UNDERSTANDING

PoS 5b
Examine styles from past
and present

The fabric-dyes that were available 150 years ago were basically the same as those used in the fifteenth century. All the dyes were made from natural products – plants, shellfish and insects. By 1980 the number of dyes had risen from a few hundred to three million, with 9000 available commercially. The discovery in 1856 of a colour-fast dye (mauve) made from coal-tar derivatives was the precursor of many new dyes.

By 1910, Diaghilev was able to make his sets and costumes for the Ballet Russe using a riot of synthetic colour. This event caused a surge in demand for the bright colours of synthetic dyes and the demand continues today. Natural dyes are still used by a few textile artists who value their more subtle hues.

AGES AND STAGES

Adding colour to fabric can be done at all ages and stages, but young children often prefer to make multi-coloured patterns by dipping the fabric in several dyes. This is a useful opportunity to talk about mixing colour since the dyes merge together instantly and dramatically. Older children are often more concerned to make colour-fast dyes so that they can wear what they dye.

Dyes made with local objects

H & S

Trying out home-made dyes introduces children to early dye-making techniques and creates a subtle range of earthy colours. These dyes can only be made if there is a safe place to boil a pan of water. Add a little alum to the water to help release the dye. Alum is safe to use with children and can be bought at a chemist.

INVESTIGATIONS

If you can obtain parents' co-operation, give the children scraps of white paper and see what coloured marks they can make from things they find in the garden and the kitchen. This needs adult supervision because of danger from poisonous berries and some materials found in the kitchen. Pool the information and then ask children to bring the most promising items to school the following day.

The following materials produce satisfying colour: red cabbage; cochineal (crushed beetles); turmeric; blackcurrant juice; coffee; cocoa; peat; crushed berries (alder, blackberries, blackcurrant, sloe berries, bilberry); flowers (marigold, broom, geranium, alder catkins, dahlia and golden rod) and leaves (privet, new bracken fronds, ivy, lily of the valley).

Some experiments need to be done at school by the teacher: onion skins, walnut shells and wood chips only release colour when they are boiled. Red cabbage causes some interesting reactions. Pick up some soap with a paint brush and mix it with red cabbage juice; it will turn a green/blue. Add lemon juice to the juice and it will turn pink. Test the best dyes on two pieces of cloth and label where the dyes came from with a marker pen. Wash one of the cloths to test for colour-fastness.

MAKING A DYE-BATH

PoS 8d
Experiment with tools and develop techniques

H & S

Use plain white cotton cloth and boil the dye in a safe area away from children. Tie-dyeing (page 148) will give a satisfying contrast between the old and new colours.

1 Chop up a source of dye into tiny pieces and wrap and tie the pieces in a piece of very thin cotton cloth or gauze.

2 Put the dye bag in a pan of cold water and bring to the boil. Simmer very gently until the water is a strong colour.

3 Use a ball-point pen to initial each piece of cloth in a corner. Wet the cloth and add it to the dye. Simmer very gently until the cloth has been dyed to the desired colour intensity. (It looks darker when it is wet.)

4 Let the fabric cool and then rinse repeatedly until the water runs clear. Untie any string. The dye can be kept in a cool, dark place for a few days.

Commercial dyes

Commercial dyes are easier to use than natural dyes and give brighter colours and stronger contrasts in tie-dyed fabric. Commercial dyes are supplied in a powder form in a packet or tin. Hot-water dyes resemble most closely the commercial dyeing techniques, but these are not recommended because they involve pans of boiling water. Cold-water dyes are safer and easier to use.

H & S

To mix cold-water dye add a small tin of powdered dye to a litre of hot water. Stir in a tablespoon of salt and a packet of dye-fix or a tablespoon of cleaning soda. The salt opens the fibres and aids absorption of the dye by the fabric. Soda fixes the dye. Add enough cold water to cover the cloth. As this process involves hot water, the teacher should mix the dyes.

ORGANISING THE DYEING AREA

Protect clothing and skin by wearing waterproof aprons and rubber gloves when mixing the dyes and dyeing the cloth.

Put dyes in deep plastic trays or buckets. Tape the name of the colour to the outside or line the containers up under a blackboard and chalk the names there. Place a bucket of water to the left of the dyes so that children can wet the tied cloth before it is dyed. Put old paint brushes or sticks by the dyes for stirring the fabric. Organise a drying area outdoors where the fabric can drip and not stain flooring.

DYEING WITH A SINGLE COLOUR

1 Wet the fabric to help the dye spread evenly.

2 Submerge the fabric in the dye. Stir with a stick for a minute and then leave the fabric to soak for one hour.

3 Repeatedly rinse the cloth in running water until the water runs clear. Take it to a drying area in a bucket.

DIP-DYEING

Dipping fabric in more than one dye creates striking multi-coloured patterns. The dyes are not given as much time to take so the colours are not colour-fast.

ACTIVITY

1 Use sponges held with peg handles to paint on irregular areas of dye (Y1–Y2).

2 Make lines of colour (Y1–Y6). Roll up the fabric. Curve the roll so the two ends meet and dip the centre into dye. Then, holding the centre with a peg, dip the two ends in different colours.

3 Make circles of colour (Y1–Y6). Pinch the fabric in the middle and pick it up in one hand. Smooth it down with the other hand. Dip the centre in one dye, clip on a peg and dip the ends in a different colour.

4 Make diamond and triangular shaped areas of colour (Y1–Y6). Fold a piece of fabric into a rectangle or triangle and secure the folds with pegs. Use the pegs as handles to dip the corners in differently coloured dyes.

PoS 4a
Investigate pattern and texture

Figure 6.25
Simple fan fold tie-dye technique on a T-shirt. Y5

KNOWLEDGE AND UNDERSTANDING

AGES AND STAGES

PoS 8f
Review and adapt the work

Tip!
Finding which child has done which tie-dye is not always easy. Write the names after the cloth has been tied to make sure it is not hidden in a fold and use a waterproof marker pen or a ball-point pen.

Tie-dyeing

Tie-dyeing is a very simple process – fabric, dyes and string only are required – yet the results are very dramatic. Tie-dyeing plain white cotton T-shirts can make your class into a walking art gallery.

Tie-dyeing is a popular craft throughout West Africa where indigo blue is traditionally used. Tie-dyeing became very fashionable in Europe and America in the 1960s and most children will have seen examples of tie-dyed T-shirts.

Tie-dyeing techniques range from the very simple to very elaborate. Try to keep a sample of cloth from each of the tie-dye methods as a reference to help children to review the options. Fabric and dyes are rather expensive to experiment with, so children new to tie-dye could start with paper and inks.

Tying tight knots is a problem for young children, so where necessary, substitute pipe cleaners, wire twist ties and strong elastic bands for string. If children in Y1 need to see results very quickly use the speed-dyeing method described on page 153.

Children at KS1 could start with circular patterns and then try simple stripes and marbled patterns. In Y3 and Y4, children could extend stripes and circles to include chevron and star patterns. If children work in pairs they will be able to make a rucking or squared pattern. Repeat patterns can have the centre of each shape marked in pencil on the fabric before the ties are made.

Even so, a very dark dye will cover a written name. In this case, leave a long piece of string dangling from one of the ties on each fabric piece and staple a name to the end. Hang it out of the dye bath.

By the end of KS2 children could try knotting fabric for quick results; threading fabric on safety-pins or yarn allows children to take full control over the shapes they produce.

It is very important that children at every stage should untie their own tie-dyes. Encourage children to unravel the string slowly and carefully to allow them to examine how the ties relate to the patterns.

Paper tie-dyes

Use thin paper for the 'fabric' (paper towels or white tissue paper) and coloured inks for the 'dye'.

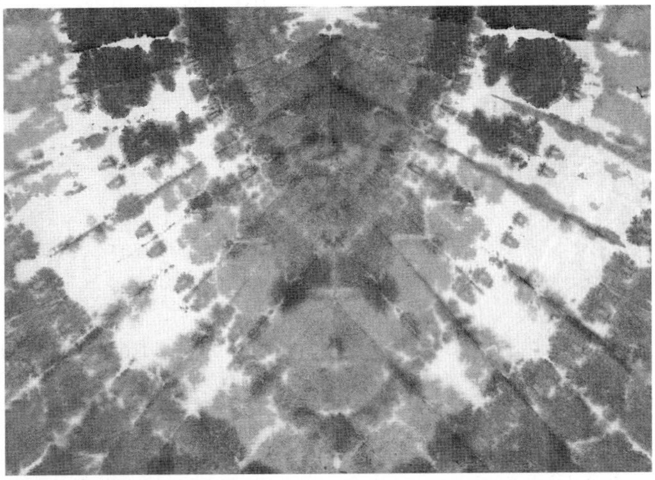

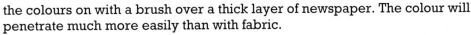

MAKING A TIE

Figure 6.26
Tie-dyed tissue paper. The paper was folded in half and then pleated diagonally with fan folds to produce a chevron pattern. Ink was used. Y1

1 Fold the paper into squares and triangles; make fan pleats; or roll or twist the paper. Use pegs or wire ties to hold the folds in place.

2 Dip the paper into coloured inks or dab the colours on with a brush over a thick layer of newspaper. The colour will penetrate much more easily than with fabric.

3 Leave the paper to dry before untying it. Wet paper tears very easily.

4 Open up the paper very carefully and smooth out the folds. Iron sideways to remove all of the creases without tearing.

ACTIVITY

1 **Use paper tie-dyes to make butterflies, flowers, greeting cards and wrapping paper (Y1–Y6).**

2 **Cut out interesting sections from less successful experiments (Y1–Y6). Use them for collage work and paper weaving.**

PoS 8d
Experiment with tools and develop techniques

Different tie-dye patterns

Tie-dye ties vary considerably in the time they take to complete. A marbled tie-dye takes one to two minutes. A pattern of small circles may take more than half an hour. It is helpful to combine a tie-dye lesson with some other activity, such as weaving or soft sculpture, so that children are occupied when they have finished their tying.

TYING THE STRING

If the tie is not tight enough the dye penetrates into the fabric under the string with disappointing results. To allow tight bindings, trap the start of the string in the binding but leave a small tail sticking out. As the string nears its end, work back to the beginning and tie the two ends together. Children at KS1 will find it easier to undo the ties if they use strong yarn in a contrasting colour to the dye. Children at KS2 could use string and recycle it as weaving yarn. Cutting the string in one or two places, just enough to loosen it, will make sure the string is long enough to be re-used.

MAKING STRIPES

ACTIVITY

*PoS 4a
Investigate pattern and
texture*

1 **Gather, roll or fan fold a piece of fabric into a narrow band (Y1–Y6). Use pegs to keep the ends in place and bind with string.**

2 **Fold the fabric in half and then pleat it diagonally with fan folds to make a chevron pattern (Y3–Y6).**

Fan folding | Rolling

Figure 6.27
Tying fabric to make stripes.

MAKING CIRCLES

a Single or multiple circles (Y1–Y2)

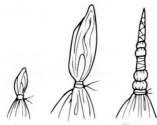

Pick up a point of fabric and stroke downwards. Bind near the point for a small circle; further away for a large circle

b Even circles (Y3–Y6)

Tie individual marbles, dried beans or small pebbles inside fabric to produce regular, small circles

c Solid circles (Y3–Y6)

Figure 6.28
Tying fabric to produce patterns based on circles.

Cover the fabric over each marble with polythene before binding to produce a solid circle of white

d Star shapes (Y3–Y6)

For a star-shaped pattern pick up a point of fabric, twist it around itself several times and bind

MAKING MARBLED AND RUCKING PATTERNS

1 Tying a small piece of fabric (Y1–Y6)

Bunch up the cloth to make a ball and bind string around. Tie the ends of the string tightly together. This makes a random but very attractive pattern

Tying a large piece of fabric (Y5–Y6)

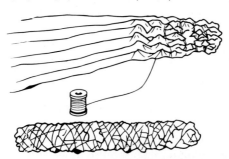

Figure 6.29
Tying fabric to produce marbled patterns and rucking patterns.

If a large piece of cloth is gathered up in a ball to make a marbled pattern, the result is disappointingly plain because the dye does not penetrate to the centre. Therefore, place the fabric flat on a table. Working from side to side, gather up the cloth in peaks using a 'clawing' action. Loosely bind the fabric up into a roll as progress is made, and then tie firmly with additional string

2

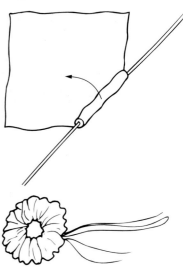

Roll fabric along string and then ruck it tightly

RUCKING   Rucking is a beautifully intricate design that reminds children of the ripples on sand and water (Y3–Y6).

MAKING A SQUARE PATTERN

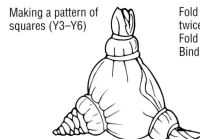

Making a pattern of squares (Y3–Y6)

Fold a square of thin fabric twice to make a smaller square. Fold again to make a triangle. Bind all three corners tightly

Figure 6.30
Tying fabric to produce a square pattern.

KNOTTING   Knotting might seem an easier alternative to tying string, but a knot needs to be tied very tightly to be effective and untying it is also difficult. Keep it as a quick tie on large areas for Y5 and Y6.

Roll or twist the fabric and tie the 'ends' together in a knot. Pull very tightly. After dyeing and drying, twist the cloth on each side back into the knot. This loosens the knot enough to untie

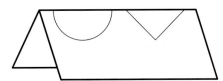

Figure 6.31
Knotting fabric, an alternative to tying.

MAKING GEOMETRIC SHAPES

*PoS 4d
Investigate shape, form and space*

Making geometric shapes (Y5–Y6)

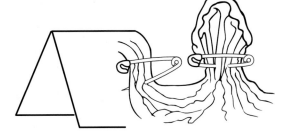

Fold a piece of fabric in half. Draw half-ovals or diamonds on the fold approximately 7 cm in length

Weave a nappy-pin in and out along the pencil line. Tie the string beneath the pin. Remove the pin and make more ties along the fan shape towards the fold

Repeat for each shape

Figure 6.32
Making geometric shapes.

'Tritik' comes from the Javanese word for sewing and is a method of gathering up cloth through stitching. It gives a high degree of control over the resulting shape and is used for motifs and initials (Y5–Y6). Pencil a design on the fabric. Use strong thread to sew a double row of small tacking stitches along the pencil line. Pull both ends of the thread and ruche (gather) the fabric tightly. Tie the two ends of the double thread tightly together.

Figure 6.33
Flower motif for a cushion, using the tritik method. Y6

ACTIVITY

1 Use a variety of bindings (Y1–Y6).

  • Use different thicknesses of string.

  • Vary the binding patterns – use narrow lines, bands of solid binding and areas of criss-cross binding.

2 Add printed details to finished tie-dye fabrics (Y1–Y6).

  • Print petal shapes around tie-dye circles to make a flower pattern.

  • Print fish or other sea shapes on linear patterns.

  • Print shell or other beach shapes on rucking patterns.

3 Sewing. Small tie-dyed circles make an ideal base for sewing stitches that radiate from the centre (Y2–Y4).

Dyeing the tie-dyed cloth

PoS 4b
Investigate colour

Tie-dyed fabrics can be dyed once, dip-dyed or passed through several stages, using a progressively darker dye.

DYEING WITH ONE DYE

Tie the fabric and then follow the instruction for home-made and commercial dyes on pages 147 and 148.

DYEING WITH TWO DYES

Soak the tied cloth in one dye, rinse, dry and then make new ties before soaking in a second dye. This takes two separate sessions but it creates exciting colour combinations and contrasts. Colours that combine well are red and brown, turquoise and brown, pink and purple, blue and purple, yellow and blue, blue and brown, blue and red. Black as a final colour gives a darker version of the first colour.

1 Use the lighter of the two colours for the first dye. After tying, soak the fabric in the dye and then rinse off the colour.

2 Undo one or two ties to obtain a pure second colour in those areas. Tie up more areas – these will stay the colour of the first dye. The remaining cloth will be a blend of the two colours.

3 Place the cloth in the second, darker dye and allow to soak.

4 Rinse and dry.

ACTIVITY

1 Use a mixture of tie-dye techniques (Y2–Y6).

- Crunch up fabric that has been already tied and wrap string loosely around the whole fabric. Then wet and dye it. This adds a marbled background to the design.

- Start with marbling, undo the ties and then tie circles for a second dye colour.

2 After the first dyeing, try untying all the ties and make a complete new set (Y4–Y6). The areas where the ties overlap remain white. This works particularly well with striped patterns. Fan fold (see page 000) the fabric diagonally one way for a first dye and diagonally the other way for a second dye.

INSTANT MULTI-COLOURED TIE-DYE

PoS 8d
Experiment with tools and develop techniques

The following methods do not produce fast colours but are useful when time is limited and children would like to use several dyes. It is also useful for children at KS1 who often need to see the outcome of their ties as soon as possible.

SPEED DYEING

Instead of soaking a fabric in a dye for one hour; place it in the dye stirring briefly and then rinse off excess dye. Add more ties and put it in a second dye for a similarly short time. Rinse off excess dye and then immediately untie the string.

PAINTING DYE

Lay the tied fabric on a thick layer of newspaper. Put the dyes in waterpots and use a brush to liberally dab on colour.

This method produces more white areas than dip-dyeing (see page 000) or speed-dyeing but it does allow a whole class to make quick multi-coloured tie-dyes at the same time.

Figure 6.34
Stripes using a fan fold. Y5

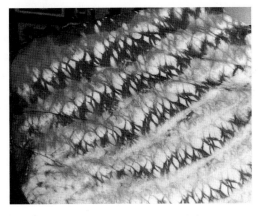

Figure 6.35
Ruching pattern. Y5

Batik

PoS 2c
Design and make creative images

Batik techniques are very similar to tie-dye. Instead of protecting cloth with tied string, hot wax is used. This means children have greater control over the results. The designs can be simple line drawings or complex patterns; it is the dramatic contrast between the waxed lines and the dyed areas that makes this such an attractive dyeing method. Safe alternatives to hot wax are shown on page 159.

The traditional batik, or true batik, method is to apply a pattern in hot wax or cold resist and then immerse the whole cloth in dye. The cloth is re-waxed and re-dyed several times.

Batik painting or false batik is a more recent development. It uses wax or resist lines as a wall or a barrier to stop different colours of dye bleeding into each other. This leaves pools of colour within the design and allows different colours to be painted on at the same time.

When all the wax is removed the colours are revealed in an exciting and highly textured design caused by small cracks in the wax allowing a little dye to penetrate some of the waxed areas.

EQUIPMENT

Bags of wax pellets can be purchased from educational suppliers. These are ready to use and melt quickly. Alternatively, melt down white candle stubs or buy specialists' batik wax in solid form – the traditional mix is three parts beeswax to one part paraffin wax.

H & S

Electric wax pots are specially made for heating up wax for batik. The wax has to be at a high enough temperature to penetrate the cloth but not so high as to burst into flames. The wax pots are designed to reach the correct temperature.

Tjantings are traditional tools for applying wax to the cloth. They have a pipette (small pipe) leading from a metal reservoir on the end of a long wooden handle. The long handle allows them to be left in the wax pot ready for use. In storage, the wax will block the pipette. Just put them in the hot wax to clear the blockage at the beginning of each lesson.

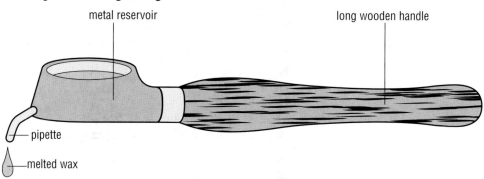

metal reservoir

long wooden handle

pipette

melted wax

Figure 6.36
Tjanting tool, used in batik to spread wax.

Paint brushes can also be used to apply wax, although the lines produced are thicker. Brushes are particularly useful for applying wax to large areas. Use old brushes that can be labelled and kept for batik only as wax is very hard to remove. If wax has to be removed, soak the brushes in boiling water and detergent.

Collect old polystyrene fruit trays and hold one under the tjanting to catch any drips as the wax is carried to the fabric.

White cotton sheeting is cheap, thick enough to absorb dye and thin enough to let wax sink through easily. Muslin is good for beginners because it is thin and wax penetrates it easily. The colours are not as intense as with cotton sheeting. Silk looks wonderful but is very expensive and will need special silk dyes (see page 160).

Frames help to keep a fabric taut. The fabric can be taped to a wooden frame or over an empty icecream tub. Embroidery hoops can also be used. Alternatively, paper, cut to the same size as the cloth and clipped to the back, supports the fabric and prevents wax and dye from reaching the table.

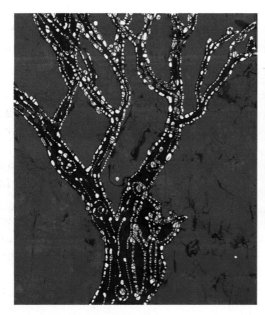

Figure 6.37
Tree, using a traditional batik method. Y5

Figure 6.38
Goose, using batik painting. Y5

KNOWLEDGE AND UNDERSTANDING

PoS 5c
Examine styles from a variety of cultures

The Indonesians, famous for their batik cloth, produce intricate and dramatic patterned fabrics, textured with a distinctive 'crackling' unique to batik. In the past, only Indonesian royalty could wear particular patterns and it was seen as a fabric for the wealthy. Now batik is made and worn all over South East Asia.

Not all traditional batik relies on hot wax. In India, mud is used as a resist to the dye; the Yorubas in Nigeria use starch. In these countries the tradition is to use only one dye, relying on a striking contrast between white resist areas and dyed areas.

Batik techniques have spread worldwide and range from the traditional intricate patterns of sarong lengths to innovative pictorial designs (Tunde Odunlade *Oranmiyan festival*, Goodwill, Contemporary African Art).

 Acorn's computer program *Art in the National Curriculum Key Stage Two* contains pictures of Indonesian batik.

AGES AND STAGES

Children at KS1 should avoid hot wax and start with wax crayon or resists (page 23). Beginners with hot wax should use a paint brush for the main lines and a tjanting for fine lines and dots (see page 154). Use very thin fabric so the wax penetrates the cloth easily. When the work is finished, back the batik on white card to brighten the colours. Start with small areas of cloth and make simple napkins, cushion covers, pictures or fabric for fabric sculptures. As the children become more skilful they can make a sarong or a wall-hanging.

Making a batik design

AGES AND STAGES

Many children find it difficult to grasp that colour does not appear where they spread wax with a tjanting. This is very different from their experience in drawing and painting when colour appears where they draw. A wax-resist drawing can help to show how it works on paper. Make a simple design with a white candle on white paper, then brush over with the first colour to show how the wax rejects colour. Leave the paper to dry and when the children are ready for the second dyeing, use the same drawing and make more lines with the white candle. Paint over with a darker colour to show how the wax protects areas from the next dye.

PLANNING A DESIGN

PoS 2c
Design and make creative images and artefacts

Keep a design simple, large and linear; small shapes are easily reduced to wax blobs.

Beginners should avoid planning their designs in advance and instead gain experience in drawing directly in the wax.

ACTIVITY

1 'Use the drips' (Y1–Y6). Drips are inevitable when children first attempt batik. Beginners could make a batik pattern entirely from drips.

Tip!

If children need to plan a design, use a thick black pen on paper cut to the same size as the cloth. Staple or paper-clip the cloth on top of the paper. The design will be seen through the cloth and this avoids visible pencil lines appearing on the batik.

Figure 6.39

Patterned cloth made into a sarong. A stencil was used to make white and then yellow palm trees. Additional small patterns were printed with wire; before a final marbled dyeing in blue. Y6

- Drip over the cloth with hot wax from a tjanting, dye, drip again and re-dye (Y3).

- Make simple, exploratory patterns using lines and drips and then dye the fabric (Y3–Y4).

- Create scenes that absorb drips. Starry nights, sparkling candle-lights or snow scenes (Y3–Y4).

2 Use a very simple positive stencil (see page 72) to make a repeat pattern in wax (Y5–Y6). Place the stencil on a piece of fabric and dab with hot wax using an old, thick paint brush. Limit to one dab for each dip to ensure the wax is very hot. Wax makes card stencils very strong and durable. Save them for future ink prints.

ORGANISING WAXING

Planning and dyeing can be carried out as a class lesson. Waxing needs to be performed in small, well-supervised groups,

H & S

Place wax pots on a table pushed against a wall that has a plug socket. Tape down any loose electrical wires. The wax should be heated with the lids on for 20 minutes. Remove the lids and place brushes or tjantings in the pots to melt the wax. Have a maximum of two children to a pot.

Establish the following firm rules.

■ Only an adult should move or touch the wax pots.

■ No stretching across the pots.

■ No picking at hardened wax (dropped wax can make the floor very slippery).

■ If wax splashes on the skin, ask the child to pick off the wax and immediately suck the area (saliva is an excellent balm).

APPLYING THE WAX

PoS 8d
Experiment with tools and develop techniques

1 Ask children to cover their name (written in pencil on the side of the cloth) with hot wax before they begin the main picture. This gives them a little practice in using the wax and protects their name from dye.

2 Lift out a tjanting, tip out excess wax and carry it quickly and smoothly to the fabric holding a polystyrene tray under the tjanting to catch any drips. Dribble hot wax along a line. Only cover a short length before going back for more hot wax. If a brush is being used, make a short dabbing action, rather than the usual long, painting stroke, because the wax soon grows cold on the brush.

3 The wax should stick to the paper underneath and look transparent. If the wax looks milky on the surface of the fabric, it has been allowed to go cold. Because it has not penetrated the fabric it will not act as a barrier to the dye. If this happens, turn the cloth over and apply wax on the back. Keep holding the fabric up to the light to check the wax has penetrated the fabric.

Dyeing batik in the traditional way

Wax on fabric hardens instantly so it can be dyed as soon as a design has been made. Plunge the fabric in dye and the waxed areas will remain white.

USING TWO DYES

PoS 4b
Investigate colour

1 Make a simple design in wax and dye the fabric in the lighter of the two colours. Rinse and dry the cloth (see page 152).

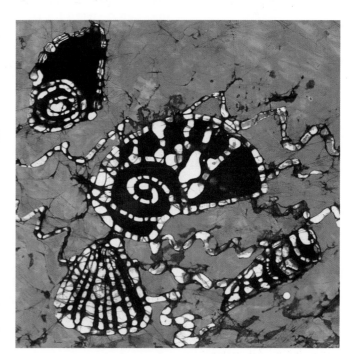

2 Use a brush to dab hot wax over all the areas that need to be kept the colour of the first dye. Children at the end of KS2 could try waxing the background instead of the main shapes. This takes a long time to complete, but the white textures and dark dye in the centre produce an image with dramatic contrasts (see figure 6.40).

Figure 6.40
Shells, on a waxed background. Y5

3 Put the cloth in the second darker dye and soak.

4 Rinse the fabric and allow to dry.

REMOVING THE WAX

The cloth is an unsightly mixture of coagulated wax and cloth before the wax is removed. Let the children watch the wax-melting process, even if they are too young to do it themselves. The colours glow through in a very exciting way as the wax melts to reveal patterns and textures.

H & S

1 Place the fabric between two sheets of white newsprint and then two sheets of newspaper. Iron across the top newspaper so that the heat melts the wax in the fabric and the wax is absorbed by the paper. Keep changing the top and bottom sheets of newspaper as they become full of wax.

2 Even after many ironings, the fabric is a little stiff with residual wax but this can be an asset if the fabric is to be mounted or embroidered. If the batik is going to be used as a sarong, scarf or cushion cover and needs to be softened, wash it separately in warm water and detergent.

3 Mount the work on white card or, if possible, display it against a light source for maximum contrast and brightness in colours.

ACTIVITY

1 Combine batik with dip-dyeing (Y3–Y6). Fold and dip the waxed fabric in different colours.

2 Combine batik with tie-dyeing (Y5–Y6). Be careful not to overwhelm the batik design. Use simple textural patterns such as loose marbling, or very small circles. Make the ties after the first dyeing. This way the new patterns do not compete with the white lines of the batik.

PoS 4b
Investigate colour

Batik painting

In batik painting the fabric is not dipped in the dye in the traditional manner, instead dyes are painted on. If the cloth is not going to be washed, coloured inks can be used for bleeding and blending and thicker fabric dyes used for areas of solid colour. The white outlines, bright colours and subtle blendings make this a very attractive medium.

KNOWLEDGE AND UNDERSTANDING

PoS 5c
Examine styles from a variety of cultures

Batik painting is a fairly recent art form that has developed from traditional or 'true' batik techniques. In South East Asia, batik paintings are mass-produced in factories for T-shirts and beach-wear. They are also made individually and sold as paintings in art galleries.

AGES AND STAGES

Children who are new to batik painting could draw lines in wax and then sweep over the lines with colour. Once children have practised making continuous wax lines, find subjects which do not demand precise areas of colour, or small gaps in the wax lines may ruin the picture. Landscapes are very forgiving subjects; colours can bleed and blend a little, without spoiling a design.

PoS 4b
Investigate colour

Figure 6.41
'Space'. There have been leaks of dye but they enhance the effect. Y5

Children at KS2 should mix colours from hues that are related on the colour wheel. The white lines of a batik painting make a pleasing foil to subtle changes in colour.

MAKING THE PICTURE

PoS 8d
Experiment with tools and develop techniques

1 Draw a linear design in pencil on thin white cotton or place a design on paper under the fabric. Try to create self-contained shapes.

2 Apply wax along the lines using a tjanting or brush. The wax lines act as waterproof barriers to paint so it is very important that there are no gaps. Keep lifting the cloth to the light to check that all the wax lines are transparent.

3 Paint colours in the separated areas starting at the centre of each section so that colour can spread to a wax barrier. If the dye gets too near to a wax line, it can flow over. If there are major problems with gaps in the wax lines, sweep dyes or inks over the fabric. The waxed lines will appear as a white design in a multi-coloured picture.

4 Use strong dyes for the centre of interest and weaker dyes for background. Start with the more dilute background colours. If there is a leak in one of the wax lines the background colour will seep into the foreground. The seepage can be covered to some extent by cautiously applying a stronger, foreground colour while keeping away from the break in the line. Keep the fabric on a piece of paper to absorb excess dye and do not move the wet fabric on and off the support paper underneath or colours will smudge.

5 When the colour is dry, remove the wax by ironing the painting between sheets of old newspaper. Keep sheets of white newsprint paper next to the fabric to protect it from the newsprint, and keep changing the newspaper on either side as it absorbs the wax.

ACTIVITY
PoS 4a
Investigate pattern and texture

1 Add textures to a painting (Y3–Y6).

- Paint on wet fabric for a smooth gradation from one colour to the next. This is a very useful technique for skies, calm water, smooth fabrics or receding landscapes.

- Paint on dry fabric to leave brush-stroke lines. These can be used to show texture creating hills, foliage, waves, feathers, fur, scales or folds in fabric.

- Sprinkle a little salt on areas of wet ink or dye. This makes an interesting pattern as the colour is gradually drawn to the salted areas. Brush off the salt when the ink has dried. Use it for rocks, soil, foliage or fur.

Figure 6.42
Kingfisher. The brush strokes in the background give an interesting texture to the sky. Y5

2 Use a direct observational drawing as the basis of a design (Y3–Y6). The image should be simplified or stylised to accommodate the strong batik lines.

3 Diffuse dilute ink over the background, after the wax lines have been drawn (see page 158) (Y5–Y6). Then paint the foreground shapes using stronger colours. Alternatively, mask the foreground shapes with paper before spraying.

ALTERNATIVES TO HOT WAX
PoS 8d
Experiment with tools and develop techniques

POLYFILLA AND FLOUR PASTE

Both of these act as a resist on the surface of the fabric. Mix the Polyfilla with water; or mix one cup of white flour, one cup of water and four teaspoons of alum (from the chemist) into a paste. Squeeze lines on thin cotton cloth after putting the paste into empty plastic ketchup bottles. Rub off when dry.

A little paint will soak under the lines giving the outlines a blurred appearance. To reduce this effect, paint the paste on thickly and allow to dry overnight before painting with cold-water dyes. Remove the resist after painting by scraping off as much as possible and then washing in warm water and detergent.

WAX CRAYON

1 Draw a linear design in pencil on thin white cotton, creating self-contained shapes.

2 Go over the lines in wax crayon, pressing hard to obtain a thick layer of wax. Black crayon highlights the dyes and can be easily seen. White wax crayon or a candle roughly mimics the batik technique.

3 Place a sheet of newspaper under and over the fabric and run an iron over the surface. This melts the wax which penetrates the fabric.

4 Paint colours in the separate areas.

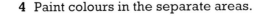

Figure 6.43
'The beautiful princess' – wax crayon batik. Y1

PoS 3
Ideas, feelings and meanings are communicated in different visual forms

Silk painting

No dyed fabric can match the luminosity and subtlety of colours that can be achieved with silk. Silk is certainly expensive, but very small areas of the cheaper, thin silk can be used and, if the painting is mounted on white card, the colours will still look strong and vibrant.

Figure 6.44
Flower in bottle. Direct observation was used for the image of the flower and the bottle; the flowing lines and colour blends were imaginary. Y6

KNOWLEDGE AND UNDERSTANDING

PoS 5c
Examine styles from a variety of cultures

Painting on silk developed in China during the Chou Dynasty (1030–771 BC) before paper was invented. The Chinese first painted banners and then scrolls, fans, screens and clothing fabrics (Chinese scroll painting *Emperor Qianlong*, Goodwill 3(26)). The Japanese adopted silk painting and in the seventeenth century invented ways of separating colours with a paste. This paste has now been replaced by gutta, but the techniques are the same. The art of painting on silk came to Europe via the silk fans which were imported from the East and through the Japanese contribution to the Paris World Exhibition of 1878. Degas, Gauguin and Signac and later artists of Art Nouveau enjoyed painting on silk (Mackintosh *Stylised tulips*, Goodwill 3(30)).

AGES AND STAGES

Although this is an expensive medium it is safe to use at all ages and even a tiny piece of silk can give beautiful results. Begin by experimenting with different techniques on small strips of cloth. Children could make a small oval or rectangular picture-frame mount and then move it over the silk to find the most interesting area and glue the fabric under the frame for a birthday card or brooch. Any trimmings can be saved for collage.

The next stage is to use the gutta to make very simple shapes. Start with transparent gutta; gold, silver and black gutta are harder to use. By the end of KS2, children could be learning to vary the width of gutta lines, to produce more intricate shapes and spaces and to work within a limited colour range.

EQUIPMENT

Special silk paints are needed. Fabric paints on silk give a very dull finish. The paints are expensive, so store any leftover mixtures in small, plastic containers.

Gutta is a resin that acts in a similar way to wax in batik paintings – it prevents paints from merging. The advantages of gutta are that there are none of the dangers of using hot wax and there is more control over a line.

Pipettes are small plastic bottles that can be bought to use with the gutta. The nozzle on the pipette has a small hole that allows a little of the resin out at a time. Children will need to practise drawing lines – a slow pace produces thick lines, a fast pace produces thin lines.

MAKING A SILK PAINTING

PREPARING THE SILK

Plan a design on paper cut to the size of the silk. Make sure a design fills the paper to minimise waste. Work from direct observation if possible but whatever the source of ideas, keep the design simple.

Put the paper underneath a piece of silk and lightly trace along the lines to transfer the design.

Tape the silk to a frame, pulling it taut. Pipe gutta along the lines and allow to dry overnight.

PAINTING THE SILK

PoS 4b
Investigate colour

Use a very clean brush to dab out the silk paints into a mixing palette. Encourage colour mixing of a limited colour range. Colours become paler but retain their brightness if they are diluted slightly with half water and half alcohol (available from chemists).

Paint light-coloured areas first. Keep away from the gutta lines to prevent paint from spilling over the edges.

DEALING WITH SERIOUS LEAKS

If there is a leak in the gutta wall, let the area dry and add more gutta. Over-paint the leaked colour if the background is dark. If the leaked area is too dark to over-paint, incorporate it into the design by making a gutta wall around it.

ACTIVITY
PoS 4a
Investigate pattern and texture

1 Create interesting textures (Y2–Y6).

• Paint on wet silk to blend colours. Paint on dry silk to leave brush-stroke lines.

• Sprinkle a little salt on the wet-painted silk to make patterned areas of colour. The size of the salt grains affects the size of the pattern.

2 Introduce differently coloured guttas (Y5–Y6). Black gutta is not as resistant as the transparent gutta so use it in landscapes where a slight leak is not disastrous. Reinforce the back with transparent gutta in places where it is essential colours remain separate.

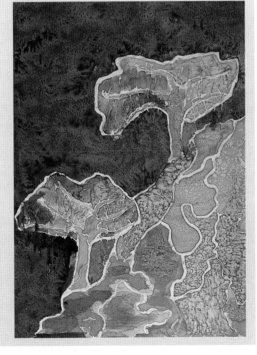

Figure 6.45
Silk painting with areas textured with salt.

ART ELEMENTS

Main NC focus

KS1 PoS 9b
Pupils should be taught to recognise visual elements, e.g. pattern, texture, colour, line, tone, shape, form, space, in images and artefacts

KS2 PoS 9b
Pupils should be taught to identify how visual elements, e.g. pattern, texture, colour, line, tone, shape, form, space, are used in images and artefacts for different purposes

Introduction

The term visual elements refers to aspects of art that can be seen – pattern, texture, colour, line, tone, shape, form, space; while tactile elements refers to aspects that can be felt – texture, form and materials. When teachers show their pupils how to recognise and use visual elements in their work, they increase the children's visual literacy.

This chapter suggests a variety of strategies that teachers can use to increase children's awareness of art elements.

- Colour (page 163)
- Showing form through tone (page 169)
- Textures and patterns (page 172)
- Composition – arranging shapes, lines and colours (page 183)
- Recording shapes and forms – proportion (page 186)
- Recording shapes in space – perspective (page 193)

PoS 8a
Record what is experienced, observed or imagined

Ages and stages through art elements

The Programme of Study states children at KS1 should learn to recognise art elements, rather than be taught consciously to use them. This is to safeguard each child's individual expression.

At the end of KS1 and the beginning of KS2, children begin to view the world more objectively. They often feel unable to formulate and to express their feelings as their private visual language of KS1 grows increasingly inadequate.

Artwork at KS2 sometimes reflects this inadequacy by becoming inhibited, safe and dull. Knowledge of visual and tactile elements therefore becomes an important resource for children at this stage, allowing them to regain some of their former artistic creativity and confidence.

Teaching points involving art elements can be easily integrated into most art lessons. They may only take a few minutes to cover and substantially increase the quality of the work. Teachers may sometimes decide to make an art element the prime focus of a lesson. Examining and mixing warm and cool colours, for example, could take most of a lesson. The mixed colours could be used to make a landscape of a hot or cold planet.

Figure 7.1
This fabric collage picture of a Victorian house involved knowledge of the elements of space, shape, texture, pattern, line and colour. Y6

Looking at art works

PoS 3
Visual literacy

Most art works contain examples of many visual and tactile elements so finding examples of suitable images and artefacts to show children is relatively easy. If resources are short, a few well-chosen reproductions and artefacts can demonstrate all the art elements; although children benefit from applying their knowledge to as many different images as possible.

Reviewing and modifying work

KS1 and KS2, PoS 7d
Pupils should be given opportunities to review and modify their work as it progresses

Once an art element has been introduced, it is useful to make brief references to it whenever possible. At the end of the clearing up, children enjoy discussing what they have learned and done. Did the work come out as they intended? What will they try next time? Children could show their work, describe the source of their ideas and how they adapted these as the work progressed. Discussing each other's work is an important part of the lesson for children but it needs to be done sensitively. Children in the audience should be encouraged to focus on what they like about the work and the owner of the art work could explain how that effect was achieved. This is valuable for language and social development as well as for visual literacy.

Colour

PoS 8e
Experiment with and use ... colour ... to make images and artefacts (for different purposes [KS2]) using the range of media

Colour is central to most areas of the art curriculum and it is also probably the visual element that gives children most pleasure. As children respond so personally and emphatically to colour, it makes an excellent starting point for teaching art elements.

<u>**KNOWLEDGE AND UNDERSTANDING**</u>

PoS 9b
Recognise visual elements in images and artefacts

Artists use colour in many ways. Harmonious hues can act as a unifying theme (Constable *Weymouth Bay*, Shorewood 205); clashing colours produce visually stimulating pictures (Matisse *Interior with eggplants*, Shorewood 1108). Isolated contrasting colours focus attention on an important area of the painting (Goya *The execution of the rebels of the 3rd May*, 1808, Shorewood 1052); a line of contrasting colour directs the eye across a painting (David *Oath of the Horatii*, Shorewood 1269).

Figure 7.2
Hornbill, still-life, in oil pastel. Y6

Children are often attracted to pictures and artefacts with bright colours but they can also learn to appreciate subtle tonal variations by looking at such work as Klee *Sinbad the sailor*, Shorewood 1202, and Berserick *Mother and child*, Goodwill 1(3); Kokoschka *The mandrill*, Shorewood 1210.

ACTIVITY

1 Collect labels and see which colours are used as trademarks for certain products (Y1–Y6). For example yellow and black for Kodak; green, white and black for Heinz; red, yellow and blue for Bird's custard. Children at the end of KS2 could discuss why certain colours predominate on supermarket shelves.

2 Analyse the colours used in artists' work (Y3–Y6).

- Make colour strips to match the colours used by an artist. Cut colours from magazines or fabrics or mix the colours using pastels, pencil crayons or paint and apply them to the strips.

- Arrange the coloured strips into warm and cool colours, or light and dark colours.

Children at KS1 frequently paint patches of colour or overlayer different colours purely for aesthetic pleasure. This spontaneous use of colour is an important asset at this stage and should be encouraged by teaching children how to widen their working colour range through careful colour mixing. They can also be made aware of hot and cool colours, light and dark and seasonal colours as well as colours that make them feel happy or sad. Vocabulary related to colour could include: mixing, matching, dark, light, bright, dull, pale, strong, weak, bold, rich, primary colours, colour wheel, warm, cool.

Figure 7.3
Landscape, made from fabric-collage using harmonious colours. Y5

While young children are very attracted to the vibrancy of strongly contrasting colours, children at KS2 should gradually learn to appreciate the vast and subtle variations in harmonious colours. By Y3 and Y4 children become more skilled in matching colours and in understanding the uses of complementary colours. Their vocabulary could expand to include: tone, tint, hue, shade, opaque, transparent, pure, vivid, secondary colours, complementary colours.

Mixing colours

The British Colour Council recognises more than 6000 colour tones and children need to be taught to recognise that there is a wide variation within each hue. A tree trunk, for example, is usually painted brown by children but on closer examination they will find that most trees have bark with subtle variations of grey–green. It is also useful for children to see colours used by painters, print-makers and fabric designers who have depicted trees – some colours are realistic, others are symbolic.

ACTIVITY

1 Collect old colour charts from DIY shops, art suppliers and printers that show subtle variations in colour (Y1–Y6). Sort and classify them, along with coloured paper, fabrics and objects such as buttons, beads and counters. String the beads into patterns or arrange them according to tone from the palest to the strongest.

2 Make colour jars (Y1–Y6). Collect nine transparent wide-necked jars. Plastic containers from sweet shops are ideal. Make them into colour jars for red, blue, yellow, orange, violet, green, brown, white/cream and black/grey, by putting in items of the correct colour – fabric scraps, pieces of paper from coloured magazines folded and sides glued together, buttons, yarns, leaves, bark, paint samples, shells, stones, small classroom and household objects, such as counters and pegs. Large zip-lock plastic bags make good substitutes for plastic jars.

   • Draw a section of the colour jars (Y3–Y6). Tape a window frame to the outside of one of the colour jars and draw or paint the colours in that section.

3 Collect coloured advertisements with large areas of one colour (Y2–Y6). Cut them into strips and move them around to make a harmonious composition of shapes and tones, or use them to make a paper weaving.

4 Invent names for different tints and tones (Y2–Y6), for example custard-yellow, sandstone-yellow, daffodil-yellow, ice-cream-yellow, dirty-yellow. Young children may need reminding that they are not for eating.

H & S

THE COLOUR WHEEL

PoS 4b
Investigate colour

It was as late as the eighteenth century that a German engraver called Jakob Le Blond discovered that all colours were derived from blue, yellow and red. Soon afterwards, in England, Moses Harris published *The Natural System of Colour* in 1776 with the diagram of a colour wheel. This simple plan showed the exact relationship between the colours.

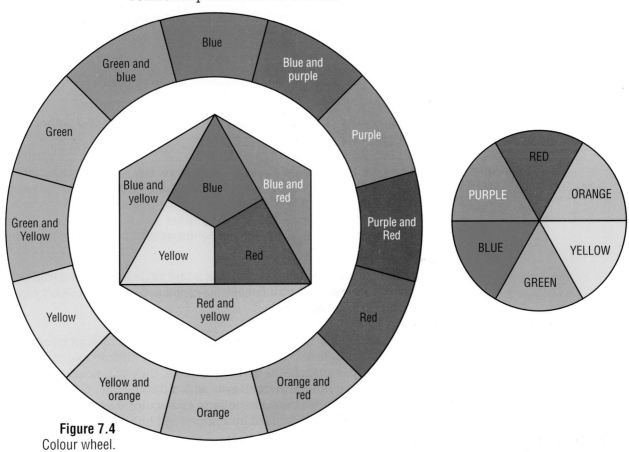

Figure 7.4
Colour wheel.

COLOUR TERMS

PRIMARY COLOURS
The primary colours are red, blue and yellow. They are the basic colours on the colour chart from which all other colours are made.

SECONDARY COLOURS
Each of the secondary colours is a mixture of two of the primary colours:

- red + blue = purple
- blue + yellow = green
- yellow + red = orange

TERTIARY COLOURS
Each tertiary colour is a mixture of a primary and a secondary colour:

- blue + purple = blue-purple
- red + purple = red-purple
- red + orange = red-orange
- yellow + orange = yellow-orange
- yellow + green = yellow-green
- blue + green = blue-green

Other colour terms to know are:

- the hue is the name of a colour
- the intensity of a colour refers to its brightness
- the tone of a colour describes its lightness, or darkness

■ tints are gradations from the original hue to white

■ shades are gradations from the original hue towards black

■ saturated colours are intense primary and secondary colours

■ unsaturated colours are subtle variations of colour obtained by mixing primary and secondary colours. There are about 48 gradual colour changes as you work around the colour wheel

■ local colour is the colour of an object without highlight or shadow

■ harmonious colours are those that are close to each other on the colour wheel

■ complementary colours are those that are opposite to each other on the colour wheel.

ACTIVITY

1 Make colour-mixing bottles (Y2–Y4). Collect three very wide-necked transparent plastic containers from a sweet shop. Fill each one with a diluted ink in a primary colour, leaving space at the top. Fill three narrower bottles with primary colours and insert them into the wide necked jars. If there are no bottles narrow enough to fit, use zip-lock plastic bags. Put the colour bottles against the light to observe the colour mixes.

2 Make coloured spinning tops (Y2–Y4). Cut a card circle and colour it with two primary colours. Push a pencil through the centre and spin. The colours mix to make a secondary colour.

PRACTISING MIXING COLOURS

Paint is the easiest medium in which to practise colour mixing because it can be mixed and tested before it is put on paper. When children use wax crayons, pencil crayons, pastels, chalks and soft pastels, they will need to cover the paper with a light colour and overlayer with a darker one. Children have much less control over colour mixing in collage and sculptures, but knowing how the dyes were mixed in fabrics, card and paper will help them make informed colour choices (see page 164).

PoS 4b
Investigate colour

Relating colours to each other

Colours are never in isolation – they react strongly to the colours near to them. The white of this page is not neutral; white will subdue yellow and heighten red whereas black would heighten yellow and isolate and brighten red.

Pictures that use harmonious colours are very pleasing because the colours support each other and give each individual hue vibrancy and depth.

ACTIVITY

1 Make a colour chart to show how colours react to each other (Y3–Y6). Cut squares of coloured paper and fabric and stick them on a chart. Keep a box of smaller coloured squares near the chart with some Blu-tak (paint samples are ideal). Place the small squares on the larger squares and see whether the background colour increases or decreases the impact of the colour. Red, for example, looks most vibrant on its complementary colour green, but also shines on the black and the white squares. The orange, yellow and purple squares subdue its brightness.

2 Use black outlines to highlight pools of colour in the style of stained-glass windows (English twelfth-century window, Goodwill 1(2)).

3 Use complementary colours to make vibrant pictures (Y3–Y6). When a colour is placed next to its complementary colour, both colours look strong and vibrant. Place a red dragon in a green cavern or an orange snake in a blue lake.

4 Subdue competing complementary colours.

  • If one colour appears to be too dominant in a painting or drawing, 'knock it back' by adding a little of its complementary colour (Y3–Y6).

  • Use a neutral grey or brown to separate complementary colours that are producing a jarring effect because they are too close (Y5–Y6).

Colour groups

Seasonal changes bring dramatic variations in colour which are affected by the light and growth patterns.

ACTIVITY

PoS 2c
Design and make creative images

1 Use coloured fabrics, paints or pastels to create a character from each season (Y1–Y6), for example a spring sprite, Queen Mab in summer, an autumn forest giant, a winter Jack Frost.

2 Mix paint or match paper to seasonal colours and create a seasonal landscape (Y1–Y6).

3 Design a personal wardrobe from seasonal colours (Y1–Y4). An autumn leaf coat, a spring flower skirt, an icicle winter hat.

Figure 7.5
Spring scene, made from paper-collage. Y1

Red, yellow and orange are warm colours. Blue, green and purple are cool colours. Each primary colour has a cooler and a warmer hue. The hot red is the orangey red and the cool red is the more purple red. The warm yellow is the orangey yellow and the cool yellow is the greenish yellow. The warm blue is the purple blue and the cool blue is the greenish blue.

ACTIVITY

1 View the world through coloured cellophane filters (Y1–Y6). Go for a walk and look at the sky and trees. The filters change the scene dramatically; from a stormy day to a forest fire. The children could paint a similar scene when they return to the classroom.

2 Use tints and shades of a hot or a cool colour and then add a touch of a contrast colour as a focal point (Y3–Y4). Reds could be used for a volcano, a fire, a dragon, a phoenix or Venus. Blues could be used for an icy picture of the Ice Queen, Antarctica, swirling water, an ice cave or the North wind.

3 Set up a still-life in warm/cool colour contrast for children to draw or paint (Y3–Y6). The warm hues of tomatoes and bananas, for example, will contrast with the cool greens, of leafy vegetables.

4 Make a grid of curved lines using a curved-edge stencil (Y5–Y6). Start at the centre and use felt-tip pens to colour shapes the warmest colours. Graduate to cooler hues for the shapes nearer to the edges of the grid. This can then be reversed.

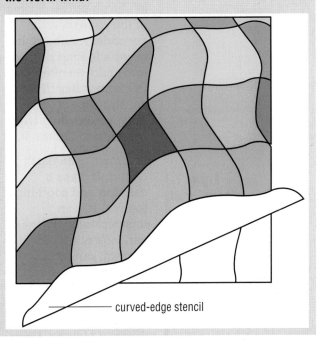

curved-edge stencil

Figure 7.6
Making a colour grid.

LIGHT AND DARK COLOURS

The lightest colours are yellow, yellow-orange and yellow-green. The darkest colours are purple, blue-purple and blue-green.

Cool, pale colours make objects in a picture seem to recede; while warm, bright colours seem to bring objects forward. The receding quality of blue, especially pale blue, is often used by artists to give apparent depth to their pictures.

ACTIVITY

1　Use light and dark colours for dramatic contrasts (Y3–Y6). Use light colours for foreground figures and dark colours for the background. Children in Y5 and Y6 could make a second picture using a reverse colour scheme.

2　Cut out squares of red and blue and stick them next to each other (Y3–Y6). The red appears to project while the blue appears to recede. Try it with other colour combinations. Children at the end of KS2 could use this information when they plan out a colour scheme for a painting.

3　Cover a sheet of white paper with a multi-coloured ink wash (Y3–Y6). When the wash is dry, use pencil to outline simple shapes (leaves, dancing figures). Paint around the shapes to make a black background. The colours of the ink-wash, inside the shapes, glow dramatically in contrast to the black.

COLOURS AND MOODS

PoS 2a
Express ideas and feelings

Colours are powerful conveyers of emotion. Show art works that are predominantly one colour and discuss the mood of the picture – Rothko *Orange and yellow*, Shorewood 1409; Picasso *Mother and child on a beach*, Goodwill 3(25); Delacroix *Frightened horse*, Shorewood 1225.

■　Blue is cold and serene. Together with red, it is the colour most people prefer. It recedes into the distance and has a feeling of calmness, mystery and sometimes sadness.

■　Yellow is hot and the lightest colour. It is warm and bright but becomes much more sinister when slightly muddied.

■　Red is a lively, emotional colour associated with celebrations. Children love its energy and strength. With a slight addition of blue, it is transformed into a colour of danger and anger.

■　Green is a tranquil colour that reminds children of growth and vegetation. It has quite cool and dark overtones.

■　Orange is very warm and full of life and joy. Many fruits are this colour. It evokes a feeling of wealth and confidence.

■　Purple is the darkest of the primary and secondary colours. It gives a feeling of power and children often use it to express fear. This sinister aspect disappears when white is added to lighten it.

■　Brown is an earth colour. It gives a calming and soothing feeling. It is an unsaturated colour and can look neutral beside vibrant, saturated, primary and secondary colours.

Figure 7.7
House and landscape, made using fabric-collage and predominantly brown colours. Y4

 Use Chameleon on 4ANIMATIONS 4M23 and Flare on the Silica Software System, both by Acorn, to experiment with different colour combinations.

1 Use inks, coloured pencils or felt-tip pens to add colour to black and white photographs from magazines (Y4–Y6). Transform stately homes into ice palaces by using cool colours and sunlit meadows into threatening landscapes by using purples and cool reds.

2 Make a picture of a swamp of death and a spring of life; a sunny autumn day with all the leaves bright and shining and a misty, grey autumn day; a still life in tranquil colours muted by white and the same still-life in pure, bright colours (Y5–Y6).

KS1 PoS 4c
Throughout their work, pupils should be taught about . . . how images are made using line and tone

. . . different qualities of line and tone in images (KS2)

Showing form through tone

Form describes the space that objects occupy. It implies a more three-dimensional (3D) element than shape. We can tell the form of a 3D object by the distribution of light and dark on its surface and this can be encouraged in sculpture by constantly turning the model to view it from all sides. In a picture, tones are used by artists to convince the eye that a flat surface is three dimensional.

KNOWLEDGE AND UNDERSTANDING

PoS 3
Visual literacy

Tone can be used for a dramatic or subtle effect in art works. Photographers use stark differences in tone to highlight texture in black and white close-up images. Goldsworthy's *The maple patch*, Ginn 17, shows subtle highlights and shading on a ball of leaves which would otherwise blend into the background of fallen leaves.

When painters contrast very dark shadows with strongly lit areas it is called 'Chiaroscuro', from the Italian for 'clear and obscure'. *Experiment with an air pump* by Joseph Wright, Goodwill 1(7), and *The newborn child* by La Tour, Goodwill 1(7), use this technique. Other artworks have more subtle tonal differences – Vermeer's *Woman in blue*, Shorewood 522; Bening's *Illumination from the Da Costa Book of Hours*, Ginn 15.

ACTIVITY 1 Turn a small sculpture or relief plaque slowly around under a lamp and notice how the tonal areas alter with the movement (Y5–Y6).

2 Ask the children where the light must be coming from in a painting – the sun, a lamp, a candle, a light bulb? Is the light strong or filtered through leaves? (Y2–Y6). What time of day is it? Where are the shadows and what do they tell us about the lighting? (Y3–Y6). Is the light broken up on many surfaces or concentrated in one area? Do the tones contrast sharply or blend together? (Y5–Y6).

AGES AND STAGES

PoS 8e
Experiment with visual elements

Children start drawing and painting at KS1 by using lines and areas of flat colour. The local colour or real colour is recorded without any deeper colour to indicate shadow or lighter colour for highlights. It is only later, during KS2, that children try to make their pictures take a more three-dimensional form by introducing tone.

Any formal teaching on tone and form would not be appropriate at KS1, but children can be made unconsciously more sensitive to tone through direct observation. They could be asked whether one side of an object is lighter than the other and why they think this is. See if the children can locate the main light source in a picture. Young children are fascinated by shadows and this can be a very good starting point for discussions on the source of the light.

In KS2, very simple, light shading and subtle highlighting could be introduced in response to direct observation. By the end of KS2, after studying objects under controlled lighting, some children will be able to include tonal variations in their illustrative and imaginative work.

PoS 4c
Images are made using
line and tone

Shading

Shading can be shown in most two-dimensional art materials. It is easiest in pencil, charcoal, crayon, chalks, pastels and paints, and more difficult in ink drawings, printing, paper collage and fabric collage. Shading in pencil and charcoal is achieved by applying more pressure to achieve a deeper tone. Off-setting is shading (in pencil, charcoal or chalks) which has been rubbed to soften and blend tonal divides. Use a finger or a cloth for large areas and a cotton bud for small areas. For more subtle off-setting, make patches of solid colour on a scrap of paper. Pick the colour up with the finger or a piece of cotton wool and apply it as shading in the drawing. A piece of paper on the outside edge of the shape will give a clean line to the shading.

Children can mix darker and lighter tones of local colour with paints, pastels, felt-tip pens, crayons and chalks. Paper collage and fabric collage are usually left as flat areas of colour but children in Y6 might try tearing or cutting small pieces of gradually darkening tones to suggest shading on a large curved object.

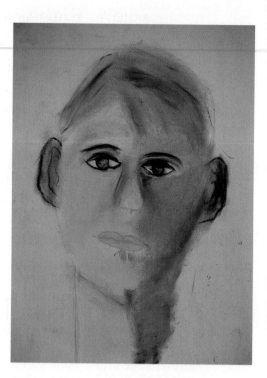

Figure 7.8
Portrait. Direct observational drawing using shading in soft pastels. Y6

AGES AND STAGES

Using increased pressure on pencil, charcoal and chalk to produce areas of darker tone is quite difficult. Children need a great deal of practice before they feel at ease with the flow and rhythm of the movement. In general it is best to introduce it towards the end of KS2. Practise on scraps of paper immediately before using the technique in a drawing. Children at this stage could also use differing pressure on coloured pencils, or overlayer the colours with different greys.

Shading with different colours is much easier to achieve than shading with one colour. Children at the beginning of KS2 can make natural shapes such as trees appear more realistic by using darker tones along one side of the trunk. Children at KS1 could also use different tones of green to show the shadows in foliage.

ACTIVITY

1 Practise reproducing five gradations of tones (Y3–Y6). Go through the tones in a continuous movement, using hard pressure at first and then gradually decreasing it. Keep one gradation as a reference in a sketchbook.

2 Use warm colours (yellow, yellow-green and orange colours) to show highlights and cool colours (blue, purple and green) to show shade (Y5–Y6).

3 Use two complementary colours, in opposite positions on the colour wheel, to represent light and shade (Y5–Y6).

Figure 7.9
An imaginary landscape painting using complementary colours to show light and shade, in liquid gouache. Y6

PoS 2b
Record observations

Highlighting

Highlighting uses patches of light colour to show where light gleams on a surface. A few well-placed highlights can create a strong illusion of form.

AGES AND STAGES

Children at KS1 and the beginning of KS2 should be encouraged to observe gleams of light on shiny surfaces but introducing highlights into their own drawings and paintings needs more caution. If it is introduced too early mechanistic highlights can result in a rash of badly observed white patches. Children at the end of KS2 can be encouraged to record exactly the highlights they see in direct observational work. Use white with a painting, leave patches of white in a colour drawing or use an eraser to remove areas of tone in a pencil drawings. Scraperboard (see page 23) makes an ideal medium for creating dramatic areas of highlights.

ACTIVITY

1 Make direct observational drawings of bottles (Y5–Y6). Their smooth surfaces make simple, easily recorded highlights.

2 Draw shiny metallic surfaces (Y5–Y6). Find a black and white photograph of a shiny metal object, such as a kettle or coffee percolator. Place a piece of thin paper over the photograph and trace over the areas of darkest tone; ignore the light areas. Colour these areas in solid black and leave the remaining area without tone. This will give the drawn surface a very shiny, hard texture.

PoS 2b
Record observations

Shadows

Shadows help to orientate an object on a surface. The shape of a shadow can show whether it is being cast on a rough, smooth, horizontal or vertical surface. Reflections show the presence of water or other 'shiny' surface.

AGES AND STAGES

Although shadows can be discussed in KS1, in general children do not have the skills to place a shadow accurately in a picture until the middle of KS2. A shadow can make a very valuable contribution to a picture but it is very easy to ruin a sensitive drawing or painting with a heavy or badly positioned shadow. Children may need to be reminded to sketch a shadow very lightly and to proceed with caution.

ACTIVITY

1 Outdoor shadows (Y1–Y4). Ask children to observe their own shadows and see how they join to their feet. Show how a shadow does not always fall vertically from the body like a reflection. Notice what happens when a shadow reaches a wall.

2 Draw shadows (Y3–Y6). Take a piece of drawing paper and fold it in half. Draw a figure with feet on the fold and draw the shadow, or reflection, in the other half.

3 Use muted complementary colours to show shadows (Y5–Y6). Give a yellow banana a purple shadow or a red ball a green shadow.

Recording tone in children's work

AGES AND STAGES

PoS 2b
Record observations

When children look around the classroom, the light sources are often numerous – windows on different walls, strip lighting or light bulbs. This makes it very difficult to demonstrate clearly the position of highlights and shading on any object. If the weather is fine, go outside where the sole light source is the sun.

In Y4 or Y5, children may be ready for more formal work of looking at and drawing simple geometric objects in conditions of controlled lighting. The transition from light to dark will look very sudden in straight-edged shapes and very gradual in curved shapes.

In illustrative or imaginative pictures, children at KS2 could use their knowledge from direct observation to decide the location of shading. If they decide on which side of their picture the sun is, subsequent recording of shade and highlights is easier. If there is no sun in the picture, an arrow in faint pencil can act as a reminder of the position of the light source.

SETTING UP LIGHTING IN THE CLASSROOM

In the classroom, switch off the artificial light, locate the main natural source of light and use a desk-light to increase its power. If the room is easily darkened, switch on one overhead light and use a desk-light as the main light source. Light coming from the side of an object, rather than from the back or front, is easier to record.

ACTIVITY

1 Use grey paper as a background for a drawing or painting in white and black (Y4–Y6). This helps children to focus on the white highlights and the dark shadows, leaving grey paper for mid-tones.

2 Record shapes in a sketchbook as a reference for more complex objects (Y5–Y6). A tree trunk, neck and fingers are basically cylinders; skyscrapers are cuboids. They can all be shaded and highlighted in a similar way to the mathematical shapes.

Figure 7.10
Drawing a cylinder, cone and bowl using a stencil.

3 Rub inside positive stencils to make soft gradations of colour within well-defined edges.

Textures and patterns

Main NC focus

PoS 4a
Throughout their work, pupils should be taught about . . . pattern and texture in natural and made forms (KS1)

. . . the use of pattern and texture in designing and making (KS2)

Figure 7.11
Flowing water pattern, in batik. Y4

Patterns are sometimes defined as shapes arranged in repetition across a page. Repetition is certainly an important aspect of pattern making, but irregularities within repetitions can also add excitement. Patterns can be flowing and soothing, jagged and strident, with a regular beat or with an irregular rhythm. Line, shape, space and colour can all be used to create the rhythms.

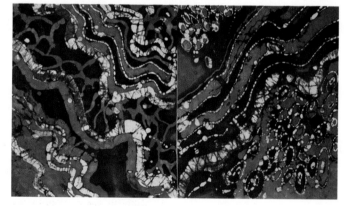

Texture is easily confused with pattern. Texture is purely what can be felt, (although it often has a pattern to it). Bark on a tree has a pattern which is also a texture. Polished wood has a pattern of grain but this is not reflected in the texture of the smooth surface.

KNOWLEDGE AND UNDERSTANDING

PoS 3
Ideas, feelings and meanings are communicated in different visual forms

In three-dimensional work an artist can create an actual texture (West Indian Carnival Costume, Ginn 21). In two-dimensional work the impression of texture is created by using line and tone. Drawings of a basketball, a tennis ball and a golf ball all have the same basic shape. It is the artist's depiction of texture that informs the viewer of what the object is.

Artists also use texture to create atmosphere. Smooth textures have a peaceful effect, whereas jagged textures convey energy. The dramatic jagged rocks in Patenier's *Saint Jerome on a rocky landscape*, Ginn 24, are dominant and give a forceful image of nature's power in a wilderness setting. An unexpected or sharply contrasting texture can also focus attention. A smooth circle of red in Gottlieb's *Brink* is placed in opposition to a spiky texture in the lower section of the painting, Shorewood 1406.

There are many examples of beautifully patterned fabrics in portraits: Bronzino *Eleanore and son*, Shorewood 112; Oliver *Two little girls*, Ginn 33. Islamic art also provides a rich resource for ideas on pattern making. Islam does not allow any representational figures, so creative energy in the visual arts is often channelled into pattern making (Turkish ceramic tiles from Iznik, Ginn 42). In Britain, William Morris and the nineteenth-century Arts and Crafts movement recognised the aesthetic value of pattern.

ACTIVITY

PoS 7f
Respond to and evaluate art

1 Supply a variety of textures for children to feel and match with textures in art works (Y1–Y6). Compare a piece of brocade with rich fabric in a portrait; a jagged stone with a rocky landscape; a smooth pebble with a picture of a marble statue.

2 Questions to ask about art works (Y3–Y6). Are the lines thick or thin, light or heavy, straight or twisting, isolated or overlayered? Is there a variety of textures and patterns or is there a unifying theme? Is there a repeated motif and does it have any significance for the picture?

3 Make a border using Islamic or nineteenth-century motifs (Y5–Y6).

4 Isolate an area of an art work (Y3–Y6). Choose a rectangle of pattern in a portrait or a painting by Matisse and make a similar pattern in pastels, collage or paint.

AGES AND STAGES

Exploring texture is a valuable starting point for many art lessons. In general once children have explored the texture of wood they feel much more confident about completing a direct observational study of a piece of bark.

Pattern making is accessible to children of every ability and age level – even the simplest of designs can be very satisfying. Children who feel unsure of their abilities in other areas of art, craft and design frequently gain confidence through the pride they take in their pattern-making skills.

Most children at KS1 use pattern intuitively in their paintings and drawings. Experimenting with different arrangements of objects, shapes and colours is a vital phase before the more disciplined work of repeat patterns.

Pattern making can be very closely linked with children's work in mathematics at all stages. At KS1, pattern making reinforces children's concepts of line, shape, symmetry and sequencing. At KS2, pattern and mathematics share an interest in , rotating and repeat patterns, regular and irregular shapes, lines, angles, and curves and making logical sequences.

Figure 7.12
Corkscrew, using a cut-shape print. The slight break in rhythm adds interest to an otherwise static pattern.

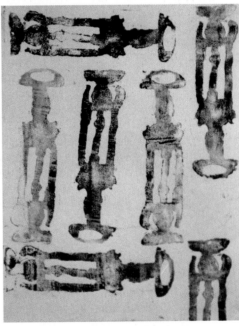

PoS 2b
Record observations

Looking at textures and patterns in the environment

Rocks, wood, fur and feathers, figure drawing, shells and cut fruit and vegetables all make interesting subjects for studying texture and pattern. Arrange the objects in still-life studies to make a striking contrast between the different textures and patterns.

AGES AND STAGES

The more children explore things through touch, the more they will represent texture in their art work – a smooth table top, rough bark, the undulating surface of a shell. Ask them to describe the texture. Is the surface soft and silky or hard and bristly? Is it pitted or smooth? Is it coarse-grained or shiny?

Children at KS2 could discuss any practical function that a pattern might have. A fence needs the vertical pattern of shapes for height and the horizontal pattern for rigidity; bricks are arranged to give maximum strength to the wall. Study shop windows and supermarkets and observe how objects are arranged in visual patterns to attract the shopper. Patterns can communicate – many motifs have a cultural significance – the flowers on narrow boats, the repeated images in Aboriginal paintings.

Figure 7.13
Squirrel with a fluffy tail, drawn using scraperboard. Y4

ACTIVITY

1 Spray a cabbage leaf with a metallic paint to highlight the texture (Y1–Y2).

2 Make a feely-box (Y1–Y6). Tape up a large box and use a craft knife to cut a large flap at the front. Post interestingly-textured objects into the box. Ask children to lift up the flap and feel the objects, to describe them and then try to identify them. If they guess the object quickly, ask them to explain why they knew it was that object.

3 Use different media to record textures and patterns (Y1–Y6).

   • Take prints or rubbings of objects with interesting surfaces and patterns. Wood with a pronounced grain, textured anaglypta paper, a whole fish, a hand, slices of a mushroom, green pepper, onion or cabbage.

   • Use modelling materials, such as clay or playdough, to record both dramatic and subtle texture changes.

4 Draw the textures of the body (Y3–Y6).

   • Draw a pencil line around the front and the back of a hand placed on a piece of paper. Children at the end of KS2 could draw the shape from direct observation. Look carefully at the marks on the back of the hand and record them in the first outline. Do the same with the front of the hand in the second outline.

   • Draw hair (Y3–Y6). A whole class can participate in a drawing lesson by sitting in a large circle, facing the back of the head of the child in front. Support the paper on clip-boards.

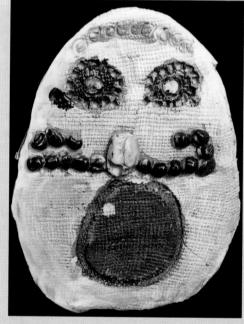

5 Make a reference page of patterns and textures in a sketchbook (Y5–Y6).

   • Divide pages of a sketchbook up into small squares and make a chart of patterns and textures from direct observation and from imaginative doodles. Use a variety of drawing media and use the squares as references for future art work.

   • Use a sketchbook to draw and analyse in detail the textures and patterns in an object (Y5–Y6). A flower could be sketched as a simple motif, as a silhouetted shape, as a set of linked shapes, or with the stamens enlarged and exaggerated. Use coloured pencils to experiment with different colour combinations. Decide on a design task and develop the most suitable pattern.

Tip!

Keep the feely-box under close supervision. Timid children (and most adults) need to have the security that nothing alive or unpleasant is inside.

Figure 7.14
Mask, made from clay. Fabric was rollered on to the clay to produce interesting texture. Y2

PoS 4c
Images are made using line and tone

Line in texture and pattern

Line is an important element in art, craft and design. The eye is drawn along the path of a line and any break in the rhythm focuses the attention.

<u>KNOWLEDGE AND UNDERSTANDING</u>

PoS 5c
Examine styles from a variety of cultures

Figure 7.15
Wood grain, in ink. Y1

To show the way artists and craftspeople use line, look at pictures of gravel patterns created in Japanese gardens, the flowing lines of O'Keeffe's *Grey line with black, blue and yellow* and *From the lake no. 1*, Shorewood 1760 and 1779, and the great arcs of dripping paint in Pollock's *Mural*,

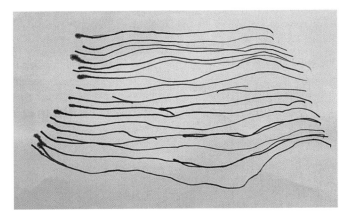

Shorewood 1412. These flowing lines could be contrasted with Mondrian's *Composition no. 2*, Shorewood 596, which demonstrates the strength and stability of straight lines.

ACTIVITY

Paint flowing lines using dripping paint (Y1–Y6). Any paint can be used but gloss or household enamel paint has the best flow and density of colour that make it ideal for this technique. When the paint is dry, children love to ripple their hands over the raised glossy surface. Use paint cleaner to remove any spots.

- Use a stick or a brush to make sweeping lines and patterns (Y1–Y2).

- Drip paint on to the paper and then tilt the paper in various directions (Y3–Y4).

- Make Lissajous curves (Y5–Y6). These were named after a French physicist who studied the science of movement. Max Ernst enjoyed using this technique in his paintings.
a) Cut the bottom off an empty plastic washing-up bottle. Cut three holes near to the edge of the cut. Thread three pieces of string through the holes and draw them together to make a pendulum.
b) Create a space between two desks and tape a metre rule across the gap. Cover the floor with newspaper. Tie the pendulum to the ruler. Tape two large sheets of black paper together and place them under the pendulum.
c) Keeping the cap tightly in place, fill the

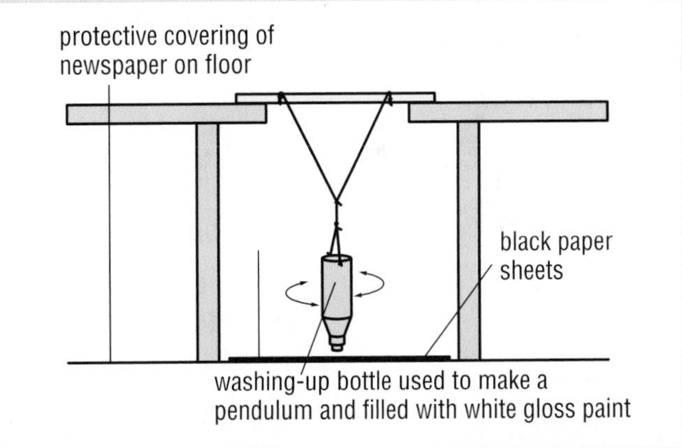

Figure 7.16
Making a pendulum.

protective covering of newspaper on floor

black paper sheets

washing-up bottle used to make a pendulum and filled with white gloss paint

Figure 7.17
Lissajous pattern. Y4

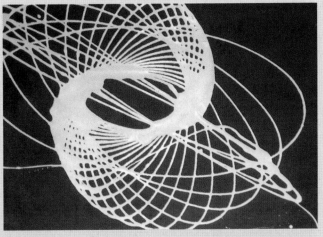

bottle up with white gloss paint. Using rubber gloves, uncap the hole and quickly swing the pendulum, altering its course at intervals to create an interesting design. Stop up the hole when enough curves have been made.

AGES AND STAGES

Drawing or painting a line in KS1 is usually a dynamic process. It can be made with speed or with deliberation, with twists and turns, smoothly and lightly, heavily and sombrely, jerking, weaving or falling and rising.

In KS2, children can be encouraged to continue with this spontaneity of line, using tone to show the depth of the texture, and different pressures and directions to indicate changing surfaces.

Figure 7.18
Wood, in pencil. Y5

ACTIVITY

1 Make patterns with straight lines (Y1–Y6).

- Make radial 3D patterns (Y1–Y2). Press art straws into a ball of softened clay or Plasticine to make a sculpture with radiating lines.

- Cut out paper strips with scissors or a paper cutter (Y1–Y6). Arrange patterns in horizontal or vertical lines, or a mixture of the two. Frame the pattern in a contrasting shape, such as a circle or a triangle.

2 Create sweeping linear patterns (Y3–Y6).

- Dip a comb, scrubbing brush, sponge or a feather in paint and pull it across a page or create circles (Y3–Y6). Do the patterns remind the children of anything – a flowing stream, a mop of hair, a windswept sky, a grizzly beard? One of the patterns could be used as a focal point for an imaginary scene.

- Cut notches into the side of a piece of chalk and pull the cut side over the paper in swirling patterns.

- Use felt-tip pens held together with an elastic band. Make sweeping movements on a paper of a contrasting colour.

- Make a pattern of lines around shapes in the style of a Japanese garden.

Decorative patterns and borders

Decorative art aims to make everyday objects attractive and memorable. Patterns are used by designers to decorate walls, furniture, containers, fabrics, floors and even the soles of shoes.

KNOWLEDGE AND UNDERSTANDING

PoS 5a
Examine styles in the locality

Examples of decorative design can be brought into school – furnishing fabrics, curtains, wallpaper, a cushion, apron or a shopping bag. Children at KS2 could discuss whether the object's function has influenced the pattern design. The school's outside walls may provide interesting examples of pattern being used to make a building attractive. Windows are necessary to let in light but an architect usually arranges the windows to provide a pleasing pattern on the outer structure (Durham Cathedral and the buildings in Lorenzetti *The effects of good government*, Ginn 39 and 53).

PoS 5c
Examine styles from a variety of cultures

Look at examples of decorative art from other cultures (*Traffic art: Rickshaw painting*, Goodwill 1(4)). The paisley design originated in India; Mendhi patterns are made in henna to decorate hands and feet during celebrations in North Africa, India and Pakistan. Look at illuminated letters for ideas on decorating inside shapes (French fourteenth century illuminated letter A, Goodwill 2(11); *St Matthew, Book of Kells*, late eighth century, Trinity College Dublin; *The initials B and C*, thirteenth-century manuscript, British Museum).

ACTIVITY

1 **Create decorative letters (Y3–Y6).**

- **Make patterns inside paper cut-outs of children's initials and interweave them to make a monogram. Children with short first names could pattern all of their name.**

- **Make clay plaques with decorated letters in relief.**

2 **Study designs from different times and cultures and adapt their motifs (Y3–Y6).**

- **Use a net for a cuboid to design a medieval chest or Victorian jewellery box .**

AGES AND STAGES

PoS 2c
Design and make creative artefacts and images

Creating patterns that will be used for decoration is a very important part of the design process. Children at KS1 could make patterned wallpaper for the playhouse or a patterned fabric 'magic carpet'. They could create patterns for calendars, greetings cards, carrier bags, decorated paper plates or napkins or they could wrap patterns around tins to make Winnie the Pooh 'useful pots' for pencils, pens or string.

Children at KS2 should relate their designs more closely to the function of the object they are patterning – a leaf pattern for the cover of a book on conservation, a personal motif on gift wrapping. Y6 pupils could also use regular, close-patterned designs for differentiating areas in map-work.

Border patterns are very attractive but time consuming, so it is probably best to restrict them to special pieces of written work. Y1 children could make simple zig-zag lines, while children in Y5 and Y6 might use an italic pen to make scrolls and graceful, curving lines.

ACTIVITY

PoS 4a
Investigate pattern and texture

1 **Make random, decorative patterns (Y1–Y6).**

- **Sprinkle powdered fabric dye or Easibrush ink powder on wet, white cartridge paper (Y1–Y4). There will be a dramatic explosion of colours and shapes.**

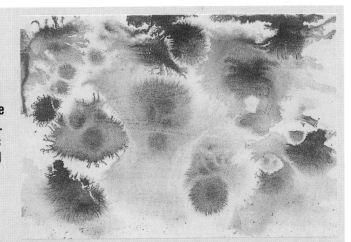

Figure 7.19
Powdered fabric dye on wet paper. Y1

- **Marbling inks make attractive swirls of colour (Y2–Y6).**

2 **Make decorative overlapping shapes (Y2–Y6). Ask children to make a card template of an interesting shape, such as a leaf or use a hand. Draw around the shapes and overlap them. Retrace the lines in heavy wax crayon. Colour in some spaces and overlaps and wash over with coloured inks.**

3 **Design richly decorated clothes, patterns for trainer soles, skateboards or rollerblades (Y3–Y4).**

4 **Make decorative borders (Y1–Y6).**

- **Draw border patterns on both sides of a strip of card (Y1–Y6). Cover the card on both sides with wide Sellotape and use it for a bookmark or a wristband.**

- **Mark the boundaries of a border (Y3–Y4). Draw along the top and bottom of a narrow strip of thick card. Draw patterns inside the lines.**

Poster 4MATION 4M13 is an Acorn computer program that produces 15 borders for written work. The computer program *Islam* on Junior Maths 2 Disc by EARO, Acorn's *Tiling* program in TOPOLOGIKA TOP011 can be used for tessellating shapes. Use EDG GRAPHICS on the BBC AVP program to create shapes and to multiply and arrange them in patterns.

Patterns based on symmetry

Children's knowledge of mathematical shapes can be extended and reinforced through making patterns based on symmetry.

KNOWLEDGE AND UNDERSTANDING

PoS 5a
Examine styles in the locality

Figure 7.20
Symmetrical butterfly, in paper-collage. Y6

Islamic patterns are a rich source of symmetrical designs but there are also many examples in everyday objects. Faces, bodies, insects, leaves, flowers, fruit, shells, coral, fishes, all have axes of symmetry that can be related to pattern making. Bath towels often have large and colourful symmetrical patterns. Some designs have perfect symmetry (Pre-Colombian figure pendant, Ginn 23); others initially look symmetrical but on closer examination children find that they incorporate small variations (Peacock brooch by Lalique, Ginn 22).

PoS 5c
Examine styles from a variety of cultures

Circular patterns often use more than one axis of symmetry. Many ancient patterns from Egypt and South America were based on a circle because it symbolised the continuity of life. Christian portraits of holy figures often showed decorative halos (Bondone *Madonna and child*, Shorewood 125). 'Mandala' comes from the Sanskrit for 'circle' or 'round'. Hindus and Buddhists use mandala patterns for ritual dancing, meditation and protection.

Look for patterns based on a circle in the immediate environment – wheels, watch faces, the patterns on plates, brooches, buckles and stained-glass rose-windows in churches. Examine natural patterns that radiate from a centre – sections of kiwi, starfruit and all the citrus fruits; spiders' webs, shells and spiral staircases. Use a magnifying glass to look closely at the whorls of lines on the fingertips.

ACTIVITY

1 **Make designer watches in paper-collage (Y2–Y6). Fold the paper to make symmetrical, circular and duplicate shapes and arrange them along a strap and on the watch-face. Fix the hands of the watch with split-pins (see Figure 4.10 on page 89).**

2 **Make symmetrical Maori facial patterns (Y5–Y6).**

   • **Cut out front views of faces from magazines and draw symmetrical facepaint patterns with felt-tip pens.**

   • **Use face paints to make symmetrical face patterns on a friend's face.**

Acorn's program *Pattern* in TOPLOGICAL TOP011 makes patterns by joining dots on a grid.

AGES AND STAGES

PoS 4d
Investigate shape, form and space

Symmetry is a theme that can be explored at all stages. At KS2, PE lessons could be used to make symmetrical shapes with a partner. Once the concept of symmetry is secure, children can break away from the static nature of a symmetrical pattern by introducing an element of the unexpected.

Children at KS1 find it quite a challenge to arrange a pattern in a circle.

Children at this stage are very responsive to background shape, so a circular background stimulates circular patterns. By the beginning of KS2, children become sufficiently confident to make a circular pattern within a rectangular background. More complex circular patterns can be made with compasses or with a card template fixed with a split-pin to the centre of the paper.

MAKING SYMMETRICAL PATTERNS

ACTIVITY
1 **Make symmetrical weaving patterns (Y2–Y6).**

Fold a piece of white paper in half and cut from the fold to within 2 cm from the edge in a series of wavy lines. Open the paper to make a paper loom. Cut black strips of paper in various widths and weave them through the lines. Push the pieces closely together to maximise the flow of the pattern. Look at paintings of rippling water and use similar colours in the warp and the weft.

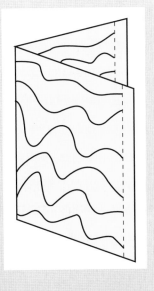

Figure 7.21
Cutting and weaving paper to show the warp and weft.

2 **Use carbon paper to draw a symmetrical shape (Y2–Y4).**
a) Fold over a piece of thin paper. Place a piece of carbon paper inside, folded in the same way making sure that the inked sides touch the paper.
b) Draw a shape from the folded edge. A ball-point pen gives crisper lines than a pencil. The carbon will transfer the image to the other side. The pattern can be opened and examined at any time.
c) Open the paper and trace over the faint lines made by the carbon to make a complete symmetrical shape.

• Fold the paper and the carbon paper into quarters to make a pattern with two axes of symmetry (Y3–Y4).

• If carbon paper is not available, make a simple symmetrical shape by drawing one side of a design on thin paper with a dark line. Hold the folded paper against a light source and trace the other side of the design (Y5–Y6).

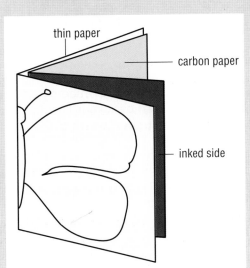

thin paper

carbon paper

inked side

Figure 7.22
Using carbon paper to draw symmetrical shapes and an Egyptian head example of the technique. Y3

ACTIVITY

3 Explore patterns with more than one axis of symmetry (Y5–Y6).

- Arrange printed or cut shapes in circles and semicircles (Y1–Y6).

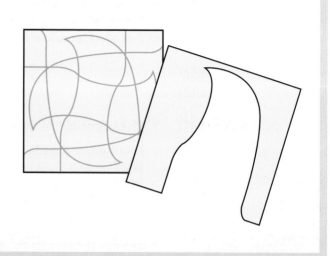

- Rotate a template inside a shape (Y3–Y4).
  a) Cut out two identical regular shapes, one in card and one in paper – a square, an equilateral triangle, a star or any polygon.
  b) Cut into one side of the card shape to make a simple shape that reaches well over half way across to the other side.

Figure 7.23
Using a rotating template.

  c) Place the card over the paper shape and draw around the cut internal shape. Rotate the card and draw the shape against the next edge. Keep rotating until all the sides have been reached.
  d) Retrace the lines in black ink or colour areas of the pattern with paints, pastels, crayons or felt tips.

- Use mirrors to plan the pattern (Y6). Set up two mirrors at an angle of 90° and fix them with Blu-tak. Arrange shapes in front of the mirrors and the pattern will be multiplied by four. Use the best design to make a pattern.

Repeat patterns

An extremely simple pattern of repeated, interesting shapes looks striking as long as a sequence is followed through. Patterns that consistently repeat the same image are called translated designs. These repeated images can also be rotated to form more complex patterns.

Figure 7.24
Paper collage pattern with an interesting break in sequence. Y4

Variety can be added to a simple sequence by changing the colour or size of a shape. If the rhythm of a repeat pattern is becoming dull, children can always introduce an irregularity or sudden break in the rhythm.

KNOWLEDGE AND UNDERSTANDING

PoS 9a
Identify local artists, craftspeople and designers

Children should be able to find repeat patterns in buildings, drain covers, tiled floors and ceilings, wallpapers, containers, watches and electronic equipment. Look at simple grids formed by graph paper, wire mesh, fruit boxes, tiles, pigeon-holes and fabric prints.

Repeat patterns are often based on simple grids but an artist may add interest with complex sequences (from Nigeria *Adire cloth*, Shorewood 1804). The *Turkish ceramic tiles from Iznik*, Ginn 42, have interesting examples of repeated patterns extending into adjacent shapes.

ACTIVITY 1 Make brick patterns (Y1–Y6). Children at KS1 and the beginning of KS2 often find it easier to draw brick patterns than print or glue them.

- Make a monoprint (Y1–Y2). Roller out printing inks, draw in a brick pattern, lay over a piece of paper and take a print.

- Use a firmly drawn wax crayon line and wash over with coloured inks (Y3–Y4).

- Experiment with more complicated brick designs using the side of a brick, as well as the front (Y5–Y6). Use a 1 cm grid to plan a sequence first.

AGES AND STAGES

Tip!

Shapes that touch are easier to make into an accurate pattern. Encourage the children to make a note of where the shapes touch and try to duplicate that position.

Simple translated designs are suitable for KS1 when children need practice in aligning shapes, or in KS2 when a complex design needs a simple setting. In Y1, priority is usually given to working from left to right in horizontal lines in order to reinforce writing patterns. Children could then try diagonal, vertical, curved or undulating lines. Children at KS1 can also be introduced to rotating patterns. Work with the three elements: shape, size and colour. Start by keeping two of these art elements constant and vary the third, usually colour.

By the beginning of KS2 children will be able to vary two of the elements of shape, size and colour, keeping one constant. Children at the end of KS2 could learn how to plan a repeat pattern on a three-dimensional object so that the images are equally distributed and also plan repeat designs where the lines flow from one motif to the next.

SIMPLE SEQUENCES

PoS 2c
Design and make creative images

Figure 7.25
Diamond shapes, using incised Polyblock print. The lines across the corners join to form the diamond shapes. Y3

Shapes can be arranged in a line. Visualising the direction of a line before beginning a pattern helps to maintain a strong, well-positioned composition. Simple horizontal lines give a pleasing gravity very suitable for marching figures. Diagonal lines add lightness and movement.

A grid can be used to divide up paper in regular shapes to help align a pattern. Fold a square of paper vertically and horizontally to make a grid. Children at the end of KS2 could use a ruler to measure and lightly draw a grid. Alternatively, use square-shaped printing blocks or paper shapes that are based on a square; place them slightly separated for a tiled effect or close together to blend into one flowing pattern (see Figure 7.25).

Staggered repeat patterns follow a pattern similar to a brick wall; one line of shapes is placed underneath and between the shapes above. The axis can be straight or tilted.

ACTIVITY Transfer a complex design with tissue paper (Y5–Y6). Draw a design on tissue paper and prick over the lines with a pin. Hold the smooth side of the tissue paper next to the surface to which the design is to be transferred. Rub over the tissue paper with cotton wool dipped in powdered chalk and repeat the design. The chalky deposit acts as a guide for the drawing or painting medium.

ROTATING GRID PATTERNS

PoS 8e
Experiment with visual elements

Simply rotating the repeated shape through 90° or 180° at each square makes an exciting pattern. Start with a very simple shape and record the sequence on the side of the pattern, as a future reference. For collage patterns use multiple copies of the same shape. Lightly number the sides of the first square on the grid. Choose a sequence of, for example: 1, 3, 1, 3. Place the base of the shape to side one for the first square and to side three for the second. Carry on the sequence.

For printing, number each side on the back of the printing block.

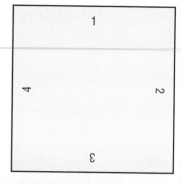

Figure 7.26
Numbers on a square for use in repeat patterns.

ACTIVITY

1 Create a swirling effect with a linear pattern by overprinting the original pattern with a different alignment (Y3–Y6). Start the second print with a different side and use a new colour.

2 Experiment with different sequences (Y3–Y6).

• Try the same sequence with an odd number of squares at the top and then with an even number. In general an odd number makes a more varied and interesting pattern.

• Try to anticipate which designs will result in interesting patterns. Lines that go diagonally across a square produce patterns with strong movement.

Figure 7.27
Rotating pattern using incised polyblock and printing inks. Y3

COUNTER-CHANGE PATTERNS

Use 1 cm square graph paper for a grid and felt-tip pens or pencil crayons for colouring the squares.

a The simplest pattern is made by colouring alternate squares

b Divide squares horizontally or vertically and colour alternate rectangles

c Divide each square diagonally, but alternate the direction of the shape

d Colour the left-hand triangle on each square

e Colour alternate sides

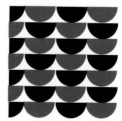

f Use curved shapes to divide the squares

Figure 7.28
Counter-change patterns.

 Patterned tiles in the Acorn computer program TOPOLOGICAL TOP011 give the chance to explore a vast range of patterns that can be made from four two-coloured squares.

Composition – arranging shapes, lines and colours

Main NC focus

*KS1 PoS 4d
Throughout their work,
pupils should be taught
about . . . the use of shape,
form and space in images
and artefacts*

*. . . how shape, form and
space are presented in
images and artefacts (KS2)*

Good design is dependent on harmonious relationships between shape, form and space. Discussing composition encourages children to think about these visual elements in their own work.

AGES AND STAGES

Most children at KS1 naturally place images to achieve a beautifully balanced composition. In Y1, children often put in extra fingers on hands, or legs on animals just to fill in spaces and balance a picture. Discussions about composition can take place in an informal way when looking at artists' work or discussing why a child's picture has been particularly successful.

Moving paper shapes around on a contrasting background helps to introduce children in Y3 and Y4 to the basic elements of composition. Limiting colours to black on white or white on black helps children to focus on space and shape which are the most important visual elements – a weak shape that is badly placed causes a design to fail, no matter how strong the colour arrangement. Colour could be introduced as an additional factor at a later stage.

At the end of KS2, children benefit from briefly discussing elements of line and shape and the value of a focal point before beginning a composition. As work progresses, children could hold their picture sideways, upside down and even look at it through a mirror. This helps to obtain a fresh view, and to see a picture as an abstract set of shapes, colours and spaces that need to be in balance. If children are taking such care with their compositions, it is important that any trimming of the work reflects the balance that has been achieved – a white area at the side may be an important part of a composition.

KNOWLEDGE AND UNDERSTANDING

*PoS 9e
Describe and express
opinions about works of
art*

Art works provide the most valuable basis for discussions on composition. Non-representational art is particularly useful in demonstrating the impact of a skilful arrangement of line, shape and space. What part of the picture or sculpture do we look at first? Are the forms balanced, symmetrical; or deliberately unbalanced? Are the shapes large or small, in flat colour or detailed; isolated or joined? What are the lines that join the shapes together and how do they affect the mood? The triangle shape made by the figures in Labasque's *Eating on the lawn*, Goodwill 1(3), gives a feeling of calm and stability to the composition and also points to the trees in the background.

Symmetrical and asymmetrical compositions

*PoS 3
Visual literacy*

Some artists achieve balance in their compositions using symmetry (when the two halves of a work are identical or very nearly identical) (the Master of the Saint Bartholomew altarpiece *The virgin and child with musical angels*, Ginn 44). Symmetrical compositions have a balance that can be very attractive despite being static. Slight adjustments can create interest without spoiling balance (Grünewald *The small crucifixion*, Shorewood 566).

Symmetrical objects look best placed near to the centre of a piece of paper slightly to one side. This reflects the balance of the shape (Botticelli *Birth of Venus*, Shorewood 110) but avoids cutting the page in two. In general artists avoid lines that cut a composition in half, either vertically, horizontally or diagonally. A division of two-thirds to one-third is a conventional proportion (Van Gogh *Starry night*, Shorewood 1399).

Asymmetrical compositions have a long tradition in Asia and greatly influenced European and American artists at the end of the nineteenth century. Artists achieve balance, not because the two sides have very similar shapes or colours, but because the two halves' visual weight is the same. This visual weight is determined by colour, texture, size and number.

A dark shape appears to be heavier than a light shape – a small dark shape can balance a large light shape.

A textured shape appears to be heavier than a smooth shape – a small, textured shape can balance a large, smooth shape.

A large shape is heavier than a small shape, although a collection of small shapes can balance a large shape (Degas *La classe de dance*, Goodwill 3(23)).

Space can balance an object so moving objects, such as a runner or a spaceship, are often given space to move into. (Degas *Two dancers on stage*, Shorewood 1200).

In general it is better to use odd numbers when deciding on how many objects to put in a composition. It is not known why this is – perhaps an unpaired object focuses the eye.

Sometimes artists deliberately create an unbalanced composition for a feeling of unease, movement or humour (Tanguy *The rock palace*, Shorewood 1389).

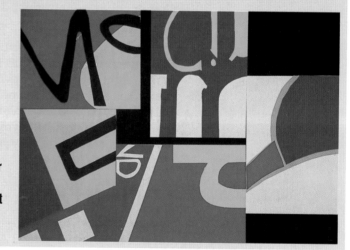

ACTIVITY

PoS 7e
Use knowledge of artists' work

1   Isolate small sections of an advertisement, package or famous painting by moving a rectangular frame, cut from card, over the surface (Y3–Y6). Use this viewfinder to select an area with an interesting balance of colour and shape and reproduce the shapes and colours on a larger scale.

2   Make paper-cuts in the rough size, colour and geometric shape of the objects in paintings (Y5–Y6). Move the paper shapes around to experiment with different compositional arrangements.

Figure 7.29
These paper collage designs are enlarged sections of drink cans.

 Use the BAYEUX section of SPA to move the figures, boats and horses around to compose a version of the Bayeux Tapestry. Move rubber-stamp images around to make lively compositions on KID PIX and KID PIX COMPANION borderbund 165005 and 165006.

Support shape

PoS 9d
Respond to and compare different styles and traditions

The shape of a support also influences the balance of a picture. Artists traditionally refer to a piece of paper as being in the landscape position or portrait position. In general landscapes are on rectangles with the longest sides horizontal. In Dyce's *Pegwell Bay*, Ginn 51, long horizontal lines give a broad, sweeping view and promote feelings of peace and tranquillity. Portraits are usually drawn on rectangles where the longest side is vertical. This generally fits the shape of a person and a vertical line leads the eye upwards towards the face (da Vinci *Mona Lisa*, Shorewood 509). Not every portrait or landscape has to conform to this practice. A figure lying down needs to be drawn landscape (Goya *Maja clothed*, Shorewood 308). A landscape with a lot of sky or featuring a tall tree or building will often be on paper placed the portrait way (Vermeer *Little Street*, Shorewood 534). Other shapes are also used. Circles are very popular in Chinese paintings and are also used in western portraits and landscapes (Raphael *The Alba Madonna*, Shorewood 101; Avercamp *A winter scene with skaters near a castle*, Ginn 25).

ACTIVITY

1 Give practice in selecting portrait or landscape positions for supports (Y1–Y6).

2 Work in the round (Y1–Y6)

• Give out circular pieces of paper or fabric for children to work on.

• Cut circular frames inside square pieces of paper to lay on top of a painting, collage or drawing.

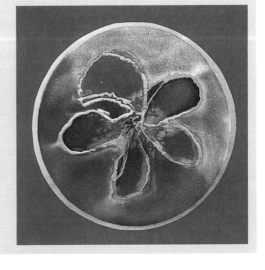

Figure 7.30
Orchid, painted on silk and worked on an embroidery hoop. Y5

'Invisible' lines

PoS 3
The way ideas, feelings and meanings are communicated in visual form

Artists often position shapes and lines so that they form a kind of internal structure. Seurat believed that a vertical line symbolised gaiety (*Le cirque*, Goodwill 2(13)). A diagonal line usually gives movement and drama to a design (Rousseau *Tropical storm with a tiger (surpris!)*, Ginn 5). Horizontal lines give a feeling of harmony and peace. Sometimes it is necessary to disturb this slightly to add interest. In Devis' *Family group in a garden*, Ginn 46, the long lines of a terrace and family group are broken by the standing father. A curved line makes a graceful movement and encourages the eye to keep within the picture. In Botticelli's *Birth of Venus*, Shorewood 110, the curve of the shell is reflected in the curve of the surrounding figures. A triangle gives a feeling of balance and harmony. It can also be used to direct attention to a focal point. The sides of the hill in *The virgin and the child with musical angels*, Ginn 44, form a triangle at whose apex lies the Christ Child.

ACTIVITY

Observe art works and see if children can pick out the 'invisible lines' in sculptures and paintings (Y3–Y6). Discuss children's work that shows a good use of line.

Focal points

PoS 7f
Respond to and evaluate art

Artists use visual and tactile elements to focus attention on important aspects of an art work. The craggy, white rocks in Patenier's *Saint Jerome in a rocky landscape*, Ginn 24, are grouped together and lead the eye downwards to the figures. Strong lines such as a horizon, fences, hedges and walls are often used to lead the eye towards a focal point. In general the eye 'reads' from left to right, so artists tend to lead the eye from the left into the picture (Degas *Dancing class*, Shorewood 1134). Contracting perspective lines of paths, roads, railway lines, rivers or canals often lead the eye from the outside of a drawing into the centre (Monet *Beach at Trouville*, Shorewood 1713).

Window frames, mirrors, doorways, the arch of a bridge or the overhanging branches of a tree can all be used to frame a focal point and draw attention to it (Friedrich *The chalk cliffs of Rugen*, Shorewood 603).

ACTIVITY

1 Look at artists' and children's work and discuss where the focal point is placed and what attracts the eye to it (Y1–Y6).

2 Position a focal point carefully (Y5–Y6).

• Divide a piece of paper into thirds; either horizontally, diagonally or vertically. Place a focal point on one of the imaginary lines.

Figure 7.31
Landscape, in paper collage. The eye focuses on the red roof and then follows the path of the stream in an inwardly direction. Y2

• Form the imaginary dividing lines into a grid. Wherever the lines intersect makes a good focal point.

3 Frame a focal point with shapes such as trees (Y5–Y6).

Main NC focus

KS1 and KS2 PoS 2 In order to develop visual perceptions, pupils should be taught . . . the practical skills needed to . . . record observations (and) design and make images and artefacts

Recording shapes and forms – proportion

To portray form convincingly the proportions of a composition need to be fairly accurate. Probably the form children most frequently want to represent is the human form. The first exploratory circle painted in playschools is usually changed to a person by the addition of arms, legs, eyes and a big smile. Adults, too, are fascinated by images of people; in a landscape even the smallest figure will attract the attention of the viewer.

Unfortunately, the human figure is perhaps the most challenging form to depict. While a picture of a piece of bark or a plant will look convincing even if the proportions are slightly inaccurate, it is obvious when body proportions are wrong and some children at KS2 start to avoid including people in their designs and three-dimensional work. For this reason, this section concentrates mainly on how to portray the human figure, but the ideas can also be used with other, easier forms.

AGES AND STAGES

Children begin making figures by drawing a big head with legs. Gradually the legs are lengthened as the head is made smaller. Parts of the legs then become joined to make a body that often becomes triangular. A figure may be drawn as a series of loops but it is invariably shown from the front, with straight limbs.

At KS1, children's images of people are predominantly expressions of their feelings about the people but open-ended investigations and brief discussions of proportions can increase their observational skills without imposing an adult view.

Figure 7.32
My Nana, painted in gouache . Y1

During KS2, children can be guided towards comparing different lines and shapes within the forms. The aim of

teaching proportion at KS2 is to allow children to represent more accurately the way that they see the world. So children who still 'see' heads bigger than they are in reality will need to portray them that way, perhaps until the end of KS3.

KNOWLEDGE AND UNDERSTANDING

PoS 9c
Relate art to its time and place of origin

There is a wealth of exciting art works of the human form to study. Named portraits fascinate children, especially if they can find out information about the model in addition to the artist (Velázquez *The infant Philip Prosper*, Ginn 34). Self-portraits are easier to collect information on.

Show as many different examples of portraiture as possible – photographs, paintings, drawings, sculptures or collage. The character and situation of a person are often shown through facial expression, pose, use of dominant colours, costume, nearby objects and background.

Exaggerated or distorted proportions have always been considered to be artistically valid. Portrait painters used to elongate a figure to make it appear more elegant. This tradition has continued in fashion illustrations. El Greco, the Renaissance painter (*Fabula*, Goodwill 1(7)), and the modern sculptor, Giacometti, both developed artistic styles with lengthened figures.

ACTIVITY

PoS 7e
Use knowledge of artists' work

1 Look at Isaac Oliver's miniatures of *Two little girls*, Ginn 33, and discuss the differences between his portraits (Y2–Y6).

  • Cut out a photograph from a magazine of a famous person's face or, if possible, use a photograph brought from home (Y2–Y6). Glue it to white paper and draw or paint an elaborate costume around it.

2 Make a self-portrait or a portrait of a friend in the style of famous artists.

  • Create elongated faces and figures in the style of African masks, Modigliani's portraits, Shorewood 162DR; Giacometti's sculptures or modern fashion drawings (Y2–Y6).

  • Examine Cubist portraits (Picasso *Woman with a hat*, Shorewood 1360; Goodwill 847) and try a self-portrait in the same style) (Y5–Y6).

3 Look at paintings and drawings by Lowry and create a playground scene with figures in the same style (Lowry *Good Friday*, O&B A5) (Y5–Y6). Children often think these are merely stick figures, but Lowry's style needs careful study and drawing. Children should practise on a scrap of paper, thinking of each drawing as a character with a story to tell.

Art in the National Curriculum Key Stage 2 Acorn AVP COM5002 shows portraits of the human face from Ancient Egypt to the present day.

PoS 4d
Investigate shape, form and space

Looking at structure beneath the surface

Looking at the structure of an object helps to simplify it and encourages an assessment of rough proportions.

AGES AND STAGES

Figure 7.33
Tiger, using mod-roc on a wire armature. The skeleton had to be studied before making the wire armature.
Y5

Children from Y1 to Y6 are fascinated with skeletons which provide an ideal starting point for work on body proportions. A skeleton avoids all the distractions of clothes, hair and muscle; it can also perform actions – a high kick, for example,

can graphically demonstrate the equal lengths of the leg and the torso. A plastic desk-top model is ideal, or use a joke-shop skeleton. Some primary science books have skeleton pictures with movable limbs.

Examine the structure beneath the surface in other forms – animals, buildings and furniture. Children at the end of KS2 may find it useful to lightly sketch this shape before painting or drawing surface layers.

At the beginning of KS2, simple fractions can be used to compare lengths. At the end of KS2 children are capable of quite accurate miniaturisation. A doll's house offers endless scope for reducing observed objects to tiny proportions.

ESTIMATING MEASUREMENTS

ACTIVITY

PoS 8d
Experiment with tools and develop techniques

1 Divide the page horizontally and vertically into quarters with light pencil lines (Y4–Y5). Then do the same with the mind's eye looking at the object. This helps to centre the drawing and obtain the correct proportions.

2 Look for horizontal and vertical relationships and lightly mark them on the drawing paper (Y5–Y6). Use visual estimates to obtain the relative scale of parts accurately. Try to judge accurately the angle of points that are not directly above, or to the side. Mark those lightly as well.

3 Place internal details by imagining lines, shapes and angles within the shape itself (Y5–Y6). Look for vertical and horizontal relationships.

4 Hold a pencil at arm's length and use it to measure the comparative lengths of different parts of the body (Y5–Y6). Close one eye and line up the top of the pencil with the top of the part that is to be measured. Slide the thumb down until it is in line with the base. Keep the thumb in position and move the pencil, still at arm's length, to another part of the body to compare the lengths.

ESTIMATING AND COMPARING BODY PROPORTIONS

PoS 7a
Record responses

Children can make useful comparative measurements on their own bodies. Hold a hand against the face to compare sizes; pull an elbow into the waist to compare the length of the upper arm; notice where the finger-tips touch the leg to see the length of the full arm. Child-safe mirrors can be used for examining facial proportions. Working in groups of three gives the opportunity for more thorough comparisons. Revise some of these body proportions whenever a portrait or figure is being made.

BODY PROPORTIONS
The following are some useful comparisons and measurements made by Y4 children, working in groups of three.

1 The top of the legs is half way up the body.

2 The head is roughly one-sixth of the body.

3 The shoulders are twice the width of the head.

4 The arms are as long as the legs.

5 The feet are as long as the head.

6 The hands are as long as the face.

7 The hands reach mid-thigh.

8 The elbow is at the centre of the arm length.

9 The knee is at the centre of the leg length.

10 The body is symmetrical.

The following additional information needed some input from the teacher.

1 Limbs can only bend at the joints.

2 Arms are joined to the shoulders and do not sprout from the neck.

3 When someone sits down, the distance from shoulder to seat is the same as from the back of the seat to knee.

HEAD PROPORTIONS

Sweep back the hair so that the extent of the forehead can be seen on the head. Y2 children may find only one or two of the following proportions; Y6 children might be able to find them all.

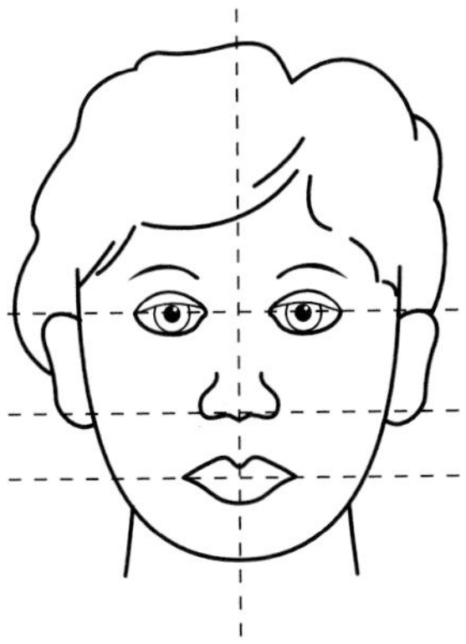

1 The head is roughly oval in shape, with slightly flattened sides.

2 The face is symmetrical.

3 The eyes are in the centre of the head.

4 The nose is half-way between the eyes and the chin.

Figure 7.34
Facial proportions.

5 The mouth is half-way between the nose and the chin.

6 The top of the ears are level with the eyes and the bottom of the ears are level with the base of the nose.

7 The eyes are roughly one eye's width apart.

8 The iris is not a round shape. It is partially covered by the top and lower lids.

ACTIVITY

1 Cut out the area surrounding the eyes of a face in an old magazine or newspaper (Y1–Y6). Glue the eyes to a piece of paper and complete the face.

2 Draw stick-figures (Y3–Y6). Children often long to make their figures act out exciting movements but find it difficult to achieve. A stick-figure based on the skeleton can be a useful starting point.
a) Draw a line for the spine. Next draw rough ovals for the head, ribs and hips. This gives the body bulk to separate the legs from the arms. Make sure the legs come from the sides of the hips and the arms from the shoulder.

Figure 7.35
Drawing a stick-figure.

b) Draw small circles at the joints to help to remember that they are the only places where the limbs can bend.
c) Draw in the hands and feet, remembering that they are as big as the face and the head. Flesh out the skeleton with fabric, paint, collage or use drawing tools such as pencils and pastels.

Life portraits

AGES AND STAGES

PoS 8a
Record what is experienced, observed and imagined

Children from Y1 to Y6 can all make highly individual and perceptive portraits. Children at KS1 tend to add well-observed details to largely symbolic portraits; presenting models in an unusual way can encourage young children to observe details more carefully.

The younger the model, the easier the pose should be. Sitting on a stool is easiest and gives an interesting view from all sides. Older models could stand or kneel on a padded surface. Children at KS2 often develop a style of drawing people that never varies, so discussing the individual variations and poses of each model is very important at this stage.

Making models in 3D is too lengthy a process for a model to pose. Children at KS2 could pose briefly for each other to view different positions and check the proportions.

ORGANISING THE CLASSROOM

Children can draw their own portraits if enough mirrors are available (use safe-foil mirrors from the science cupboard).

For a full figure portrait a model is needed. Move the desks in a circle around the model. If the desks cannot be easily moved, pose the model in a seated position on the teacher's table. Draw a line around the model's feet so that she or he can move away, have a rest, and then find the same position again.

Gather the children around the model. Not all the children will be able to sit at a desk, so some children will need boards as rests. Children are often reluctant to draw a back view, until it is pointed out that this avoids the difficulty of drawing a face.

Palettes of mixed drawing materials – charcoal, pastels, pencils, chalks – allow children to change the medium easily from one drawing to the next.

CHOOSING A MODEL

Despite the difficulty of sustaining a pose for any length of time, there is generally no shortage of eager volunteers to be models. Keep modelling sessions short and make frequent changes of model to ensure every child has a chance to draw and to prevent the modelling from becoming tedious. It is worth warning the class of a changeover a few minutes beforehand so that drawings can be finished off in time.

Elderly people make ideal models. They have more patience and can sit for long periods of time. Find someone who will not mind references to their interesting lines and wrinkles.

The ultimate patient model is a doll, ornamental figure or puppet. It can provide a useful aid for learning about body proportions and an interesting model for a drawing. Even the distorted proportions of a Barbie doll could make a useful basis for a discussion on the length of legs relative to the rest of the body.

ACTIVITY

PoS 7b
Use resources to stimulate ideas

1 Dress a model in a costume to fit in with current history or geography subjects (Y1–Y6). Use a hat as an accessory or surround the model with unusual props.

 • Use a Victorian half-mask to cover the top half of the face on a self-portrait (Y5–Y6).

2 Use poses that show emotion (Y4–Y6). These will need to be completed very quickly as the model will tire, but this can contribute to the vigour of a drawing.

3 Draw a tableau of several overlapping figures (Y5–Y6).

4 Ask a model to make a series of repeated movements as slowly as possible (Y5–Y6). At first make it as simple as lifting a glass up to drink. Encourage children to spend more time observing and studying than drawing. Make quick sketches in charcoal on newspaper to explore the different poses. Then make a more finished drawing on drawing paper.

Figure 7.36
Standing figure, in charcoal.
Y4

DRAWING A MODEL

Encourage children to draw the figure first and then the seat. It is much easier to adjust a seat to fit a figure. The background needs to be left quite sparse if children are to give enough time to the portrait – just a few lines are needed to suggest the position of a seat or corner.

Hands and heads are the hardest parts of a body to draw but give the most character to the portrait so children should be encouraged to complete these parts even if the rest of the body is only sketched. Encourage children to think of the figure in 3D rather than as a series of flat planes. Use tone to suggest form and avoid hard lines around the nose and mouth. The eyes are sunk in an eye socket, so there is usually an area of shadow there. Highlights on the iris in the eye give expression to the whole face. Hair should be observed as a solid shape, with highlights and shaded areas.

ACTIVITY

PoS 1
Work individually, in pairs or as a class

1 Use mirrors to make distorted images (Y3–Y6). Use concave and convex child-safe mirrors or the surface of a shiny spoon, a kettle or a school sports trophy. Encourage children to 'pull faces' and draw the strangest of images.

2 Make drawings of a hand (Y5–Y6). Think of the fingers as short cylinders, linked by joints. Cut out an object from a magazine and trim it down so that it fits into the drawn hand. The hand will look as though it is holding the object.

3 Cut out a head-and-shoulders portrait very carefully and mount it on a sheet of dark-coloured paper (Y5–Y6). This gives instant prominence to the head. Add sparse detail to the background to give character to the portrait.

Making portraits without a model

USING PHOTOGRAPHS

PoS 7b
Use resources to stimulate ideas

Artists have not always been able to afford models and since the nineteenth century, photographs have provided a useful reference for portraying people. Use black and white pictures or coloured photographs from magazines as a reference. Craggy faces provide a more interesting subject than the bland perfection of fashion models so it is worth collecting faces from colour supplements rather than from women's magazines.

Figure 7.37
Portrait, in soft pastel giving subtle gradation of tone. Y6

ACTIVITY

1 Complete a mystery portrait (Y3–Y6). Tear two pieces out of a face cut from a magazine. Glue the sections on to separate pieces of paper and give them to different children. They should complete the portrait without looking at each other's work and then see how closely the faces resemble each other.

2 Put a mirror on a photograph vertically (Y3–Y6). Turn it so that the features become distorted – the face becomes wider or narrower; the mouth alters in size and the space between the eyes grows and contracts. Draw one of the images.

DRAWING FROM MEMORY

PoS 2a
Express ideas and feelings

Each child develops a formula for portraying faces and it is particularly difficult to break away from this 'same look' in imaginative work. Here are several ideas to encourage children to think imaginatively about faces.

ACTIVITY

1 Use the symmetry of the face (Y3–Y4). Fold a piece of paper in half vertically. Paint on one side of the paper and fold the paper over to make prints of the colours. This makes the facial proportions totally symmetrical and any smudging can be adjusted when the paint has dried.

2 Try out ideas on photocopied drawings of heads (Y3–Y4). Photocopy a page of identical heads. Use wrinkles, facial hair, hair styles, eyebrows, jewellery and clothing to make different characters. Choose a combination of features to make a portrait of an imaginary aunt or uncle.

3 Link animal and human characteristics in a single portrait (Y5–Y6).

• Use a picture of an animal's head to develop into a face – a 'thug' could be made from a gorilla's face, a haughty duchess from a giraffe, an aggressive pensioner from a bull dog.

• Look at a picture of a face closely and see if it resembles an animal. Exaggerate the characteristics to create an imaginary face.

PoS 8d
Experiment with tools and develop techniques

Using a grid

A grid allows children to copy a picture very accurately. The shape can be copied the same size, or it can be enlarged or reduced to fit the children's own designs. The original picture should be fairly simple and also dispensable – from a comic, newspaper or magazine; if not, take a photocopy. (Take care not to break any copyright laws. Avoid all Disney characters as they enforce very strict copyright rules.)

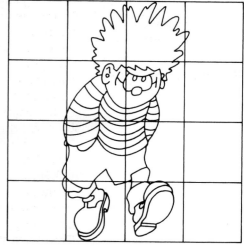

Figure 7.38
Grids for 'Dennis the Menace' and a print. Y6

© D. C. Thomson & Co. Ltd.
Acknowledgement:
The Beano

AGES AND STAGES

Children in Y4 could start with an exact copy of a very simple form using a four-squared grid. Gradually increase the complexity of the form and the number of squares in the grid and the difference in scale between the original and the drawing. A 3 cm-square cartoon can be accurately transferred to a drawing 36 cm square by children in Y6.

The constant searching for horizontal and vertical relationships in grid-drawing makes excellent training for looking at forms in direct observational work.

MAKING A GRID DRAWING

1 Mount a picture on paper and trim it into the shape of a square.

2 Fold the picture vertically and horizontally until there is a grid of 16 squares. Do the same on the drawing paper.

3 Use the position of the lines on the grid of the original drawing as reference points and transfer the lines to the same position on the grid.

Some children find it useful to turn a drawing upside down so that the shapes are unfamiliar. This enables them to concentrate exclusively on aligning the shapes and lines.

ACTIVITY

1 Draw a mirror-image (Y4–Y5). Cut a simple symmetrical object, landscape or cartoon face in half. Fold a square piece of drawing paper into a 4 × 4 grid. Place the cut out shape to one side of the fold – left for right-handed children and right for left-handed. Draw the other side of the picture. If the picture is coloured, mix colours to match the original.

2 Make a distorted face (Y6). Draw curved gridlines to make the shapes in the centre either very small or very large. Choose a picture of a well-known face and draw a conventional, straight-lined grid on top of the face. Carefully copy the positioning of the lines of the face from the photograph to the distorted grid.

Figure 7.39
Making a distorted grid.

Recording shapes in space – perspective

Main NC focus

KS1 and KS2 PoS 2 In order to develop visual perceptions, pupils should be taught . . . the practical skills needed to . . . record observations (and) design and make images

Some teachers avoid teaching children about perspective because of its associations with vanishing points and perspective lines. In practice only some children at the end of KS2 need to know about these technical aspects of perspective. Other, easier, rules of perspective can be discussed earlier. These will help children to represent three dimensions more convincingly on a flat surface.

<u>**KNOWLEDGE AND UNDERSTANDING**</u>

PoS 5b Examine styles from past and present

PoS 9b Recognise visual elements

A picture with plenty of action and detail such as Avercamp's *A winter scene with skaters near a castle*, Ginn 25, provides an interesting basis for looking at uses of perspective. The foreground skaters are large in size, are positioned low in the painting, overlap those behind and have more textural detail than those figures further away. In Delacroix's *Entry of the crusaders*, Shorewood 1270, distant hills look paler and bluer. Artists in Ancient Greece knew about perspective in the sense that they knew that a figure was smaller the further away it was, but they had not discovered the rules that would 'tell' them the size of a figure at a known distance. In the Middle Ages, paintings had no foreground and lacked depth. Gradually subjects became more dramatic in content and composition and artists wanted to represent form as though it were in 3D. The Renaissance gave them the techniques to do this. At the beginning of the fifteenth century, Filippo Brunelleschi discovered how to calculate the size of figures using a vanishing point and perspective lines. There are strong perspective lines in Botticelli's *Adoration* leading to the infant Christ (Shorewood 102) and also in Devis' *Family group in a garden* (Ginn 46) where lines give a feeling of distance and space.

<u>**AGES AND STAGES**</u>

Figure 7.40
Direct observation was used to record the foreshortening in the arms. Chalk drawing. Y4

At first, children at KS1 will separate each object in their pictures and avoid all references to perspective and even gravity. Later a base-line appears and the relationship between the objects becomes more ordered. Children learn most of the simple rules of perspective quite unconsciously through looking carefully at the world and by looking at pictures. Discussing what they can actually see, rather than what they know to be there, is a valuable preparation for drawing with perspective, but it is not something that every child will respond to at this stage.

Often children at KS2 know that something looks 'wrong' in their picture but cannot locate what it is. This is when a knowledge of the basic rules of perspective can be very liberating. Most of the rules can be explained in very simple terms using stick drawings on a blackboard, paper cut-outs pinned to a board or by looking at art works that show perspective. Introduce the terms: foreground, middleground, background, horizon.

When some children, at the end of KS2, need a more exact measure of size and positioning, they could learn about perspective lines, a vanishing point and how to draw the sides of objects. The more technical rules should be introduced only to children who are ready and eager to learn them so they will mostly be taught in small, informal groups rather than in class lessons.

Perspective – basic rules

There are four basic rules of perspective that children usually learn through experience but which might need reinforcing.

1 SHOWING PERSPECTIVE THROUGH SIZE (PERSPECTIVE OF SCALE)

PoS 8a
Record what is experienced, observed and imagined

Perspective of scale makes things smaller the further they are away and this can be demonstrated quite easily in the classroom. Ask two children of roughly the same size to stand together at the front of the class. Ask one child to take six steps forward towards the class and the other child six steps backwards away from the class. Children at KS2 could measure the two figures with a ruler held at arm's length.

Next, show how this works on a picture. Draw a large stick-figure and then an identical, but smaller, stick-figure slightly higher on the blackboard. Use paper cut-outs from magazines as an alternative to drawing. Which person looks further away?

ACTIVITY

1 Place similarly shaped objects of different sizes in a picture.

   • Make a paper-collage landscape (Y3–Y4). Cut out a small and then a large balloon and place them on a landscape to show perspective. This can also be done with hot-air balloons, aeroplanes or houses.

   • Look at a painting or print which uses this method of showing perspective (Shosun *White birds in snow*, Shorewood 416) (Y5–Y6). Cut out similar shapes, placing them in a different setting.

2 Frame a picture (Y3–Y6). A tree on a grassy bank, placed at the side of a picture and reaching to the top of the page, frames a landscape and provides a dramatic perspective reference for smaller, distant trees.

3 Cut out differently sized figures from magazines and move them around on a paper to create a crowd scene (Y5–Y6).

2 SHOWING PERSPECTIVE THROUGH POSITION (PERSPECTIVE OF CONTOUR)

Figure 7.41
Line of trees. The black trees look further away even though they are the same size. It is because they are higher on the page and overlap. Y4

Perspective of contour means that things that are nearer are placed in front of, and lower down the paper than things that are further away. Look outside the classroom and notice how things look higher if they are further away.

Draw a large tree next to a small tree. They both look to be in the

foreground because perspective of contour (placing things up or down on the page) is even stronger then perspective of scale (making things larger or smaller). Move the small tree higher up than the larger one and it will instantly appear to be further away. Even larger objects will often look further away if they are placed higher up.

ACTIVITY

1 Draw simple objects piled on top of each other such as buttons, pebbles, marbles in a jar (Y1–Y2). Some children will draw each one separate from the other but others may discover how things can overlap.

2 Use printing to place the same image in different positions to create a sense of perspective (Y3–Y6).

3 Draw overlapping groups of figures (Y4–Y6), for example people sharing a secret, children in the playground.

4 Work as a group to create a picture of a landscape (Y3–Y6). This involves useful discussion and comparisons of size for perspective. Map out a skyline and main physical features together. Decide where the foreground, the middle ground and the background are positioned and draw a figure to scale in each area. Add other overlapping figures and details, checking against the original three figures that the scale is approximately correct.

5 Cut out and arrange children's self-portraits in a group according to perspective of scale and contour (Y4–Y6). Look at pictures of football crowds to observe the differences in head size.

3 SHOWING PERSPECTIVE THROUGH TEXTURE AND DETAIL (TEXTURAL PERSPECTIVE)

Textural perspective makes an object look nearer by giving it greater textural detail than things in the distance. If possible, go outside and compare detail that can be seen on things that are near with detail on objects further away.

ACTIVITY

1 Encourage children to show detail in objects in the foreground of their pictures (Y3–Y6).

2 Work with large sweeps of a brush or the sides of crayons or pastels when making a background and use a small brush or the points of the drawing tools to create fine detail in the foreground (Y3–Y6).

4 SHOWING PERSPECTIVE THROUGH COLOUR (AERIAL PERSPECTIVE)

Aerial perspective gives paler, bluer tones to things in the distance. The air acts as a filter for the other colours leaving things in the distance looking fainter, paler and bluer. The blues of the sky also pale towards the horizon. If the school grounds have a long view, look at the way things in the distance look a grey-blue.

ACTIVITY

1 Encourage children to use greyer, bluer colour tones for distant hills in paper- and fabric-collage and painted landscapes (Y3–Y6).

2 Cover black paper strips with varying depths of white chalk. Cut them into skylines showing trees, hills or buildings and arrange them so the palest is at the back (Y4–Y6).

3 Give children different charcoal greys so that they can use paler greys for distant objects (Y5–Y6).

Figure 7.42
Landscape, in charcoal, showing the use of paler greys for distant objects. Y5

PoS 8d
Experiment with tools and
develop techniques

More technical rules of perspective

The more difficult rules of perspective are best taught individually or in small groups, generally at the end of KS2. They are very helpful for children who are ready to learn them but can be intimidating for others who are not.

Drawing the edge of a cylinder

Children often want to draw objects that are basically cylindrical in shape. Using an ellipse will make any roughly cylindrical shape such as a cup, bottle, vase, plant-pot look much more convincing.

Put elastic bands around a large transparent cylinder-shaped jar. As the eye level changes, so does the ellipse shape of the elastic bands.

Find a large cube and stick a large circle on each surface. By changing the angle of the cube the children can see how the circle becomes an ellipse at the sides, as well as on the top and bottom.

Hang up a hoop from the ceiling, if possible next to a plain wall. As the hoop rotates the shape will change from a circle, through narrowing ellipses to a line and back again.

ACTIVITY

1 Practise drawing curves and ellipses so that they become smooth and even (Y3–Y6).

2 In a still-life, draw the whole of the ellipse of a vase lightly; even if part of it is obscured by leaves (Y4–Y6). This produces a better shape than working round the leaves. Ignore the 'invisible' parts of the ellipse as the drawing evolves.

3 Break the rules of perspective in the manner of Braque, Shorewood 1729 (Y5–Y6). Create a still-life on a circular table.

Drawing the sides of a cuboid

When children want to draw the sides of box-shaped objects accurately, introduce the simple but very effective idea of parallel lines. Technically speaking, the lines on the side of a cuboid are perspective lines that lead to a vanishing point. The vanishing point, however, is so far away, it hardly affects the angle of the perspective lines and they appear to be parallel. This means that the technique can be introduced without any reference to a vanishing point.

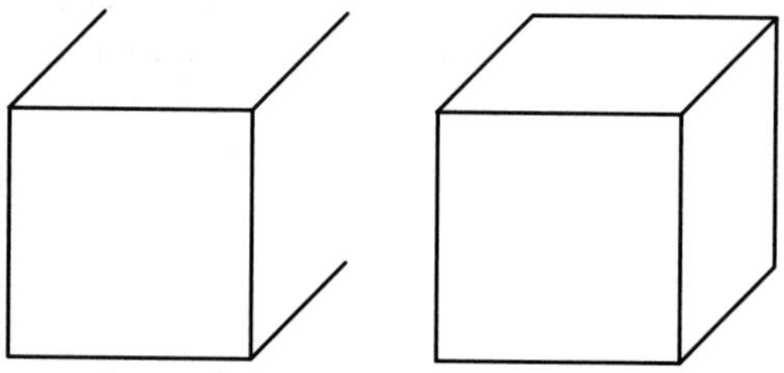

Figure 7.43
Drawing a cube.

Ask the children to draw a rectangle and decide which way the side lines will go – up to the right or up to the left? Draw faint parallel lines out from three corners so that they are all approximately equal in length. Draw faint lines parallel to the top and the sides of the original rectangle.

Figure 7.44
Travel bag, in soft pastel. The lines for the bag were based on an approximate cuboid shape.

This method works for any object that is approximately cuboid in shape – vans, houses, books, desks, chairs, travel bags.

ACTIVITY
1 Use transparent plastic cuboids or boxes for direct observational drawings (Y3–Y6). Use them as a basis for drawing buildings.

2 Use mathematics paper with diamond geometric shapes to draw side lines consistently (Y3–Y6). When the drawing is completed, go over with a dark line and the diamond guidelines will not be noticed.

3 Draw modern buildings (Y5–Y6). Start with one building at the front and to the side of the paper and gradually work to the other side and higher up the page. Add smaller cuboids to the top of buildings. Use light lines so that mistakes can be erased. It is easier if all the buildings face the same way so that the side lines are all to one side.

Lines of perspective and the vanishing point

A straight, flat road appears to disappear into the distance as the sides of the road become closer and closer. The sides of the road can be drawn along perspective lines and the place where they appear to meet is called the vanishing point.

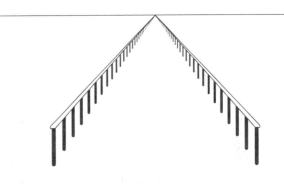

Figure 7.45
Drawing the vanishing point.

ACTIVITY
1 Start to draw fences, roadside trees and walls, which can all recede in a similar way towards the vanishing point (Y4–Y6). The perspective lines slope so children tend to make the lines of the trees and fences lean in sympathy. Encourage them to check all vertical lines with the edge of the paper.

2 Try drawing a building using a vanishing point (Y6). The walls should stop before they reach the vanishing point and have to be drawn vertically if the building is to look convincing. The windows and doors should also be drawn with the aid of perspective lines.

Figure 7.46
Street scene using perspective lines in charcoal. Y6

HEALTH AND SAFETY

Carving tools

Always work under close supervision and teach children to work away from the body. The holding-hand should always rest near to the body and away from the direction of a tool.

Contact glue

Work in a well-ventilated room to avoid build up of fumes.

Craft-knives

A craft-knife is extremely sharp. Its use is more suitable for children at the end of KS2 and continual supervision should be given. Place card or paper on a thick wad of newspapers to protect the table.

Dyes

Teachers should prepare the dye bath away from the children. Avoid inhaling the powder while it is being mixed and wear rubber gloves and an apron.

Fixatives

The fine air-borne spray can be an irritant, especially to asthmatic children. Spray outdoors or next to an open window and avoid breathing in the fumes. Do not spray near a flame and do not throw an empty can on to fire.

Irons

If possible children should see procedures involving ironing. This will need an extra adult working with small groups.

Marker pens

The fumes from marker pens can be overpowering if used in a confined space for any length of time. Marker pens from educational suppliers do not have this problem.

Oil paints and turpentine

Keep children with asthma away from these materials and supervise their use carefully. Use only at the end of KS2.

Needles

Teach children to look where others are seated and pull their needles and thread into an empty space – usually to the front of them.

Paste

Check that a paste does not contain fungicide if purchased locally. Educational supplies are safe.

Plaster of Paris

Powder from the plaster can cause irritation to the lungs if inhaled. Use a scoop, rather than pouring out the plaster, and keep children with asthma away from the mixing process.

Put a container of water in the centre of the table so that tools can be washed as soon as they have been used. Once hardened, plaster cannot be removed.

Cover all surfaces with newspaper sheets and fold sheets up carefully at the end of the lesson to contain all waste plaster. Place old wet towels at the doors of the classroom for children to wipe their feet before leaving.

Never wash plaster of Paris down the sink. Even a small amount can set solid and block drainpipes. Wash in a bucket and throw waste water down a gutter.

Wax pots

Hot wax can cause serious burns. Position the pot against a wall. Secure electrical leads with tape. Make it clear that only an adult can touch the pot or the lid. Encourage children to suck any areas of the skin splashed with wax as the saliva acts as a balm.

Wire

Teach children to hold the ends of wire firmly in each hand if possible. Any loose ends should point away from themselves and any other children.

3D forms 104–5

abstract painting 33
acrylics 45, 48–9, 51, 67
additive monoprints 69–70
armatures 111–12, 115, 117
art elements 162–97
art galleries 28
art jigsaws 29
art works, looking at and
discussing 1–2, 27–30, 103, 163
artificial fibres 131
asymmetrical compositions 183–4

ball-point pens 18
batik 154–9
batik painting 158–9
block printing 56–66
body proportions 188–9
border patterns 176–8
brushes 42, 43, 47, 49
bubble prints 70

candlewick 136
card construction 104–7
card looms 144
card-relief blocks 57
cardboard boxes 107
cartoons 9–10, 11
carved sculptures 119–21
carving tools 120, 198
chalks 6, 20–1, 74
charcoal 6, 18–20
Chinese dry brush technique 42
circular patterns 178, 179
clay 97, 121, 122–3, 124
clay presses 123
clay printing blocks 61
coil-pots 127–8
cold clay (Newclay) 97, 122, 124
collage and relief 82–101
collaged blocks 57
colour 163–9
    choosing paints 45, 47, 48
    in drawing 14–15, 20, 21–2, 26
    mixing 36–8, 164–6
    and painting 33–8
    and perspective 195
    in printing 65
colour wheels 165–6
coloured pencils 6, 14–15
commercial dyes 147–8

composition 182–6
cones 106
construction 103–18
contact glue 198
contour drawing 5
cords 133–4
counter-change patterns 182
craft-knives 198
cuboids
    constructing 106
    drawing 196–7
    slab-pots 124
cylinders
    constructing 106
    construction with 108
    drawing 196
    slab-pots 124, 125

decorative art 176–8
diffusers 75, 76
dip-dyeing 148
dip-pens 16-17
direct observation
    drawing from 4–6, 20
    painting from 31–2
    and printing 53
direct prints 53–5
doughs 97, 121, 122
drawing 1–26
drawings, discussing 1–2
dye-baths 147
dyeing textiles 146–59
dyes 41, 51, 147–8, 198

embroidery 91–6
emotions see feelings and moods
environment, pattern and texture
    in 173–4
erasers 12, 19, 21
estimating measurements 188
Expressionists, use of colour 35

fabrics
    collage 91–6
    dyeing 146-59
    painting on 41
    for printing 51–2
    soft sculptures 96, 116–18
    transfers 80
    see also quilting; silk
        painting;

feelings and moods
    conveyed by colour 168
    expressing 8, 31, 33
felt-tip pens 6, 17
figure drawing 186–7 see also life
    portraits
finger painting 43
finger paints 45, 51, 67
firing clay 128, 129
fixatives 19, 198
flour paste, as resist 159
focal points 185–6
form and tone 169–72
found objects and materials
    armatures 115, 117
    collage 90
    colours from 34
    construction 107–9
    painting with 44
    printing with 53–5
fountain pens 16
frames, embroidery 92
French knitting 138
frottage 59–60
fruit and vegetable carving 120

geometric shapes
    constructing 106–7
    tie-dye 151
glazing 128–9
glove figures 118
glue 57, 84–5, 90, 92, 104
glue and string blocks 58
God's eyes 132–3
gouache 44, 45, 46
greys 37
grids 192–3

head proportions 189
high relief (in collage) 86–8
highlighting 171
home-made colours 34
home-made dyes 147

illustrative drawings 7–8
illustrative paintings 30–1
imaginative paintings 30–1
Impressionists, use of colour 35
ink drawings 15–18
inked transfer prints 79–80

inks
    drawing 16
    printing 51, 67
    in resist drawings 23
'invisible' lines 185
irons 198

kilns 128
knitting 140–1

laminated paper 98, 114–15
landscapes 6, 32–3, 86, 98
layering colours 14
life portraits 189–93
light and dark colours 36, 168
lighting 172
line 2, 8–9, 175–6
lino-cuts 63-4
Lissajous curves 175
looms 143, 144–5

macramé 138–9
marbling 67, 71
marker pens 17, 198
masked monoprints 68–9
masks (face) 86, 88, 98, 106
masks (for printing) 66
Matisse, use of collage 83
mixing colours 36–8, 164–66
mobiles 110
mod-roc 99, 112–13
modelling 121–9
    in relief 97–101
monoprinting 67–71
moods see feelings and moods
moulds
    for clay 125
    for plaster of Paris 120

natural fibres 131
natural objects
    drawing 4–5
    sculptures 108–9
needles 92, 199

oil paints 198
oil pastels 6, 21–3, 74

painting 27–49
painting dye 41, 153
paintings, looking at 27–30
paints 44–9
    printing with 51
palette knives 43
paper
    for drawing 12, 16, 19, 20, 22
    for painting 39, 46, 47, 49
    for printing 51, 56, 67
paper collage 82–9
paper collections 85
paper construction 104–7
paper-cuts 84

paper tie-dyes 149
paper weaving 142–3
papier mâché 98, 114–15
paraphrasing 30
paste 198 see also flour paste
pastel pencils 20
pastels see oil pastels; soft pastels
patterns 172–82
    collage 89
    tie-dye 149–52
    weaving 142–3
pen and ink drawings 15–18
pencil sharpeners 6
pencil sketching 3, 6
pencils 3, 6, 13–15
perspective 193–7
photo-montage 83–4
photograms 77
photographs, portraits from 191
picture weaving 145–6
plaits and braids 139–40
plaster casts 99–101
plaster modelling 99
plaster of Paris 199
    carving 120
    constructions 112–13
plastic containers and packaging
    108
plastic materials 97
Plasticine 97, 121, 122, 124
Plasticine printing blocks 61
playdoughs 122, 124
Pointillists, use of colour 35
polyblock printing blocks 62
Polyfilla
    and cloth sculptures 113
    in collage 90
    relief modelling 99
    as resist 159
pom-poms 135–6
portraits 31–2, 187, 189–93
poster paints 51
potato prints 62–3
powder paints 45, 46, 51
practice paper 3
primary colours 36, 37, 165
print-making 50–81
printing areas 52
printing boards 67
printing wheels 57
problem-solving drawings 11–12
proportion 186–93
pyramids 106

quilting 95–6

rag-rugging 93
raised-relief prints 56–8
reduction printing 65
reflected images 89
repeat patterns 180–2
resist drawings 23

roller offset prints 71
roller printing 55–6
rotating grid patterns 181–2
rubbed stencil prints 73–4
rubbings 58–60

saltdough 121, 122, 124
scissors 85, 92
scraffito 25–6
scraperboards 23–5
scraperpaper 24
screen printing 72, 77–9
sculpture 102–29
sculptures, discussing 103
scumbling 42
seasonal colours 167
secondary colours 36, 37, 165
sequences 10, 181
shading 14, 170
shadows 171
shape 3, 8–9
shaped and incised blocks 60–6
sharpeners 6, 22
silhouettes 84
    card prints 60–1
silk painting 160–1
sketchbooks 6–7
sketching 3, 6–7
slab-pots 124–5
soft pastels 6, 20–1
soft sculptures 116–18
    faces 96
solid paints 46
speed dyeing 153
splatter prints 75–6
sponges, painting with 44
sprayed stencil prints 75
stages of drawing (Lowenfeld) 2
stencil prints 71–9
stencil sheets 73
stick-weaving 137
still life painting 31–2
stippled stencil prints 74
structure 187–9
stuffed shapes 117–18
styles of painting 29–30
subtractive monoprints 68–9
supports (surfaces)
    for drawing 12
    for painting 39–40, 49
    for printing 51–2
    shape of 184–5
    size of 40
symmetrical compositions 183
symmetrical patterns 178–80

tassels 134–5
technological designs (fantasy)
    12
tempera 51
tertiary colours 165
textiles 130–61

textures and patterns 172–82
threads, embroidery 92
thumb-pots 126–7
tie-dyeing 148–53
tjantings 154
tone 14, 169–72
   mixing tones 37–8
transfer prints 79–81
tribute paintings 30
tritik 152
turpentine 198

vanishing point 197
visual jokes 10
visual stories 9–10

warm and cool colours 36, 167
washes 38
watercolours 44, 46–8, 51

wax crayons
   in batik 159
   drawing with 21–3
   stencil prints 74
   transfer prints 81
wax pots 155, 199
wax scraffito 25-6
weaving 141–6
wet and dry painting 40–1
wire 199
   construction 109–12
wood
   carving 121
   construction 109
word pictures 8

yarn collage 95
yarn wrapping 131–8
yarns 131